M000237222

"Many Christians have a problem with the Christian life. For some, Christianity is just a set of beliefs, and for others a rigid set of standards. There is in the gospel a dynamic to energize and guide life along the proper paths. God has given his Word to point his people to the way of piety. Casillas has charted a course showing how the truths of the Bible must translate to life. He effectively shows that Christianity is not just a religion; it is a way of life."
—**MICHAEL P. V. BARRETT,** Vice-President for Academic Affairs, Puritan Reformed Theological Seminary

"How can an ancient book like the Bible guide us through the complexities of contemporary life? This is the question that Ken Casillas answers, and he does a fine job. This is an unusual book, and one that is unusually insightful. Casillas challenged my thinking and he fed my soul."
—**KEVIN BAUDER,** Research Professor of Systematic Theology, Central Baptist Theological Seminary, Minneapolis

"Casillas wrote this book with the heart of a pastor and with the biblically based conviction that Christ saves believers not only from God's wrath but in order that we may increasingly image God's holiness. Beyond Chapter and Verse supplies Christians with a theological framework and method for applying Scripture to our everyday lives. He suggests that our interpretive quest is to distinguish the timebound elements from the timeless truths, and he supplies a host of Old and New Testament examples that model an approach to Scripture that takes seriously the power of the gospel to save—past, present, and future. He helpfully distinguishes his approach from legalism, defines Christian liberty, and saturates his discussion with rich and careful biblical exposition. This thoroughly researched book is worshipful and will help those of us in Christ become more who we already are and who Christ saved us to be."
—**JASON S. DeROUCHIE,** Professor of Old Testament and Biblical Theology, Bethlehem College and Seminary

"Many of our problems in the Christian life are problems of how to 'apply' Scripture to ourselves. Ken Casillas helps us with a comprehensive study of the nature of application, including many specific examples. He shows how biblical writers themselves apply God's Word, and how we, in turn, ought to do it. The book is based on a strong view of Scripture's authority and sufficiency, and it shows a deep insight into the real problems we face in our walk with God. Casillas is especially concerned with sanctification—the doctrine of how the Spirit and the Word conform our lives to Christ. I hope that the book will gain a wide readership and thus be a great blessing to the church."

—**JOHN FRAME,** Professor of Systematic Theology and Philosophy Emeritus, Reformed Theological Seminary

"If you haven't encountered difficulties in applying the Bible, then you haven't spent much time applying it. Walking in a manner worthy of the gospel can seem unrealistic or, at the very least, incredibly difficult. But there is hope. This book is an encouraging aid in connecting the Bible with your life. These pages provide a helpful tool to joyfully and confidently build your life on God's Word for his glory."

—**SAM HORN,** Executive Vice President for Enrollment and Ministerial Advancement, Bob Jones University

Beyond
Chapter and Verse

Beyond Chapter and Verse:

The Theology and Practice of Biblical Application

Ken Casillas

WIPF & STOCK · Eugene, Oregon

BEYOND CHAPTER AND VERSE
The Theology and Practice of Biblical Application

Copyright © 2018 Ken Casillas. All rights reserved. Except for brief quotations in critical publications or reviews, no part of this book may be reproduced in any manner without prior written permission from the publisher. Write: Permissions, Wipf and Stock Publishers, 199 W. 8th Ave., Suite 3, Eugene, OR 97401.

Wipf & Stock
An Imprint of Wipf and Stock Publishers
199 W. 8th Ave., Suite 3
Eugene, OR 97401

www.wipfandstock.com

PAPERBACK ISBN: 978-1-5326-4534-1
HARDCOVER ISBN: 978-1-5326-4535-8

Manufactured in the U.S.A.   02/27/18

Unless otherwise indicated, Scripture quotations are from the Holy Bible, English" "Standard Version, copyright © 2001 by Crossway Bibles, a division of Good News Pub- lishers. Used by permission. All rights reserved.

Quotations designated (KJV) are from the King James Version of the Bible.

Scripture quotations marked HCSB are taken from the Holman Christian Stan- dard Bible®, Copyright © 1999, 2000, 2002, 2003, 2005 by Holman Bible Publish- ers. Used by permission. Holman Christian Standard Bible®, Holman CSB®, and HCSB® are federally registered trademarks of Holman Bible Publishers.

Quotations designated (NASB) are taken from the NEW AMERICAN STAN- DARD BIBLE, © Copyright The Lockman Foundation 1960, 1962, 1963, 1968, 1971, 1972, 1973, 1975, 1977, 1988, 1995. Used by permission.

Quotations designated (NET©) are from the NET Bible® copyright ©1996-2017 by Biblical Studies Press, L.L.C. http://netbible.com All rights reserved.

Quotations designated (NIV) are from THE HOLY BIBLE: NEW INTERNA TIONAL VERSION®. NIV®. Copyright © 1973, 1978, 1984, 2011 by International Bible Society, www.ibs.org. All rights reserved worldwide.

To my children:
Daniel, Josh, Anna Grace, Abigail, and Samuel

Contents

CONTENTS

Acknowledgments

This book reflects the unquantifiable assistance and influence of many fellow Christians. I happily thank them for their contribution to this work and to my life generally.

First I want to express my gratitude to Stephen Jones, former president of Bob Jones University (BJU), for launching the President's Writing Endowment. Those who have funded the endowment were used by God to make the writing of this book financially possible. Current president Steve Pettit remains committed to the ministry of the BJU Seminary, and I'm grateful for his supportiveness.

Thanks are due to Sam Horn and Steve Hankins, dean and associate dean at the Seminary. Their selfless leadership enables the faculty to pursue our calling. I appreciate their faithful encouragement and intercession. I also thank my colleagues Gary Reimers and Layton Talbert for reading the manuscript. They made many recommendations that strengthened my content and sharpened my presentation.

I'm deeply indebted to all my former professors at BJU for teaching me the Word of God and shaping my approach to it. Their influence pervades this book. For some years now, I've taught alongside some of them, and I praise the Lord for this privilege.

I appreciate the support of God's people at Cleveland Park Bible Church. They prayed me through this project and graciously receive my efforts to apply Scripture as I preach from week to week.

How can I sufficiently thank my family? My extended family has upheld me in prayer. My five children have endured months and months of my absorption with this book. I trust that the result will benefit them especially. The epilogue explains why I'm dedicating the work to them.

ACKNOWLEDGEMENTS

My wife Soraya has served relentlessly as prayer-warrior, cheerleader, sounding board, and behind-the-scenes facilitator. When we married I had no idea what a gift the Lord was giving me.

To that Lord belongs the ultimate praise for everything true and useful in this book and for anything good that may come from it. May his Word be obeyed and his name be honored. *Soli Deo gloria!*

Abbreviations

AOTC	Apollos Old Testament Commentary
BDAG	Walter Bauer, Frederick W. Danker, W. F. Arndt, and F. W. Gingrich. *Greek-English Lexicon of the New Testament and Other Early Christian Literature.* 3rd ed. Chicago: University of Chicago Press, 2000.
BECNT	Baker Exegetical Commentary on the New Testament
BSac	*Bibliotheca Sacra*
BST	The Bible Speaks Today
CNTUOT	G. K. Beale and D. A. Carson, eds. *Commentary on the New Testament Use of the Old Testament.* Grand Rapids: Baker, 2007.
GSC	A Geneva Series Commentary
HALOT	Ludwig Koehler and Walter Baumgartner. *The Hebrew and Aramaic Lexicon of the Old Testament.* Study ed. Revised by Walter Baumgartner and Johann Jakob Stamm. Translated by M. E. J. Richardson. Leiden: Brill, 2001.
JBMW	*The Journal for Biblical Manhood and Womanhood*
JETS	*The Journal of the Evangelical Theological Society*
NAC	The New American Commentary
NICNT	The New International Commentary on the New Testament
NICOT	The New International Commentary on the Old Testament

NIDOTTE   Willem A. VanGemeren, ed. *New International Dictionary of Old Testament Theology and Exegesis.* 5 vols. Grand Rapids: Zondervan, 1997.

NIGTC   The New International Greek Testament Commentary

NSBT   New Studies in Biblical Theology

OED   J. A. Simpson and E. S. C. Weiner, eds. *The Oxford English Dictionary.* 20 vols. Oxford: Oxford University Press, 1989.

PNTC   The Pillar New Testament Commentary

TNTC   The Tyndale New Testament Commentaries

TOTC   The Tyndale Old Testament Commentaries

WBC   Word Biblical Commentary

ZECNT   Zondervan Exegetical Commentary on the New Testament

Introduction

Kate closed her Bible with a sense of disappointment. She was glad that she had faithfully "done her devotions," yet she was frustrated that she hadn't "gotten anything out of it." Even more discouraging was that she had been asking the Lord to show her his will about a major decision, and the Bible didn't seem to provide the direction she needed.

Andrea appreciated the opportunity to counsel her friend Carla, whose marriage had hit hard times. After a while, though, Andrea didn't know what to do. She was coming up dry as she tried to think of verses that related to Carla's situation. She faced the same struggle in responding to questions and objections from her non-Christian coworkers.

Ryan, an inner-city pastor, contemplated his text for Sunday. He understood fairly well what God was telling the Israelites through this next chapter of Deuteronomy. He was committed to expounding the Scriptures, but what could this passage possibly have to do with urban Americans in the twenty-first century?

As Marsha thought back on Sunday's services, she felt spiritually energized. At the same time, though, she was a bit uncomfortable with some of the points the visiting preacher had made. They didn't seem very connected with the text for the day. Actually, they sounded more like personal opinions.

Craig was having another tense discussion with his teenage son Chris. They were back to the issue of video games. "What's wrong with this game?" questioned Chris. "The violence is only make-believe. Besides, where in the Bible does it say this is wrong? There's plenty of killing in the Bible anyway."

Nate didn't know what to think after his first semester at a Christian college. He came from a fairly conservative home and was basically following the habits and standards his parents had taught him.

But in his new environment he had been confronted with a diversity of views on Christian-living issues. He was also hearing some of his peers criticize their upbringing as "legalistic." They wanted to live a "gospel-centered" life, not one oriented toward details of conduct. Nate's online reading only added to his confusion. He wanted to develop biblical convictions but wasn't sure where to begin.

The Challenge of Application

The scenarios above illustrate just a few of the challenges related to the topic of this book: the application of Scripture to contemporary life. It's no secret that the books of the Bible were originally written to people who lived thousands of years ago. So it shouldn't surprise us that we struggle to know how the Bible guides us in today's technologized, globalized, and secularized society. Nor is it surprising that we can go too far or not far enough with application. Think back on the application problems raised in the scenarios.

In our personal reading of Scripture, we sometimes find it difficult to glean practical truths. Our devotional life can become unproductive, a mere religious routine. We may also become disheartened when we don't find answers to specific questions on our hearts.

The struggle becomes more pronounced when dealing with pressing questions from people to whom we're attempting to minister. We may find ourselves wishing the Bible were set up like an encyclopedia of ethics or apologetics.

Bible teachers and preachers face these challenges to an even greater degree. Sermon preparation doesn't end once a preacher has accurately interpreted his text. He must go on to relate the text to people's lives in a compelling way. This task involves some daunting subtasks, especially with Old Covenant material. Even with the New Testament, the preacher will need to sort through differences between first-century and twenty-first-century cultures.

Sadly, preachers aren't always as careful as they ought to be, and they can end up using the pulpit to promote views that have little or no basis in Scripture. As a result, they lose the confidence of their hearers, and this can contribute to skepticism and other spiritual struggles.

On the other hand, should we expect an explicit "chapter and verse" on every question we face? After all, God isn't reissuing the Bible for every new generation. Is it possible to take what he has said and discern his will about what he hasn't addressed? If so, how do we avoid "adding" to God's Word?

Finally, how does our responsibility in application relate to the glorious truth that God saves us by grace and not by our own works? What is and what isn't "legalism"? And how should we define "Christian liberty"?

Taking up the Challenge

These are the kinds of issues I explore in this book. Clearly, the application of Scripture is a complex topic. It's impossible to lay out a formula that will guarantee we will appropriately apply every passage of Scripture to every conceivable situation. Application is both a "science" and an "art." It requires not only that we follow a valid approach as we work with the Scriptures but also that we exercise Spirit-led discernment as we bring God's Word to bear on particular circumstances. Another way of saying this is that by its very nature application involves both objective and subjective elements.

Yet we must not allow the subjective side to discourage us or lead us to minimize application. If we believe that the Bible is our authority, we need to grasp how that authority actually functions in our lives. We should articulate a coherent theology of and method for biblical application. That is the goal of this book.

Furthermore, we ought to look to God's Word itself to help us reach our goal. That's one of my key theses—that the Bible itself requires us to apply its teachings and also guides us in developing a process for doing so. As a result, our discussion will be substantially *exegetical*—carefully examining multiple passages that relate in one way or another to the matter of application.

The book divides into five parts. Part I gives vital background material. It sketches the broad theological context of Bible application, relating it to the gospel generally (chapter 1) and to the doctrine of sanctification specifically (chapters 2 and 3).

Parts II and III form the heart of the book. They provide a synthesis of key Old and New Testament passages touching on application. Part II argues that application is necessary due to the nature of Scripture (chapter 4) as well as the scope of sanctification (chapter 5). Then Part III unfolds various biblical patterns of application, particularly as reflected in the New Testament's use of the Old Testament (chapters 6 and 7).

Part IV interacts with common objections to application. Here chapter 8 deals with appeals to the doctrine of the sufficiency of Scripture, and chapter 9 discusses charges of legalism. This leads to an exposition of Christian liberty in chapter 10.

Based on all the preceding, Part V lays out procedures for arriving at legitimate applications of God's Word. Chapters 11–14 explain and illustrate an approach for moving from the Bible to life. Chapters 15–17 show how to move in the other direction: from life to the Bible and then back again. A brief epilogue concludes the book with some personal reflections.

Ultimately, this book is merely a blueprint for what should be an ongoing building project for all Christians—a life pleasing to our Lord. As you read, I pray he will guide you, give you wisdom, and help you grow in your application of his Word. May we all be enabled to think God's thoughts after him.

Part I

The Context
of Biblical Application

Chapter 1

It's All about the Gospel

The term *application* carries various meanings in Christian parlance. Often it refers to a stage of Bible study or a component of a sermon. In this connection it means the formulation of what one ought to do in response to Scripture. This response may or may not be a tangible action. It could, for example, be a change in thinking or beliefs or attitudes. If you say, "I want to know how this verse applies to my life," you're using the first meaning of application. You are talking about what you *should* do. That is what this book will typically mean by application as well.

At other times application speaks of "follow-through," choosing to respond to God's Word in the appropriate way. It means something you *actually* do, as when someone says, "I applied God's Word by asking my brother to forgive me for speaking to him unkindly." Perhaps a better word for this idea is simply obedience.

Whatever meaning is in view, biblical application focuses on human responsibility, our doing. This simple fact raises an important and foundational issue. You may have heard it said that the world's religions can be encapsulated in the word *do,* but the Christian gospel is unique because it proclaims, "Done!" I've made that kind of statement myself, and it succinctly captures the heart of the gospel. Our relationship to God is not based on what we do, our work. Instead it is based on what Jesus Christ has graciously done, his work as our substitute. What a relieving and refreshing truth!

In our efforts to apply the Scriptures, we could easily overshadow this truth. That, in fact, is a common criticism of biblical application. So in this chapter we'll examine the general relationship between application and the gospel. This will give us necessary perspective and will help prevent misunderstanding. I trust it will do even more—minister to us motivation to pursue the application of Scripture.

The Greek term underlying the English word *gospel* (*euangelion*) means "good news." This noun and related parts of speech occur over 130 times in the New Testament. But what exactly is the good news? Often the biblical writers assume their readers know the answer based on past teaching and/or the broader context. But other times the writers provide detail. We get a sense of the breadth of the good news from phrases where the noun *gospel* is followed by "of" and then another term. In these cases, "of" tends to mean "about" or includes that idea:

- The gospel of the kingdom (Matt 4:23)
- The gospel of Jesus Christ, the Son of God (Mark 1:1)
- The gospel of the grace of God (Acts 20:24)
- The gospel of God (Rom 1:1)
- The gospel of the glory of Christ (2 Cor 4:4)
- The gospel of your salvation (Eph 1:13)
- The gospel of peace (Eph 6:15).

Some passages state blessings that the gospel brings: Christ "abolished death and brought life and immortality to light through the gospel" (2 Tim 1:10). Others condense what took place in history to secure those blessings: "Remember Jesus Christ, risen from the dead, the offspring of David, as preached in my gospel" (2 Tim 2:8). Still other texts define or describe the gospel at length. We'll be studying two of these, probably the most famous two: 1 Corinthians 15 and Romans 1.

1 Corinthians 15

The Holy Spirit led the apostle Paul to write 1 Corinthians 15 in order to defend the bodily resurrection of believers, refuting a denial of that doctrine that was having some influence in the Corinthian church. As he begins, Paul reviews the message he had originally proclaimed to the Corinthians. He calls that message *the gospel*, and verses 1–11 explain the term.

Now I would remind you, brothers, of the gospel I preached to you, which you received, in which you stand, and by which you are being saved, if you hold fast to the word I preached to you— unless you believed in vain. For I delivered to you as of first importance what I also received: that Christ died for our sins in accordance with the Scriptures, that he was buried, that he was raised on the third day in accordance with the Scriptures, and that he appeared to Cephas, then to the twelve. Then he appeared to more than five hundred brothers at one time, most of whom are still alive, though some have fallen asleep. Then he appeared to James, then to all the apostles. Last of all, as to one untimely born, he appeared also to me. For I am the least of the apostles, unworthy to be called an apostle, because I persecuted the church of God. But by the grace of God I am what I am, and his grace toward me was not in vain. On the contrary, I worked harder than any of them, though it was not I, but the grace of God that is with me. Whether then it was I or they, so we preach and so you believed.

The Gospel

Notice some key facts about the gospel in these verses, starting with its *priority*. In verse 3 Paul may be saying that he delivered the gospel to the Corinthians "first in time." But the translation "as of first importance" fits best with the fact that this chapter is a defense of the gospel against false teaching. The Corinthians should appreciate the priority of the gospel—it is the message through which they "are being saved" (v. 2). Second, consider the textual *foundation* of the gospel. Twice the apostle asserts that his message is "in accordance with the Scriptures" (vv. 3, 4). This phrase indicates that the gospel fulfills God's redemptive promises throughout the Old Testament. So we won't grasp the full significance of the gospel apart from its Old Testament background.

We come thirdly to the actual *content* of the gospel. Starting in verse 3, Paul spells out the content in what may be an early creed setting forth the foundational beliefs of the Christian Church. This gospel summary centers on certain historical events of Jesus's ministry. Yet "in accordance with the Scriptures" breaks up the structure in such a way as to suggest a particular relationship among those events.

9

Main event: that Christ died for our sins
> in accordance with the Scriptures
>
> *Supporting event:* [Gk. and] that he was buried

Main event: [Gk. and] that he was raised on the third day
> in accordance with the Scriptures
>
> *Supporting event:* and that he appeared to Cephas, then
> to the twelve . . . .

So the main events are two: Jesus's death and resurrection. His burial comes in as the evidence that he truly died. Likewise, the eyewitnesses confirm that he truly rose from the dead.[1] In any case, it is plain that the gospel is fundamentally about what Christ accomplished.

But why did he die? That's our next thought—the *purpose* of the gospel, or at least one of its purposes. Paul says that Christ died "for our sins" (v. 3). This short phrase assumes a great deal of theology: that God exists, that man owes him obedience, that man has rebelled against him, that God will punish man as a result, and that man may avert this punishment through an atoning sacrifice God has provided through Christ. The immediate connection with "in accordance with the Scriptures" points to Old Testament sacrificial ritual for more explanation and perhaps specifically to the Suffering Servant prophecy of Isaiah 53.[2]

In addition to assuming theology, "for our sins" *implies* further theology. It raises the question of a person's relationship to sin *after* he has been restored to God through Christ. Does the gospel make provision for that problem as well? We'll begin to answer that question as we look at the human *experience* of the gospel. The Corinthians had "received" (v.1), or "believed" (v. 2), Paul's message. These terms cry out for definition, but again the apostle assumes his readers understand their meanings from past experience. He does make one point about genuine faith, a warning: "and by which you are being saved, if you hold fast to the word I preached to you—unless you believed in vain" (v. 2).

---

[1] Adapted from Fee, *First Epistle to the Corinthians,* 802–9.

[2] Ibid., 803–5; Thiselton, *First Epistle to the Corinthians,* 1190–92.

Several details in this verse deserve our attention. First, the initial Greek verb is translated "are being saved" because it is in the present tense. This phraseology indicates that the Corinthian believers are experiencing ongoing deliverance from sin through the gospel.[3] Second, the Corinthians need to "hold fast" to the gospel. In fact, if the Corinthians fail to do so, their faith will have been "in vain." This ironic remark anticipates the assertions of verses 14 and 17. There, using similar words for "vain," Paul says that if the Corinthians reject the doctrine of the resurrection, they would have believed in vain in that they would be rejecting a truth indispensable to the gospel's saving power.[4]

The end of our passage shows more of what is involved in Christians' experience of the gospel. Here Paul's autobiographical comments illustrate that the gospel transforms the believer, altering his values and redirecting the course of his life. The gospel had taken a man who "persecuted the church of God" (v. 9) and turned him into someone who "worked harder than any of" the other apostles to promote the gospel and the church (v. 10). This dramatic change proved that God's grace had not been "in vain" in Paul's case (v. 10). And lest anyone misunderstand Paul's change as self-produced, he underscores the source of what had happened and what was happening in his life: "it was not I, but the grace of God that is with me" (v. 10).

Application

First Corinthians 15 brims with truth, but what does it have to do with our topic, the application of Scripture? For one, it should move us to "keep the main thing the main thing." The core of the gospel is the death and resurrection of Jesus Christ. We cannot allow our applications of Scripture to take precedence over that message. More than anything else, our lives and our preaching must be conspicuously characterized by

---

[3] Fee, *First Epistle to the Corinthians,* 800, n. 33; Morris, *1 Corinthians,* 200; Thiselton, *First Epistle to the Corinthians,* 1185.

[4] Fee, *First Epistle to the Corinthians,* 801.

a focus on Christ and his atoning work. Yet notice what I just did in saying that—I made an application! I extended to us an historical statement about Paul's ministry to the Corinthians. So even our prioritizing of the gospel constitutes an application.

In addition, since 1 Corinthians 15 teaches that we are saved by faith in what Jesus did, we must guard the gospel from any notion that our efforts—before or after conversion—somehow merit our standing with God or derive from our own ability. At the same time, is not faith itself a kind of application, our response to God's provision? And does not 1 Corinthians 15 also teach that saving faith will transform a person's behavior? Paul himself points us to the answer as he wraps up the chapter with an exhortation: "Therefore, my beloved brothers, be steadfast, immovable, always abounding in the work of the Lord, knowing that in the Lord your labor is not in vain" (v. 58).

We make a vital point when we describe the gospel as a simple message, a truth even young children can understand. We shouldn't, however, be *simplistic* in talking about the gospel. As one commentator puts it, in 1 Corinthians 15 Paul gives the "'bare bones' content of the gospel that saves."[5] The apostle limits his definition this way because that best suits his narrow discussion of the resurrection of believers. Paul doesn't intend this passage as a comprehensive statement about the gospel. And once we consider all the theology that he assumes and implies, we realize that there need be no tension between the gospel and our endeavor to apply the Bible to the specifics of life. In actuality, this endeavor is a necessary outworking of the gospel.

Romans 1

We'll find these conclusions strengthened as we study our second passage, Romans 1. Early on Paul tells the Romans, "So I am eager to preach the gospel to you also who are in Rome" (v. 15). Here the apostle could be talking about evangelizing unbelievers in Rome. In this regard, some

---

[5] Ibid., 802.

commentators hold that the pronoun *you* refers to Paul's readers in their identity as Romans not in their identity as Christians.[6]

While Paul certainly had a passion to preach the gospel to the unsaved, in this verse "you" more naturally refers to the Roman Christians without an identity distinction. The idea would be that in order to become more spiritually mature and productive these believers needed a greater understanding of the gospel.[7] Indeed, the grand exposition of the gospel that we call Romans is a Spirit-inspired letter written to people who had already embraced that gospel.

The Gospel in Romans 1:16–17

As Paul explains his reason for wanting to proclaim the gospel, he articulates the overarching thesis of Romans (vv. 16–17):

> For I am not ashamed of the gospel, for it is the power of God for salvation to everyone who believes, to the Jew first and also to the Greek. For in it the righteousness of God is revealed from faith for faith, as it is written, "The righteous shall live by faith."

This statement famously launches Paul's discussion of the doctrine of justification by grace through faith—God's way of declaring sinful people righteous while upholding his own righteousness through the substitutionary atonement of Jesus Christ.

I treasure the doctrine of justification! My heart is regularly stabilized, strengthened, and renewed by recalling this precious truth. My standing before God is secure because it rests not on my performance but on the righteousness of Christ imputed to my account. I enjoy this status because of God's pure grace—it is free to me, though it was dreadfully costly to Jesus. My earthly life and eternal destiny depend on justification by faith in Christ. This is the only way God has provided

---

[6] Leon Morris follows Frederic Godet in taking this position. See Morris, *Romans,* 65.

[7] Cranfield, *Romans,* 1:86; Kruse, *Romans,* 66; Moo, *Romans,* 62–63. Schreiner sees here both initial evangelism and ongoing discipleship (*Romans,* 52–56).

for people to be accepted by him. I love to meditate on, sing about, and preach on justification. In fact, my favorite hymn exults in this doctrine:

> Jesus, Thy blood and righteousness
> My beauty are, my glorious dress;
> 'Midst flaming worlds, in these arrayed,
> With joy shall I lift up my head.
>
> Bold shall I stand in Thy great day,
> For who aught to my charge shall lay?
> Fully absolved through these I am,
> From sin and fear, from guilt and shame.[8]

For the purposes of this book, however, my focus has to be broader.[9] What we need to ask is whether the gospel is *limited* to the doctrine of justification. We can answer this question by reading further into Romans. Paul's treatment of justification climaxes in 3:21–26. In chapter 4 he defends the doctrine using the example of Abraham's life. Then chapters 5–8 explore the absolute security of those justified by Christ's work. Here we find some new emphases.

Consider this consequence of justification by faith: "We rejoice in our sufferings, knowing that suffering produces endurance, and endurance produces character, and character produces hope, and hope does not put us to shame, because God's love has been poured into our hearts through the Holy Spirit who has been given to us" (5:3–5). Here Paul makes a connection between godly character and assurance. As our character grows through suffering, the more we become persuaded that God has supernaturally intervened in our lives. Consequently, we become more confident that he claims us as his own for all eternity.

---

[8] From "Jesus, Thy Blood and Righteousness," by Nikolaus Ludwig von Zinzendorf (1700–1760), trans. John Wesley (1703–1791).

[9] For a survey of justification, see Barrett, *Complete in Him,* 119–46. For a more comprehensive treatment, see Bridges and Bevington, *Great Exchange,* based on a classic nineteenth-century study by George Smeaton. Another classic is Bonar, *Everlasting Righteousnes.* For a treatment in the context of contemporary controversies, see Schreiner, *Faith Alone.*

Romans 6 also addresses the daily experience of those who have been justified by Christ. Verses 1–11 assert that believers have been delivered from slavery to sin and have been empowered for a new kind of life. We must therefore resist obedience to sinful impulses (vv. 12–13):

> Let not sin therefore reign in your mortal body, to make you obey its passions. Do not present your members to sin as instruments for unrighteousness, but present yourselves to God as those who have been brought from death to life, and your members to God as instruments for righteousness.

Romans 7 explains that believers have also been freed from the enslaving power of God's law. This doesn't mean, however, that we no longer need to follow the morality taught in the law. On the contrary, one purpose for which God saves us is "in order that the righteous requirement of the law might be fulfilled in us, who walk not according to the flesh but according to the Spirit" (8:4). Paul seems to have made this statement to answer Jewish critics who alleged that his gospel encouraged a lawless life. In actuality, the apostle replies, the gospel enables believers to abide by the law's ethical norms through the power of the Holy Spirit.[10] Such a lifestyle is indispensable proof that one has genuinely experienced the gospel (vv. 12-14):

> So then, brothers, we are debtors, not to the flesh, to live according to the flesh. For if you live according to the flesh you will die, but if by the Spirit you put to death the deeds of the body, you will live. For all who are led by the Spirit of God are sons of God.

We could look at more verses, but the ones I've cited are sufficient to show that Romans expounds not only the believer's legal

---

[10] Commentators differ on the meaning of the statement, "in order that the righteous requirement of the law might be fulfilled in us." The position above is defended by many, e.g., Cranfield, *Romans,* 1:383–85; Kruse, *Romans,* 328–30; Schreiner, *Romans,* 404–8; Stott, *Romans,* 221–22. Others hold that the expression refers to justification, e.g., Hodge, *Romans,* 254–55; Moo, *Romans,* 481–85. All agree that the phrase, "who walk not according to the flesh but according to the Spirit," addresses Christian living.

standing (justification) but also his divinely enabled obedience to the Lord (sanctification). The one inevitably leads to the other. Ultimately, the gospel encompasses both elements. It is in every respect "the power of God unto salvation" (1:16): salvation from the penalty *and* the power of sin, along the way to salvation from the very presence of sin.

In fact, some scholars see the structure of Romans 1–8 anticipated in 1:17's quotation of Habakkuk 2:4. The verse says, literally, "The just by faith will live," and the connection would be as follows:

> "The just by faith": 1:18—4:25, emphasis on justification
> "will live": 5:1—8:39, emphasis on sanctification.[11]

This analysis strengthens the link between the gospel and sanctification even further.

The Gospel in Romans 1:1–6

But our explanation of the gospel still isn't broad enough. We need to consider the very first statement about the gospel in Romans 1. While verses 16–17 receive much attention, verses 1–6 are not so well known. In introducing himself to his Roman readers, the author writes,

> Paul, a servant of Christ Jesus, called to be an apostle, set apart for the gospel of God, which he promised beforehand through his prophets in the holy Scriptures, concerning his Son, who was descended from David according to the flesh and was declared to be the Son of God in power according to the Spirit of holiness by his resurrection from the dead, Jesus Christ our Lord, through whom we have received grace and apostleship to bring about the obedience of faith for the sake of his name among all the nations, including you who are called to belong to Jesus Christ.

Surprisingly, this summary of the gospel contains no specific reference to sin, atonement, forgiveness, or justification. The human beneficiaries of the gospel don't appear explicitly until the end of the passage, and even there Paul focuses not on what we receive but on what we render to Christ. What is the apostle doing here?

---

[11] Cranfield, *Romans*, 1:102; Moo, *Encountering*, 86.

To begin with, he gives the same background he gave in 1 Corinthians 15: the gospel is not a Johnny-come-lately message; it had been prophesied in the Old Testament Scriptures (Rom 1:2). It brings to realization an intricate divine plan that God had been gradually revealing for centuries.

Verse 3 states that the subject matter of this plan is God's "Son." Then we read that this Son belongs to the lineage of David. This connects him with the covenant God had made with David, promising that the Davidic dynasty would enjoy permanent rule over Israel and ultimately over the entire world.[12]

Verse 4 plays a key role in this passage. It says that through his resurrection Jesus was "declared to be the Son of God in power." The Greek term translated *declared* means to designate or appoint. The expression *the Son of God in power* doesn't imply that Christ was not a member of the Godhead before the resurrection. What this statement teaches is that through the resurrection Jesus was officially appointed to a *new phase of ministry* as the Son of God. The point of "in power" would not be that the resurrection displayed supernatural power (though it certainly did) but that the resurrection elevated Jesus to a new *position* of power as the Messianic King. This translation captures the idea well: "who was appointed the Son-of-God-in-power" (NET©).[13]

The Obedience of Faith

What is the only appropriate response to this exalted figure? Paul states the response he calls for as he preaches to the nations: "the obedience of faith" (v. 5). What does this phrase mean? Some commentators read "obedience that consists in faith." This is taken to describe conversion,

---

[12] See especially 2 Sam 7; 1 Chr 17; Pss 2, 89, 110; Isa 9:6–7; 11:1–10; Jer 33:19–26.

[13] This is the standard view among recent commentators, e.g., Cranfield, *Romans*, 1:61–64; Kruse, *Romans*, 45–47; Moo, *Romans*, 47–51; Schreiner, *Romans*, 37–45; Stott, *Romans*, 49–51.

meaning that faith (though not a meritorious work) is a kind of obedience—submitting to God and his plan of salvation.[14] Others read "obedience produced by faith." This describes discipleship and means that genuine faith leads to a life of obedience to Christ.[15]

Some expositors combine the two ideas, arguing that "the obedience of faith" encompasses both conversion and discipleship.[16] I find this view compelling because it fits so well with the full scope of what Romans teaches about the gospel—that it not only declares us righteous but also empowers us to practice righteousness. A heart posture of faith-obedience is required for all of this. As a leading Romans scholar says,

> Obedience always involves faith, and faith always involves obedience. They should not be equated, compartmentalized, or made into separate stages of Christian experience. Paul called men and women to a faith that was always inseparable from obedience—for the Savior in whom we believe is nothing less than our Lord—and to an obedience that could never be divorced from faith—for we can obey Jesus as Lord only when we have given ourselves to him in faith. Viewed in this light, the phrase [*the obedience of faith*] captures the full dimension of Paul's apostolic task, a task that was not confined to initial evangelization but that included also the building up and firm establishment of churches.[17]

"The obedience of faith" was no small theme in Paul's ministry.[18] And it's vital to the message of Romans. Related expressions occur at 6:17; 10:3, 16; and 15:18. Then the phrase *the obedience of faith* (1:5) shows up again at the end of Romans (16:26). Thus the expression forms part of a "literary envelope" for the book's exposition of the gospel.

---

[14] Cranfield, *Romans,* 1:66–67; Murray, *Romans,* 1:13–14.

[15] Kruse, *Romans,* 50–52.

[16] Moo, *Romans,* 51–53; Schreiner, 34–35; Stott, 52–53.

[17] Moo, *Romans,* 52–53.

[18] See, for example, 2 Thessalonians 1:8 and the comments on the verse in Green, *Thessalonians,* 291.

This leads us to one more statement in Romans 1:5. Paul ends the verse with the ultimate purpose for which he preaches the gospel and calls people to "the obedience of faith." It is for the sake of Christ's "name," to bring him glory as more and more people rely on and submit to him. Evangelists tend to present the gospel in terms of man's need, sometimes announcing, "God loves you and has a wonderful plan for your life." While emphasizing God's love for us, the gospel more fundamentally proclaims that God loves *Christ* and has a wonderful plan for *his* life. Our experience of the gospel contributes to that bigger purpose.

Micro View and Macro View

Looking back on Romans 1, it may trouble you that the gospel in verses 1–6 doesn't seem quite the same as the gospel in verses 16–17. We can resolve the difficulty by organizing our thoughts around two categories.[19] Some passages of Scripture look at the gospel narrowly, like the telephoto or zoom lens on a camera. This "micro" view concentrates on the individual's experience of the gospel. It can be summarized in the basic truths typically used in witnessing to the unconverted:

- *God* as the holy Creator and King
- *Man* as a condemned sinner
- *Christ* as the sinless sin-bearing substitute, crucified and risen again
- Man's *response* of repentance/faith.

Passages such as Romans 1:16–17 and 1 Corinthians 15:1–10 focus on the micro level.

Other texts view the gospel with a wide-angle lens. This broad or "macro" view deals with God's plan to restore his kingdom on earth through Christ. I'll return to this later in our study, but here I'll summarize it in three points, the main movements of the Bible's storyline:

---

[19] Various contemporary writers have popularized the labels I'm using here. See, for example, DeYoung and Gilbert, *Mission,* 67–139. But the idea of the macro gospel corresponds to a long-standing emphasis on redemptive history in the discipline of biblical theology. I will be dealing with this in various places as I discuss the biblical storyline.

- God's *creation* of his earthly kingdom and human beings as his image-bearing vice-regents
- Humanity's satanically inspired *fall* and its devastating consequences
- God's work of *redemption,* which includes his preparatory work in and through the nation Israel; Christ's incarnation, life, death, resurrection, and ascension; the present unification of Jews and Gentiles in the church; and the consummation of God's redemption in the ultimate restoration of his kingdom, including the final defeat of Satan.

Romans 1:1–6 highlights this macro level. Even 1 Corinthians 15 blends into it, as verses 20–28 predict Jesus's future handing over of the kingdom to God the Father.

Sometimes the Bible uses gospel terminology for the micro level of salvation or aspects of it (e.g., 1 Cor 1:17–18; Col 1:15) and sometimes for the macro level or aspects of it (e.g., Mark 1:14–15; Eph 3:6–7). Other passages collapse the two levels somewhat (e.g., Acts 20:24–25; Gal 3:8). Yet we aren't dealing with multiple gospels. There is only one gospel, though it can be viewed from the perspective of personal redemption or from the broader perspective of cosmic redemption. The two overlap at many points. More specifically, the macro encompasses the micro. In order to enjoy the future blessings on the macro level, one must experience salvation presently on the micro level. Although we can distinguish these two dimensions of the gospel, we can't ultimately separate them.

Transformed by the Gospel

The time has come to articulate what has been emerging as the thesis of this chapter: *man's moral transformation is a key component of the gospel.* We've encountered this truth in both the macro and micro views of the gospel. On the macro level, God's plan to restore his kingdom on earth includes bringing individual people into subjection to Jesus Christ. "The obedience of faith" makes this point. Or as Colossians 1:13 says, the Father "has delivered us from the domain of darkness and transferred us to the kingdom of his beloved Son." Relative to the micro level, once God has *declared* us righteous in Christ he begins to *make* us righteous as well. Romans 6:18 states it even more strongly: believers are "slaves of righteousness." As a result, we strive to apply the teaching of Scripture to the details of our lives.

We could explore at length the connection between the gospel and moral transformation or sanctification. Multiple passages state and further develop the concepts we've observed in 1 Corinthians 15 and Romans 1. These include texts that may not use the "gospel" word family but do use related terminology such as "salvation," "grace," and "Christ." The connection between the gospel and moral transformation is implicit in passages that tie the gospel message to the themes of judgment (e.g., Rom 2:16) and God's law (e.g., 1 Tim 1:8–11). It's also implicit when unsaved people are called to repentance, an inward turn regarding the general orientation of one's life—from sin to God.[20] Similarly, in the Great Commission Jesus told his original disciples to make other disciples, followers who are taught to obey everything Christ commanded (Matt 28:18–20).

To be sure, an unregenerate person won't understand the gospel's many moral implications for his life. Yet as evident in our discussion of "the obedience of faith," conversion does include a basic posture of yieldedness to Christ. This is a radical moral shift, which is why God himself must grant people repentance and faith (Acts 11:18; Phil 1:29).

Consider some other indications of the gospel's moral transformation. The gospel brings us to experience the New Covenant (2 Cor 3:4—4:6), and one provision of this covenant is that God's law is written on our hearts (Jer 31:31–34; Heb 10:14–18). Furthermore, multiple passages declare that a fundamental purpose God has in salvation is perfecting us in his image, making us holy, enabling us to carry out good

---

[20] See, for example, Matt 3:1, 8; Mark 1:14–15; Acts 2:36–38; 14:15; 20:18–27; 26:20.

works.[21] As a result, to a significant degree our assurance of salvation flows from our progress in godliness.[22]

Naturally, the New Testament frequently links our lifestyle choices with gospel truth. Philippians 1:27 says straightforwardly, "Only let your manner of life be worthy of the gospel of Christ."[23] In this regard, theologians often distinguish between *indicatives* and *imperatives.* Indicatives declare what Christ has done for us and who we are in him. Imperatives issue commands that we should obey as a result. We must maintain the biblical balance between indicatives and imperatives. Imperatives apart from indicatives leave one demoralized and defeated. Yet indicatives alone do not accomplish God's redemptive plan.

The total gospel message includes *both* indicatives *and* imperatives. For the Christian, "God's commands have now become God's enablings."[24] Here's another way to say that: it is *good news* when God says, "Through Christ I have graciously delivered you from bondage to sin, and I have graciously given you all the resources you need to live a life of obedience. Now take advantage of those resources and obey me!" We ought to appreciate this since our whole reason for existence is inseparably tied to obedience. The gospel empowers us to do what we were created to do in the first place—live under God's benevolent rule, display his image, exercise dominion over the earth, glorify and enjoy him. We should view this all as *great* news!

We won't, of course, reach perfection in this life. "What we will be has not yet appeared" (1 John 3:2). This verse implies that struggle

---

[21] See, for example, Rom 8:28–30; 2 Cor 5:14–15; Eph 1:4; 2:10; 5:26–27; Col 1:21–29; 1 Thess 4:7; Titus 2:11–14; 1 Pet 2:24.

[22] See, for example, Gal 5:19–21; Heb 12:12–17; Jas 2:14–26; 2 Pet 1:3–11; 1 John 2–3; Rev 21:8.

[23] Parallel statements appear in passages such as Rom 12:1–2; 1 Cor 6:18–20; Eph 4:1; Col 3:1–3; 1 Pet 1:13—2:2; 2:9–11.

[24] Bruce, *Romans,* 164.

and some degree of failure will remain a sad reality until we see our Savior face to face. In fact, the more we grow the more aware we become of our sins, and the more they grieve us. I'll develop these truths further in our next chapter. Nevertheless, our overriding attitude reflects 1 John 3:3: "And everyone who thus hopes in him purifies himself as he is pure." Thankfully, the gospel provides for ongoing cleansing from sin (1:9). But we don't constantly wallow in our weakness. Believers' hearts have been changed so that we love God and our lives come to be characterized by obedience to his commands.

Some of these commands will be extremely challenging, but within the context of gospel-engendered love we won't find them burdensome (5:3). Our attitude increasingly mirrors Christ's when he said, "My food is to do the will of him who sent me and to accomplish his work" (John 4:34). To express the matter poetically,

I will not work my soul to save,
For that my Lord has done;
But I will work like any slave
For love of his dear Son.[25]

Yes, the gospel boldly announces, "Done!" Yet a one-syllable summary can't ultimately convey the fullness of God's glorious redemption. Or we could put it this way: one of the things that has been "done" is that Christ has given us a new life and a new ability to obey. We are not saved *by* our works, but we are saved *for* good works (Eph 2:8–10). Salvation is so mighty and so complete that it not only *reconciles* us to our Creator but also *rewires* us so that we find our joy in pleasing him.

A Voice from the Past

Preachers and theologians have developed this theme throughout church history, but I've been particularly helped by the teaching of the English Puritans. They spoke of "gospel holiness" or "evangelical obedience." This was their way of distinguishing divinely enabled

---

[25] Author unknown; cited in Thomas, *Romans,* 329.

sanctification from self-reliant morality that sought to gain merit with God. John Owen (1616–1683), the foremost Puritan theologian, described it as follows:

> This whole matter of sanctification and holiness is peculiarly joined with and limited unto the *doctrine, truth,* and *grace* of the gospel; for holiness is nothing but the implanting, writing, and realizing of the gospel in our souls. . . . There neither is, nor ever was, in the world, nor ever shall be, the least dram of holiness, but what, flowing from Jesus Christ, is communicated by the Spirit, according to the truth and promise of the gospel. There may be something like it as to its outward acts and effects (at least some of them), something that may wear its livery [distinctive dress] in the world, that is but the fruit of men's own endeavours in compliance with their convictions; but holiness it is not, nor of the same kind or nature with it. And this men are very apt to deceive themselves withal.[26]

Within this gospel context, God calls on believers to obey his commands. In Owen's time, however, some balked at this: "'If holiness be our *duty,* there is no room for *grace* in this matter; and if it be an effect of *grace,* there is no place for *duty.*'" Owen replies:

> It is true, our works and grace are opposed in the matter of justification, as utterly inconsistent; if it be of works it is not of grace, and if it be of grace it is not of works, as our apostle argues, Rom xi. 6. [But] our duty and God's grace are nowhere opposed in the matter of sanctification, yea, the one doth absolutely presuppose the other. Neither can we perform our duty herein without the grace of God; nor doth God give us this grace unto any other end but that we may rightly perform our duty.[27]

Later Owen ties the Christian's pursuit of holiness to the three mediatorial offices of Christ. As Priest, Christ came to remove the sin that separated us from God. So how could his people be content to remain in sin? As Prophet, Christ came to reveal God and his will.

---

[26] Owen, *Holy Spirit,* in *Works,* 3:371.

[27] Ibid., 384.

Embracing Christ entails following what he says. Finally, as King, Christ came to subdue our enemies and free us from them. Sin is one of those enemies, so when we yield to sin we are going against his kingly work.[28]

Conclusion

The gospel frees us from the impossible burden of obeying God in order to be accepted by him. But that doesn't mean that the more gospel-centered or Christ-centered we are, the less concerned we will be about our conduct. On the contrary, the more we grasp the gospel, the more intent we'll be on obeying God's Word. The gospel-thrilled heart yearns to experience more and more of the gospel's transformation.

I'm not suggesting that all our contemporary applications of Scripture belong to the definition of the gospel. What I am saying is that the gospel causes us to become serious about honoring Christ in every aspect of our lives, through the power of the Holy Spirit. Specific applications are the product of this gospel-engendered earnestness, practical implementations of gospel imperatives.

As this chapter closes, I want to share some comments along these lines from Pastor Kevin DeYoung. He has helped to popularize the "gospel-centered" movement of the early twenty-first century but has issued some striking warnings about it.

> The hole in our holiness is that we don't really care much about it. Passionate exhortation to pursue gospel-driven holiness is barely heard in most of our churches. . . .
>
> My fear is that as we rightly celebrate, and in some quarters rediscover, all that Christ has saved us *from,* we are giving little thought and making little effort concerning all that Christ has saved us *to.* Shouldn't those most passionate about the gospel and God's glory also be those most dedicated to the pursuit of godliness? I worry that there is an enthusiasm gap and no one seems to mind. . . .
>
> There is a gap between our love for the gospel and our love for godliness. This must change. It's not pietism, legalism, or fundamentalism

---

[28] Ibid., 628–41

to take holiness seriously. It's the way of all those who have been called to a holy calling by a holy God.[29]

Undoubtedly, our role in applying God's Word can be portrayed in such a way that it ends up competing with the gospel of God's grace. But the solution to that problem isn't to pit application against the gospel. Instead we must root application *in* a biblically robust gospel, especially the doctrine of sanctification. The next two chapters will consider that doctrine in some detail. For now, I encourage you to ponder the thrust of our opening chapter as expressed in another little poem:

> To run and work the law commands,
> Yet gives me neither feet nor hands;
>
> But better news the gospel brings:
> It bids me fly and gives me wings.[30]

---

[29] DeYoung, *Hole in Our Holiness,* 10–11, 21. On the gospel-centered movement, see Hansen, *Young, Restless, Reformed.* Compare Buice, *New Calvinism;* Dutcher, *Killing Calvinism.*

[30] Author disputed; cited in Bruce, *Romans,* 164. For an in-depth study closely related to the basic thesis of this chapter, see Green, *Covenant and Commandment.* For a devotional tool to help keep the pursuit of sanctification rooted in the gospel, see Vincent, *Gospel Primer.*

Chapter 2

Surveying Sanctification

"I often pray, Lord, make me as holy as a pardoned sinner can be made."[1] So testified the beloved Scottish pastor, Robert Murray M'Cheyne (1813–1843). And so chapter 1 explained: the gospel incites in us a yearning for holy living. But the good news is even better than that. God doesn't leave our longings unfulfilled. Through the gospel he provides the enabling and resources we need in order to move toward the goal of holiness. Chapters 2 and 3 develop that truth as we continue to survey the theological context for our applications of Scripture. Specifically, we will analyze the biblical doctrine of sanctification. This chapter will define terms and then overview three aspects of sanctification.

Defining Our Terms

What comes to your mind when you hear the terms *holiness* and *sanctification?* Maybe they generate a negative reaction. Perhaps you associate these words largely with annoying rules or unreasonable prohibitions. They might conjure up images of overbearing discipline or feelings of guilt and discouragement. It's regrettable if your past experience has led to these kinds of impressions. I hope you've begun to see that holiness and sanctification are profoundly positive words. And I trust this sense will grow as we define the terms more closely.[2]

---

[1] Cited in Bonar, *Robert Murray M'Cheyne*, 159.

[2] For a fuller discussion of the biblical concept of holiness, see Jaeggli, *More Like the Master*, 19–78.

27

The English words *holiness* and *sanctification* come from different roots but share a fundamental concept. That concept surfaces when we look at the biblical terms that are translated by the English terms. In the Old Testament the relevant Hebrew words are built from a single root.[3] The same is true of the primary Greek words rendered by holiness and sanctification terminology in the New Testament.[4] The Hebrew and Greek roots do not mean sinlessness or perfection. It's commonly said that their basic idea is "apartness" or "separateness." That approaches the truth but doesn't go far enough. We must ask what one is separated *to* and separated *from*.

The Holiness of God

In order to answer these questions, we need to understand the holiness of God himself. When biblical writers describe God as holy, often they're communicating the broad concept that he is incomparable or unique. For example, 1 Samuel 2:2 says, "There is none holy like the LORD: for there is none besides you; there is no rock like our God." More than any other writer, the prophet Isaiah emphasized this truth. "To whom then will you compare me, that I should be like him? says the Holy One" (40:25). "For thus says the One who is high and lifted up, who inhabits eternity, whose name is Holy: 'I dwell in the high and holy place'" (57:15a). Such verses are asserting that God is separate from anyone and anything that isn't God. In other words, he is the only one in his category, one of a kind.

In this general sense, God's holiness means the totality of what makes him God. Two verses in Amos are helpful here. In Amos 6:8 we read, "The Lord GOD has sworn by himself," or "by his person." A parallel statement in Amos 4:2 says, "The Lord GOD has sworn by his holiness." These verses equate God's holiness with his entire person.

---

[3] The main forms are the verb *qādăsh*, the noun *qōdesh*, and the adjective *qādôsh*.

[4] The main forms are the verb *hagiazō*, the noun *hagiasmos*, and the adjective *hagios*.

Due to such evidence, scholars conclude that holiness "can be used almost as a synonym of deity."[5] Some identify this meaning as God's "majesty-holiness."[6] For a New Testament example we can look at the Lord's Prayer. When we pray that God's name would be "hallowed" (passive of *hagiazō*), we're asking that his character would be honored as distinctive or unique—that God would receive the recognition that he deserves as deity (Matt 6:9).

Yet sometimes God's holiness has a narrower sense. Focusing on issues of morality, holiness can mean that God is separate from anything inconsistent with his character. Specifically, he separates from moral evil. Habakkuk 1 contains a classic text in this regard. Verse 12 describes Yahweh as "my Holy One," and then verse 13 says that he is "of purer eyes than to see evil" approvingly. Here God's holiness is connected with his moral purity. This purity leads him not only to withdraw from sinners but also to punish them if they do not repent. "Man is humbled, and each one is brought low, and the eyes of the haughty are brought low. But the LORD of hosts is exalted in justice, and the Holy God shows himself holy in righteousness" (Isa 5:15–16).

Isaiah's famous vision of God reflects both definitions of divine holiness. Several features highlight God's uniqueness/majesty. He was "sitting upon a throne, high and lifted up; and the train of his robe filled the temple" (6:1). The attending angels had no sin to make them ashamed in God's presence, yet they covered their faces because he was so much more exalted than they (v. 2). When the angels cried out to one another, "Holy, holy, holy, is the LORD of hosts; the whole earth is full of his glory!" (v. 3), "the foundations of the thresholds shook at the voice of him who called, and the house was filled with smoke" (v. 4).

Isaiah's response to this vision wasn't to burst out in a hymn of praise. Instead he felt stunned by an overwhelming sense of guilt: "Woe

---

[5] Naudé, "קדש," 879.

[6] Berkhof, *Systematic Theology*, 73.

is me! For I am lost; for I am a man of unclean lips, and I dwell in the midst of a people of unclean lips; for my eyes have seen the King, the LORD of hosts!" (v. 5). God's holiness—in the sense of his purity—made Isaiah painfully conscious of his own impurity. Thankfully, the Lord immediately responded with cleansing (vv. 6–7) so that Isaiah could remain in his presence and then be sent on a mission (vv. 8–13).

Holiness as Sacredness

Each definition of God's holiness has a counterpart in the holiness of his people. Actually, the Old Testament regularly uses the first definition even for inanimate things, and these serve as helpful illustrations of our holiness. When God places certain things in a special connection with himself and dedicates them to some special service for him, they are described with holiness terminology. We see this the first time the verb *make holy* (or *sanctify*) occurs in the Bible: "So God blessed the seventh day and made it holy" (Gen 2:3). He distinguished the seventh day from the other six. Every day belongs to him, but the seventh day came to belong to him in a special sense.

Note also the first time the noun *holiness* appears. At the burning bush Yahweh told Moses, "Do not come near; take your sandals off your feet, for the place on which you are standing is holy ground [lit. ground of holiness]" (Exod 3:5). A piece of land does not have the ability to obey or disobey God. The issue here is not specifically separation from sin. Rather, this piece of land was separate from other pieces of land—unique—because God was manifesting his special presence there.

Leviticus 10:10 tells the priests to "distinguish between the holy and the common." So the opposite of the holy is the common. In the Old Testament Yahweh removes many objects from common use and places them in a unique Godward category. The tabernacle furniture and implements are key examples (e.g., Exod 40:9–13). In such cases we can use the verb *consecrate* to express God's action and the adjective *sacred* to describe the status of what has been consecrated.

Amazingly, God consecrates his people, setting us apart as sacred. Do you view yourself in this light? We would expect that the Levitical priests would have a sacred status (see Lev 21). Yet God describes the entire nation Israel in this way: "For you are a people holy to the LORD your God. The LORD your God has chosen you to be a people for his treasured possession, out of all the peoples who are on the face of the earth" (Deut 7:6; cf. Exod 19:5–6). And the New Testament says the same about the church of Jesus Christ: "But you are a chosen race, a royal priesthood, a holy nation, a people for his own possession" (1 Pet 2:9a, adapting the language of Exod 19:5–6 and Deut 7:6).

Such passages should cause us to view holiness as a priceless privilege. If you're a Christian, God hasn't allowed you to go your own way, away from his presence and blessing. He has distinguished you, setting you apart for a unique relationship with himself. It's hard to fathom, but it's true—God views his people as sacred, as his special treasure. Marvel at the dignity of your position! Revel in the grace God has lavished on you in elevating you to this position!

But *why* did the Lord separate us unto himself? It wasn't only so that we could enjoy his acceptance. Our sacred status is tied to the broader biblical teaching that God created man in his own image (Gen 1:26–27). As I pointed out in chapter 1, when he restores sinners to himself, God begins to reconstruct that image, to reproduce in us multiple dimensions of his character.

Yahweh is targeting this purpose when he commands the Israelites, "Be holy, for I am holy" (Lev 11:44–45; 19:2; 20:7, 26). Sinclair Ferguson helpfully explains the background to this command:

> The indicatives and imperatives of the Old Testament covenant relationship are . . . not cold formalities. They have a distinctively familial connotation. They aim at reproducing the family likeness—godliness, or god-likeness—in the people. Just as the heart of the covenantal relationship is 'I will be your God, you will be my people', or 'I am your Father, you are my son', so the heart of sanctification in the Old Testament is an application of this: 'I the Lord [your Father] am holy;

therefore you [my children] are to express the family likeness and image—you are to be holy too'.[7]

Within the context of the New Covenant, Peter *applies* Leviticus' teaching to the church: "But as he who called you is holy, you also be holy in all your conduct, since it is written, 'You shall be holy, for I am holy'" (1 Pet 1:15–16). Through Christ we have been elevated to a holy status so that we can display God's holy character.

Holiness as Purity

Now we can appreciate the second definition of holiness: purity. When God sets people apart for himself and works to make them like himself, it's only natural that he calls on them to stay away from whatever displeases him. This is why Leviticus specifies its holiness motto with lengthy lists of things that the Israelites were to avoid (see, for example, Lev 19). And Peter quotes this motto to substantiate a prohibition: "As obedient children, do not be conformed to the passions of your former ignorance" (1 Pet 1:14). Paul likewise connects holiness with separation from sin. "Let us cleanse ourselves from every defilement of body and spirit, bringing holiness to completion in the fear of God" (2 Cor 7:1). According to the writer of Hebrews, holiness is so valuable that God is willing to chasten sin out of us. "He disciplines us for our good, that we may share his holiness" (Heb 12:10).

When you think about holiness and sanctification, always keep together the ideas of sacredness and purity. This is behind the statement I quoted from Deuteronomy 7. Verse 6 highlights the Israelites' "specialness" to motivate them for a sobering task: exterminating the Canaanites so they wouldn't tempt God's people away from their unique relationship with him (vv. 1–5). As it relates to the church, 1 Peter 2:9 also makes a practical connection. The glorious titles in the verse serve this purpose: "That you may proclaim the excellencies of him who called you out of darkness into his marvelous light."

---

[7] Ferguson, *Holy Spirit*, 140–41.

So holiness and sanctification have to do with being set apart as God's special possession. He has distinguished us out of humanity so that we can enjoy a special relationship with him, be made like him, and represent him to others. This requires that we separate from moral evil. We need to view this "negative" dimension of holiness in the positive light of our glorious position as God's sacred people. We'll be willing to separate *from* sin if we are in awe that we've been separated *to* God.[8]

Three Aspects of Sanctification

Now that we've covered basic definitions, we can outline the doctrine of sanctification as a whole. When we compare the various passages on this doctrine, we discover some complexity. The Christian's sanctification consists of three aspects that amount to three chronological phases.

Past Sanctification

We call the first phase of sanctification *past* because it was instituted at the time of our conversion. It overlaps with what we've already seen about the Lord's separating us unto himself. It refers to a fixed status of holiness in which God has placed us, and this status determines the Lord's overall perspective of us. According to John Murray, when the New Testament uses holiness/sanctification terminology for the believer, most of the time the focus is on the past aspect of sanctification.[9] David Peterson understands virtually all the references in this way.[10]

---

[8] These concepts appear in passages that don't use the holiness word groups. One such passage is Ezra 6:21. This verse refers to a group of people who celebrated the Passover alongside the Jews who had returned from the Babylonian exile: "Every one who had joined them and separated [*bādăl*] himself *from* the uncleanness of the peoples of the land *to* worship the LORD, the God of Israel" (emphasis added). Here again we see the "negative" and "positive" dimensions of holiness inseparably linked.

[9] Murray, *Collected Writings of John Murray, Volume Two*, 277.

[10] This is the basic thesis of Peterson's *Possessed by God*. Though Peterson overstates his case at times, his book remains a genuinely helpful corrective to views that overemphasize the believer's role in sanctification.

Some of the references are hard to interpret conclusively (e.g., 1 Pet 1:2), but many clearly speak of past sanctification. The New Testament describes Christians as "saints" or "holy ones." This includes even the Corinthian Christians, with all their failures and foibles (1 Cor 1:2; 6:1–2; 2 Cor 1:1; cf. 1 Cor 3:16–17). Paul says that these brothers and sisters were already sanctified (1 Cor 6:11). Acts 20:32 and 26:18 similarly describe believers as those who have already been sanctified.

How can this be? In view of our fallenness, how can God call us saints? Some respond by linking past sanctification with justification specifically. This is what writers sometimes have in mind when they refer to past sanctification as *positional sanctification.*[11] In other words, God views us as saints because he has forgiven our sins and has imputed to us Christ's righteousness. Hebrews uses sanctification terminology along these lines. It says that we have been sanctified through Christ's blood-shedding death, paralleling this sanctification with our forgiveness and access into God's presence (9:13–14; 10:1–10; 13:9–13).

Many explain past sanctification not in terms of justification but in terms of a crucial theme we'll take up shortly. That is the truth that through union with Christ we've been removed from the enslaving dominion of sin and have been brought under God's lordship (Rom. 6).[12] Some prefer the phrase *definitive sanctification* for this idea, though *positional sanctification* can carry this meaning as well.[13]

We should probably view past sanctification as a multi-faceted divine work. One could argue that both our justification and our transfer into God's dominion place us in a unique Godward category.

---

[11] Demarest, *Cross and Salvation,* 407–8.

[12] A standard statement can be found in Murray, *Collected Writings of John Murray, Volume Two,* 277–93. His view is echoed in several contemporary systematic theologies, e.g., Grudem, *Systematic Theology,* 747–48. Grudem argues that Hebrews' use of sanctification terminology is unique to its context and not directly related to the broader doctrine of sanctification (748, n. 3).

[13] Hoekema, *Saved by Grace,* 202–6.

Peterson, for one, concludes that "[past] sanctification involves forgiveness, cleansing, and a reorientation of life that results from trusting in Christ."[14] Whatever the precise explanation, let us be humbled and moved to worship at the thought that the holy God regards us as saints.

Future Sanctification

In the future, believers will experience sanctification in totality. Someday we'll reflect our sacredness perfectly, free from even the possibility of sinning. Paul's prayers for the Thessalonians point to this phase using holiness terminology (1 Thess 3:11–13; 5:23–24; cf. Eph 5:27). But the New Testament employs a variety of terms, general and specific, to speak of future sanctification. Philippians 1:6 provides a cherished illustration: "And I am sure of this, that he who began a good work in you will bring it to completion at the day of Jesus Christ."

Future sanctification will occur in two stages. Upon physical death the Christian's spirit enters the presence of God (2 Cor 5:8; Phil 1:23). Hebrews 12:23 describes believers in that state as "the spirits of the righteous made perfect." But at the resurrection even our bodies will be sanctified, delivered entirely from the curse of sin (Rom 8:18–23; 1 Cor 15:51–57; Phil 3:20–21). This event, known as *glorification*, will culminate God's plan to conform us to Christ's image (Rom 8:28–30; Col 3:4). "Beloved, we are God's children now, and what we will be has not yet appeared; but we know that when he appears we shall be like him, because we shall see him as he is" (1 John 3:2).

Present Sanctification

As you would expect, present sanctification occurs between the poles of past and future sanctification. Here our earthly experience becomes more conformed to the holy status we enjoy through past sanctification.

---

[14] Peterson, *Possessed by God,* 67. McCune comes to a similar position (*Systematic Theology, Volume 3,* 125–29). Hoekema objects to including justification in past sanctification because he does not want justification and sanctification to become confused (*Saved by Grace,* 206). I'm not convinced that such confusion necessarily follows.

Likewise, God moves us toward the goal that we will reach at future sanctification. When people use the word *sanctification* without a qualifier, they are typically talking about the present phase. In addition, present sanctification is often called *progressive sanctification* because it is a gradual, lifelong process of development. This process includes the possibility of sin and setbacks within a broad context of advance.

Progressive sanctification has been illustrated in various ways. Picture someone walking up a stairwell while playing with a yo-yo. The yo-yo is moving up and down on its string, but it's still going upward overall. Or remember the last time you hiked up a mountain. You were generally ascending, but along the way you went down and up several ravines. You also followed trails that zigzagged instead of taking you on a direct route. Maybe some of those trails proved to be dead ends, and you had to retrace your steps and find a better path. This happens in progressive sanctification as well.

A Gradual Process

Some views of the Christian life end up minimizing the progressiveness of sanctification. In particular, some have taught that through a post-conversion crisis experience God launches Christians into a life of more-or-less unbroken obedience to him.[15] While initially attractive, such perfectionistic theologies have left many believers disillusioned and defeated. This problem highlights the need to understand accurately the nature of present sanctification.

Several lines of biblical evidence indicate that present sanctification is a gradual process. First, the New Testament speaks of wrong attitudes and actions as an all-too-real possibility throughout the Christian's life.[16] Sanctification entails a continuing battle between sinful

---

[15] For a helpful survey and critique of these views, see Packer, *Keep in Step*, 101–37; cf. Naselli, *No Quick Fix*.

[16] This point stands whether Romans 7 is describing the struggles of a believer, an unbeliever, or both. Dealing with this passage is beyond the scope of my discussion. See Wilder, *Perspectives*.

desires and the Spirit's desires (Gal 5:17). Sin is a force that must be actively resisted (Rom 6:12–13). James says bluntly, "We all stumble in many ways" (Jas 3:2). No wonder Jesus taught his disciples to pray regularly, "Forgive us our sins" (Luke 11:4; cf. Matt 6:12).

In his first epistle John makes a strong assertion about ongoing sin, apparently in response to some who were teaching otherwise. First John 1:8 states, "If we say we have no sin, we deceive ourselves, and the truth is not in us." John's Gospel uses the phrase "to have sin" four times, and each time it refers to being guilty of committing particular sins (9:41; 15:22, 24; 19:11). That seems to be its meaning in 1 John 1:8 too: "If we say we do not bear the guilt of sin, we are deceiving ourselves and the truth is not in us" (NET©).[17] First John 1:10 restates the idea of verse 8 in different words: "If we say we have not sinned, we make him a liar, and his word is not in us." Thankfully, sandwiched between these two verses is the assurance that God forgives those who confess their sins (v. 9). John "portrays authentic Christian living as involving honest and ongoing acknowledgement of one's sins."[18]

Also pointing to the process of sanctification are the many imperatives God issues to Christians. Obedience to such directives isn't automatic. It requires a choice of the will against other alternatives. Why would the New Testament's repeated commands and exhortations be necessary if sinning were not a significant possibility?

More importantly, several key statements about present sanctification directly describe a process. Second Corinthians 3:18 speaks of "being transformed" into Christ's image "from one degree of glory to another." First John 3:3 says, "And everyone who thus hopes in him [Christ] purifies himself as he is pure." In each verse the Greek verb is

---

[17] Kruse, *Letters of John*, 66, 70. The parallels in the Gospel of John make this view more likely than the common idea that verse 8 is dealing with a claim not to have a "sin nature." See, for example, Burdick, *Letters of John*, 125, 128.

[18] Kruse, *Letters of John*, 68.

in the present tense, indicating an ongoing activity. Hebrews 12:14 commands Christians to *strive* for holiness. Many other passages depict present sanctification in terms of growing, maturing, being renewed, and increasingly abounding with virtues. As Peter urges, "Grow in the grace and knowledge of our Lord and Savior Jesus Christ" (2 Pet 3:18).[19]

Finally, consider Paul's celebrated testimony in Philippians 3. He explicitly states that he has not reached perfection (vv. 12a, 13). Nevertheless, he is "straining forward to what lies ahead" (v. 12b). The apostle also says, "I press on toward the goal for the prize of the upward call of God in Christ Jesus" (v. 14). This is not the language of arrival but of pursuit and improvement.

Conclusion

By way of encouragement, this chapter has shown that holiness is a privilege and that sanctification is a process. These truths give us the right vantage point as our study continues. They keep us both positive and realistic as we apply the Bible to daily life. They spur us on to sober-minded yet hope-filled gospel obedience.

---

[19] Other examples include Rom 5:3–4; 12:2; 2 Cor 4:16; Eph 4:13–6; Phil 1:9–11; Col 1:9–11; 3:10; 1 Thess 3:12; 4:1; Jas 1:2–4; 1 Pet 2:2; 2 Pet 1:5–8.

Chapter 3

Become Who You Are

The Christian's applications of Scripture are a function of progressive sanctification. We need a fuller view of this before getting into details of application. Building on the foundation of chapters 1 and 2, this chapter serves as a primer on progressive sanctification, drawing together various strands that have surfaced in our discussion and adding some others.[1]

The Goal of Sanctification

I've already noted the goal of sanctification, but explaining it a bit further will give it proper emphasis. As a means of bringing glory to himself, God made human beings in his image and appointed us to rule the world as his representatives (Gen 1:26–28; Ps 8). To a finite but still astonishing degree, we were created to mirror many of God's perfections. The image of God encompasses every way in which we can reflect his character. The opening chapters of Genesis suggest several of these points of similarity: our moral faculties (2:16–17), our intellectual and creative abilities (2:19–20, 23), and our capacity for fellowship with other image-bearers (2:20–24). Most delightfully, likeness to God enables us to enjoy fellowship with him (3:8–9).[2]

---

[1] For more on sanctification, the following works helpfully blend theology and practice: Berg, *Changed into his Image;* Bridges, *Discipline of Grace;* Chapell, *Holiness by Grace;* Davis, *Infinite Journey;* Ferguson, *Devoted to God;* Lane and Tripp, *How People Change.* The older work by Ryle, *Holiness,* is also accessible. For a Puritan classic, see Marshall, *Gospel Mystery of Sanctification.*

[2] For more on the image of God, see Grudem, *Systematic Theology,* 442–49. For a full-length treatment, see Hoekema, *Created in God's Image.*

Sin has separated us from God, however, marring his image and preventing us from successfully fulfilling our calling (Rom 3:23; Eph 4:17–19). So a major goal of God's plan of salvation is to restore his image in man (Eph 4:24; Col 3:10). Progressive sanctification is the way in which God is presently pursuing this goal. More specifically, we are being conformed to Jesus Christ, whose humanity constitutes the ultimate expression of God's image (John 1:14; 2 Cor 3:18; 4:4, 6).

God will achieve the goal of sanctification when he makes us as similar to Christ as it is possible for humans to be (Rom 8:29a). "This is the highest end conceivable for created beings, the highest end conceivable not only by men but also by God Himself. God Himself could not contemplate or determine a higher destiny for his creatures."[3] Yet our bliss will contribute to an even greater goal with reference to Christ: "In order that he might be the firstborn among many brothers" (Rom 8:29b). In other words, Christ will receive eternal glory for all the goodness of his own character that has been reproduced in us. Hallelujah!

The Source of Sanctification

That sanctification belongs to *God's* plan of salvation indicates that he is its source. Various biblical prayers, benedictions, and doxologies emphatically recognize that God is the one who does the sanctifying. I find Hebrews 13:20–21 especially reassuring:

> Now may the God of peace who brought again from the dead our Lord Jesus, the great shepherd of the sheep, by the blood of the eternal covenant, equip you with everything good that you may do his will, working in us that which is pleasing in his sight, through Jesus Christ, to whom be glory forever and ever. Amen.

Paul's epistles are rich with such prayers, and we should use them to feed our hope[4]

---

[3] Murray, *Collected Writings of John Murray, Volume Two,* 316.

[4] See, for example, Phil 1:9–11; Col 1:9–11; 1 Thess 3:11–13; 5:23–24; 2 Thess 1:11–12. For a helpful study, see Carson, *Praying with Paul.*

Adding to the encouragement, each member of the Godhead is involved in sanctifying believers. Paul's prayer in Ephesians 3:14–19 illustrates this handily. Its ultimate request is that the Ephesians would be "filled with all the fullness of God" (v. 19), meaning that they would fully possess God's moral character.[5] The prayer is addressed to *the Father* (vv. 14–15). But it includes a request for internal strengthening by *the Spirit* (v. 16). It also asks for a greater experience of the presence and love of *Christ* (vv. 17–19). The entire Trinity works within us and grows us!

Yet it is the Holy Spirit who especially functions as our sanctifier. The Spirit empowers us to resist sinful tendencies and display godly character qualities (Rom 8:13; Gal 5:16–26). His influence results in right responses to God and to other people (Eph 5:18—6:9). He progressively transforms us into the image of Christ (2 Cor 3:18).

The Basis of Sanctification

We come now to the foundational provision God has made so that we can grow in holiness: our union with the Lord Jesus Christ. Though often underappreciated, union with Christ has been well described as "the fundamental idea which underlies the whole range of the Epistles, and gives the specific character of their doctrine."[6] We could go so far as to say that union with Christ constitutes the essence of our relationship with God, the "heart and soul" of the entire Christian life.

Perhaps we overlook this concept because many of its biblical expressions take the form of short phrases such as "in Christ" and "in him." Such phrases occur over 200 times in the writings of Paul alone.[7] That this language is so pervasive and is connected with so many different ideas should compel us to consider it closely. As we do so, we'll appreciate why Hoekema concluded, "Once you have had your eyes

---

[5] Hoehner, *Ephesians,* 491.

[6] Bernard, *Progress of Doctrine,* 177.

[7] Demarest, *Cross and Salvation,* 313.

opened to this concept of union with Christ, you will find it almost everywhere in the New Testament."[8]

In eternity past, when the Father chose to save us he did so in Christ, in connection with him, on the basis of what he would do (Eph 1:4). What Christ did in history was to join himself with us in the incarnation (John 1:14), assuming a genuine human nature so that as our substitute he could achieve everything God required of human beings. As a man, Christ faced temptation successfully (Heb 4:15) and lived in submission to God's law (Gal 4:4). His humanity also enabled him to suffer God's wrath in our place on the Cross (2 Cor 5:21; Heb 2:14).

Then by faith—mysteriously but truly—we were personally united with Christ at conversion. As a result, all the benefits of his redemptive work become ours (Eph 1:3). Every element of our salvation we enjoy in Christ. First Corinthians 1:30 provides the classic summary statement: "And because of him you are in Christ Jesus, who became to us wisdom from God, righteousness and sanctification and redemption." As John Murray states, union with Christ

> is not simply a step in the application of redemption; when viewed, according to the teaching of Scripture, in its broader aspects it underlies every step of the application of redemption. Union with Christ is really the central truth of the whole doctrine of salvation not only in its application but also in its once-for-all accomplishment in the finished work of Christ.[9]

Here I can only sketch the relationship between union with Christ and progressive sanctification.[10] We'll divide our discussion into three categories: the positional, vital, and corporate dimensions.

---

[8] Hoekema, *Saved by Grace*, 64.

[9] Murray, *Redemption*, 161.

[10] Resources on union with Christ are numerous, and some get rather technical. For overviews, see Hoekema, *Saved by Grace*, 54–67; Ferguson, *Christian Life*, 104–14; and Murray, *Redemption*, 161–73. For more in-depth

The Positional Dimension

The term *positional* refers to our official standing before God as our Creator/Owner/Judge. According to Romans 5:12–21, the expression *in Adam* summarizes the standing that all human beings naturally have. God structured the human race so that Adam's choice affected all of us. As a result of his sin, we all stand condemned before God, separated from him on earth, and headed to eternal separation from him. Furthermore, as taught in Romans 6, sin holds a position of authority over us. Paul states the matter strongly: those in Adam are "slaves of sin."

The gospel changes all of this! At conversion God moves us from being in Adam to being in Christ. One consequence is that we are declared righteous on the basis of Jesus's work and therefore we are assured of eternal life (Rom 5:18–19). That's the blessing of justification that I've mentioned several times. But another result is that we are delivered from bondage to sin and brought under God's authority (6:17–18). Here again Paul uses strong language: we are "dead to sin" (v. 2); our old self, who we were in Adam, was "crucified" with Christ (v. 6).

This doesn't mean that we no longer have sinful tendencies or that sin isn't appealing to us or that we cannot commit acts of sin. It means that our master-slave relationship to sin has been terminated. When Christ died he became permanently separated from the realm of sin's authority, and when he rose again he began life anew in God's realm of righteousness (Rom 6:10).[11] Being united with Christ includes being united with his death and resurrection, and with the victory won through those events (Rom 6:3–4).

---

discussion, see Johnson, *One with Chris;* Letham, *Union with Christ;* Wilbourne, *Union with Christ.*

[11] This does not, of course, imply that Jesus sinned during his earthly life. Yet Christ did live in the realm over which sin has authority. Consequently, he experienced temptation. He also endured physical, emotional, and social experiences that belonged to the curse of sin. Finally, he suffered the ultimate penalty of sin on the Cross. See Moo, *Romans,* 378–79; Lloyd-Jones, *Romans, An Exposition of Chapter 6,* 102–3.

We no longer have to sin because sin is no longer our master. It has no legal claim on us. When we choose to sin, we're voluntarily submitting to a deposed tyrant. Consider this analogy:

> The story is told of a great eagle tethered to a post, walking sadly round and round. One day a new owner announced he would release the bird. A crowd gathered, the rope was removed—and the eagle continued walking round and round in the same old rut. He was free to fly and yet did not. The sad absurdity of that scene is like the Christian who continues in sin.[12]

The Vital Dimension

Yet union with Christ does more than detach us from the authority of sin. It connects us with Christ so intimately that we receive spiritual life and strength from him. That's what the adjective *vital* indicates.

Amazingly, the passages on this theme tend to speak not of our being in Christ but of Christ being in us. In Galatians 2:20 Paul declares, "I have been crucified with Christ. It is no longer I who live, but Christ who lives in me. And the life I now live in the flesh I live by faith in the Son of God, who loved me and gave himself for me." Paul's testimony recalls a metaphor in the Gospel of John: Christ is the vine through whom we branches bear fruit (15:1–11). And lest anyone think these blessings are limited to Jews, Colossians 1:27 teaches that Gentile believers have Christ dwelling within them as "the hope of glory."

Here we return to the ministry of the Holy Spirit, since Jesus also taught that it would be through the Spirit that he would minister his life-giving presence.[13] At regeneration the Spirit made us alive in Christ (2 Cor 5:17; Eph 2:4–6). Now Christ permanently resides within us through the Spirit. Paul specifically identifies the indwelling Spirit as "the Spirit of Christ" (Rom 8:9–11). The implications for sanctification are staggering. Christ's own power is ever available to enable us to please

---

[12] Ash, *Teaching Romans, Volume 1,* 232.

[13] See John 14:16–18, 25–26; 15:26; 16:7, 12–15; cf. 1 John 3:24; 4:13.

God. Conversely, we are joined to Christ so inseparably that wherever we go we take him with us—even when we sin (1 Cor 6:15–20).

The Corporate Dimension

By "corporate" I mean that when we are united with Christ, we are also united with everyone else that is united with Christ. Jesus prayed that his disciples "may all be one, just as you, Father, are in me, and I in you, that they also may be in us. . . . I in them and you in me, that they may become perfectly one" (John 17:21, 23). Positionally, this happens through "Spirit baptism." At conversion "in one Spirit we were all baptized into one body—Jews or Greeks, slaves or free" (1 Cor 12:13a).

Yet union with Christ's body is vital as well as positional. Paul's graphic descriptions in Ephesians make this point. As the cornerstone, Christ gives stability to the church as it develops into a magnificent temple (2:20–22; cf. 1 Pet 2:4–5). As the head, Christ directs the body in its growth (Eph 4:15–16). As the husband, Christ lovingly supplies all the needs of his wife-body (5:22–33). A little later in this chapter we'll begin to see that the corporate dimension of union with Christ has important ramifications for our sanctification.

The Method of Sanctification

We need to consider more specifically *how* God goes about sanctifying us. How is union with Christ practically realized so that we're changed into his image in our inner person and our outward choices? In particular, what is *our* role in this process?

Parallel to the Method of Justification

Since justification and sanctification are both divine works, we might expect that God would use the same method in each. To a degree this is true. The Lord justifies us and sanctifies us by means of faith/repentance. In dealing with 1 John 1:8–10 in our previous chapter, I touched on the necessity of ongoing repentance in sanctification. As we repeatedly grieve over, confess, and turn away from specific sins, God deepens our humility, our hatred of evil, and our commitment to obey him.

Faith is likewise crucial to our growth. It is as we believingly behold or contemplate Christ's glory that we are transformed into his image (2 Cor 3:18).[14] Growing in holiness does not mean that we somehow move away from relying on Christ. In fact, a deepening reliance upon Christ for justification advances our sanctification.

This happens in several ways. For one, recalling that we're accepted on Christ's merit alone keeps us humble when we make spiritual progress. Yet when we fail, the truth of justification also protects us from despair. At the same time, the assurance of justification inspires us to love and obey God more fervently as our hearts are filled with joy and gratitude and praise. We see these dynamics in Paul's testimony in Philippians 3 as well as in the priority and weight he gives to justification in Romans and Galatians.

But we do not trust Christ for justification only. We trust him also for victory in our daily struggle against sin. After expounding our union with Christ in his death and resurrection, Paul urges, "So you also must consider yourselves dead to sin and alive to God in Christ Jesus" (Rom 6:11). The term translated "reckon" means to take something into account or regard it to be true—to believe. As we face specific temptations, we reflect on and choose to believe that sin is not our master.

Different from the Method of Justification

Though God justifies and sanctifies us through faith/repentance, justification and sanctification differ in important ways. In justification we

---

[14] In the New Testament the Greek verb *katoptrizō* occurs only in 2 Corinthians 3:18. It could mean "reflect," but "behold" best fits the context as well as extrabiblical usage. This verb is related to a noun for "mirror" (*katoptron*), which is why many translate *katoptrizō* "behold as in a mirror." If Paul had in mind the idea of a mirror, he probably did not intend to identify the mirror as a specific item in the sanctification process. Instead his point was more general: in this life we behold Christ indirectly (cf. 1 Cor 13:12). See Garland, *2 Corinthians,* 199–200; Hughes, *Second Epistle to the Corinthians,* 118–19, n. 19. Of course, as I explain below, it is through Scripture that we have access to the glory of Christ.

remain passive as we receive the gifts of forgiveness and a righteous standing. In sanctification, however, God works through our active participation. He calls on us to engage in efforts and activities that flow from faith/repentance.

This is apparent from the biblical terms I referenced in introducing progressive sanctification, for example, "straining forward" (Phil 3:13), "strive" (Heb 12:14), "make every effort" (2 Pet 1:5), and "grow" (2 Pet 3:18). We could add many more such as "I discipline my body" (1 Cor 9:27), "train yourself for godliness" (1 Tim 4:7), and "pursue righteousness, godliness, faith, love, steadfastness, gentleness" (1 Tim 6:11). In addition, the New Testament depicts the Christian life in terms of warfare (e.g., Eph 6:10–7; 1 Tim 6:12). Romans 6 similarly emphasizes that faith must be put into action. After telling us to consider ourselves dead to sin and alive to God, Paul urges us to resist the influence of sin and to present ourselves to God for obedience (vv. 12–13). Clearly, sanctification requires our intense exertion.

You may have heard it said that in justification God does all the work, but in sanctification we "cooperate" with him. This may not the best way to state the case as it could be taken to mean that God does a percentage of the work and the Christian separately does another percentage. Philippians 2 clarifies the matter. After challenging the Philippians to display Christ-like humility, Paul writes, "Therefore, my beloved, as you have always obeyed, so now, not only as in my presence but much more in my absence, work out your own salvation with fear and trembling" (v. 12)

The Greek verb translated "work out" (*katergazomai*) is striking. It means something like "bring about."[15] The object of this verb, "your own salvation," cannot be focusing on justification. If so, Paul's

---

[15] BDAG, 531. Note some parallel usages of *katergazomai* (emphasis added): "Suffering *produces* endurance" (Rom 5:3); "sin . . . *produced* in me all kinds of covetousness" (Rom 7:8); "the signs of a true apostle were *performed* among you" (2 Cor 12:12).

statement would contradict what he himself teaches in the next chapter: our righteous standing comes by faith in Jesus Christ not by our works (3:9). In the context of Philippians 2, "salvation" has to do with salvation's goal of making us like Christ in our attitudes and actions, specifically in self-sacrificing service to others. Paul indicates that we have considerable responsibility in the accomplishment of this goal, and it demands rigor and work.

But the apostle doesn't stop there. He says we work out our salvation "with fear and trembling." What is the reason for this overwhelming reverence? Verse 13 begins with "for," explaining the reason: "For it is God who works in you, both to will and to work for his good pleasure." As we earnestly pursue Christ-likeness, we are awed by the realization that something more than human exertion is taking place. In our efforts to please God, our desire and determination ("to will") as well as our follow-through ("to work") result from supernatural energizing.[16]

So all our work flows from God's work, enabled by his infinite might. By the same token, as John Murray puts it, "The more persistently active we are in working, the more persuaded we may be that all the energizing grace and power is of God."[17] If this sounds paradoxical, then you're on the right track! Actually, Paul describes his whole ministry in these terms. Recall 1 Corinthians 15:10: "But by the grace of God I am what I am, and his grace toward me was not in vain. On the contrary, I worked harder than any of them, though it was not I, but the grace of God that is with me."

The Means of Grace

Though we can't fully explain the paradox of sanctification, we can grasp our responsibilities in the process. To begin with, we must diligently use

---

[16] The Greek verb translated "works" is *energeō*. The English word "energy" derives from the root of this word.

[17] Murray, *Redemption*, 149. For further discussion, see Melick, *Philippians*, 109–11; Silva, *Philippians*, 118–23.

the means of grace, vehicles through which the Lord strengthens us in our pursuit of holiness and through which he grows us in holiness.

The foremost of these is Scripture. "Sanctify them in the truth: your word is truth" (John 17:17). "Like newborn infants, long for the pure spiritual milk, that by it you may grow up into salvation" (1 Pet 2:2). Through Scripture the Lord keeps us from evil (Ps 119:9, 11), builds us up (Acts 20:32), and equips us for every good work (2 Tim 3:16–17). God's Word is "the sword of the Spirit" that we wield in spiritual warfare (Eph 6:17). Experiencing Scripture's many ministries requires that we faithfully meditate on it (Ps 1:2) and put it into practice (Jas 1:22–25). Can this be done without some process of application?

Second, prayer is a means of grace. As I pointed out earlier, biblical writers prayed for God to sanctify his people (e.g., Heb. 13:20–21). Paul mentions prayer in close connection with our spiritual armor (Eph 6:18). It is through prayer that we confess our sins (Luke 11:4; 1 John 1:9). In response to prayer, God gives us grace to resist temptation (Matt 26:41; Heb. 4:14–16) or spares us from it altogether (Luke 11:4). Through prayer we come to enjoy peace that overcomes anxiety (Phil 4:6–7). And through prayer we submit to God's will (Luke 22:42). Prayer and Scripture work together. One thing we pray for is divine illumination to understand the Word (Ps 119:18; Eph 1:15–18). Such back-and-forth communion with God surely has a sanctifying effect!

Finally, our fellow believers—especially those with whom we join in a local church—function as means of grace. Earlier we noted that being united with Christ includes being united with other Christians. One result of this is that sanctification is a "community project." We minister grace to one another through edifying conversation (Eph 4:29). We encourage one another to persevere (Heb 10:23–25). We hold one another accountable through various levels of church discipline (e.g., Matt 18:15–20). In corporate worship we draw near to God but also minister his truth to one another (Eph 5:19–20; Col 3:16).

As we use our spiritual gifts, God conveys sanctifying grace to our brothers and sisters (Rom 12:3–8; 1 Cor. 12–14; 1 Pet. 4:10–11).

More specifically, he sanctifies us through the ministry of our pastors and teachers (Eph 4:11–16; Heb 13:7, 17). As our study proceeds, we'll see a connection between this community emphasis and our application efforts. In applying Scripture, we do so with sensitivity to the assembly in which God has placed us.[18]

Mortification and Vivification

In addition to availing ourselves of the means of grace, we refuse to engage in sin and actively develop godly virtues. Theologians sometimes refer to the negative side as "mortification." This imagery of killing sin comes from Romans 8:13 and Colossians 3:5. It pictures the intensity—violence—that is required in resisting temptation. Jesus had such intensity in mind when he spoke hyperbolically of tearing out an eye or cutting off a hand that has become an avenue of temptation (Matt 5:29–30). The Bible uses other images in this regard. For instance, we "put off" sinful dispositions and practices like we would rid ourselves of worn-out, foul-smelling clothes (Eph 4:25; Col 3:8).

On the positive side, "vivification" refers to cultivating the qualities of our new life in Christ. One reason the New Testament recounts the earthly life of Jesus is to detail his modeling of these qualities as our pattern.[19] In addition, the Bible lists categories of godliness to develop

---

[18] For a broader survey of the means of grace, see Grudem, *Systematic Theology*, 950–65. For a fuller, practically oriented study, see Mathis, *Habits of Grace*. There is a sense in which suffering may also be considered a means of grace. Suffering is an aspect of the curse of sin (Rom. 8:18-25), but it is more than that. God turns it around for our good, employing it to make us like Christ (Rom. 8:28-30). Sometimes he uses suffering as fatherly chastening (Heb. 12:5-11). More generally, suffering is God's tool to grow our dependence on him (2 Cor. 1:8-11; 12:1-10), develop our character (Rom. 5:3-4; Jas. 1:2-4), and prepare us for ministry (2 Cor. 1:3-7). The passages cited teach that we "use" this means of grace by accepting suffering with humility and trust and patiently enduring it.

[19] See, for example, Matt 11:28–30, John 13:12–17, Rom 15:1–3, Eph 5:1–2, Heb 12:1–2, and 1 Pet 2:21–25.

as well as categories of sins to avoid.[20] In due course we'll consider the nature of such lists and their outworking in our lives.[21]

Our choices to "put off" and "put on" result from a past experience: by Gods' enabling, at conversion we decisively put off our old self and put on our new self (Col 3:9–10).[22] We then go on to express this radical change in our daily choices (Col 3:8–14; Eph 4:25–32; cf. Rom 6:1–14). But how? It's not by mere will-power to "turn over a new leaf." Progress comes as we consciously yield to the sanctifying influence of God. Mortification happens "through the Spirit," by following his leading (Rom 8:13–14). We can resist the flesh, our sinful inclinations, and grow in Christ-like traits by regularly submitting to the convicting and prompting ministry of the Spirit (Gal 5:16–26; Eph 5:18–21). Indeed those traits are called "the fruit of the Spirit" (Gal 5:23).

Conclusion

Our next chapter will have more to say about progressive sanctification, but notice that in this chapter mortification and vivification have come up at the very end. That's because holiness is not fundamentally about "do's and don'ts." Instead, this chapter has emphasized that progressive sanctification is about *becoming who we are.*

God has set believers apart as his special people. He has united us with Christ. In Christ we've been declared righteous, and we've been freed from bondage to sin. In addition, God has blessed us with "all things that pertain to life and godliness" (2 Pet 1:3). He has given us

---

[20] See, for example, Rom 12:9–21, 1 Cor 6:9–10, Gal 5:19–25, Eph 4:25—5:21, Col 3:1–17, and 2 Pet 5:1–7.

[21] For more development of mortification, see the three classic works of John Owen published as *Overcoming Sin and Temptation.* Owen's teaching has been distilled in Lundgaard, *Enemy Within.* For more development of vivification, see Berg, *Essential Virtues;* Bridges, *Practice of Godliness.*

[22] Though the grammar is more challenging, Ephesians 4:22–24 also seems to be referring to conversion. See Hoehner, *Ephesians,* 599–602; Wallace, *Greek Grammar,* 603–5.

multiple means by which we can receive sanctifying grace. Furthermore, Christ has taken up residence within us through his Holy Spirit. As we make use of these resources, we can become increasingly holy in heart and in conduct, displaying God's image so that he receives the honor he deserves. Our applications of Scripture contribute to this glorious purpose. They are specific ways through which we become who we are in Christ.

Part II

The Necessity
of Biblical Application

Chapter 4

The Nature of Scripture

Moses was stumped again. As the Israelites were preparing to conquer Canaan, the aged leader received a visit from five sisters (Num 27:1–11). Mahlah, Noah, Hoglah, Milcah, and Tirzah were concerned about their future in the Promised Land. Their father Zelophehad had died son-less in the wilderness. Upon a man's death his property would transfer to his male descendants (cf. Deut 21:15–17). In the absence of sons, the closest male relative would inherit the land. This system meant that Zelophehad's name would die out. And if his daughters remained unmarried, their economic prospects looked bleak.

Yahweh hadn't given a law for this particular circumstance, so what was Moses to do? He could just ask the Lord! And the Lord gave him a straightforward answer: "The daughters of Zelophehad are right. You shall give them possession of an inheritance among their father's brothers and transfer the inheritance of their father to them" (Num 27:7). Yahweh went on to establish this as permanent policy: if a man died without sons, his daughter(s) would get the inheritance. Only in the absence of daughters would a man's property go to other relatives (vv. 8–11).

No doubt Zelophehad's daughters walked away relieved, but that wasn't the last Moses would hear of them. In time their clan leaders approached Moses, concerned about a potential domino effect of the new ruling. If these ladies married outside their tribe, their land would be lost to their husbands' tribes. So a follow-up divine ruling was required. Because he wanted each tribe to retain its property in full, Yahweh decreed, "'Let them marry whom they think best, only they shall marry within the clan of the tribe of their father'" (36:6). Thankfully, five qualified bachelors were available (vv. 10–12).

I find this story fascinating on several levels. For one, at the time the daughters' case was settled, Israel stood on the east side of the Jordan, and the Promised Land was populated by the Canaanites. The entire debate concerned property that belonged to someone else. That Yahweh was stipulating detailed laws about the land indicated just how committed he was to enabling the Israelites to take Canaan. True to God's Word, after the conquest Eleazar and Joshua gave the daughters of Zelophehad their rightful inheritance (Josh 17:3–4). Presumably the five sisters lived happily ever after with their husbands and their homesteads.

The story of Zelophehad's daughters stands as a touching testimony to God's compassion and faithfulness, but it also raises the challenge that is driving this book. While few of us would desire the leadership role that Moses bore, surely we'd appreciate a direct line to God when we face questions that the Bible doesn't specifically address. The incident with Zelophehad's daughters was not the first time Moses approached Yahweh about matters not mentioned in Scripture. The Lord gave him detailed directions about how to handle a half-Israelite who blasphemed (Lev 24:10–16), several men who were ceremonially defiled at the time of Passover (Num 9:6–14), and another man who gathered sticks on the Sabbath (Num. 15:32–36).

But how do we proceed in our day? As we've seen, God has graciously set us apart for himself so that we can display the image of Christ and thereby glorify him. Yet how do we know what Christ's image looks like in contemporary life—especially when we face situations and issues for which there is no chapter and verse? The answer is that we need to *apply* the Scriptures. This chapter and the next present a variety of ways in which the Bible itself indicates the necessity of application.

Fundamentally, what kind of book, or collection of books, is the Bible? What qualities characterize God's written revelation? As we reflect on some key features of Scriptures, we repeatedly encounter the need for application.

Time-Bound and Timeless Truth

To begin with, every Bible student wrestles with the tension between the time-bounded character and the timeless authority of Scripture. On the one hand, there's a sense in which when we read the Bible we are "reading someone else's mail." The books of Scripture are historical records of God's dealings with people of the ancient world. These records tell us how God guided them in the process of conforming them into his image. Yet because these people's lives were vastly different from ours, the Bible often deals with issues we are highly unlikely to face. When was the last time you puzzled over whether you should glean the corners of your field (Lev 19:9) or eat meat that has been sacrificed to idols (1 Cor 8–10)?

Conversely, we face a multitude of issues that wouldn't have crossed the minds of the Bible's original addressees. They never heard of speed limits, credit cards, Hollywood, the Internet, or smartphones. Given how quickly the world is changing, how could the Bible directly address all our questions, struggles, and problems in sanctification? The Lord would have to do what computer software companies do—issue regular updates.

But that isn't how God has chosen to work. Instead biblical books present themselves as transgenerational. Even though they're God's words to historically situated individuals and groups, they hold authority over later individuals and groups. So we need to modify the idea of "reading someone else's mail." As I once heard my colleague Gary Reimers say, reading the Bible is more like reading an email addressed to someone else but intentionally carbon-copied or blind-copied to you.

The transhistorical character of Scripture surfaces throughout the Old and New Testaments. Enduring authority is built into the covenant that Yahweh made with the nation Israel and that dominates the Old Testament. In Deuteronomy Moses emphasizes this fact through hyperbole: he says that the covenant was not made with the first generation of Israelites that came out of Egypt but with their descendants (5:1–3). He extends the covenant to even later generations: "It is not with you alone that I am making this sworn covenant, but with whoever is standing here with us today before the LORD our God, *and with whoever is not here with us today"* (Deut 29:14–15, emphasis added). Finally, Moses repeatedly uses the pronoun *you* to refer to Israelites who wouldn't be on the scene until nearly a millennium later, those who would return from exile to the Promised Land (30:1–5).

> The book [of Deuteronomy] is written in a way that puts together original readers and later readers—across hundreds of years—to hear the selfsame message. . . .
>
> If we take the use of "you" seriously, we should read the book as speaking directly to a transgenerational readership, spanning the last days of Moses to the exile and, in some sense, beyond.[1]

The Mosaic Covenant would have this effect specifically as Israelite parents diligently taught the Torah to their children (e.g., Deut 6:7; 29:29). This instruction was to continue generation after generation. Yahweh himself told Joshua to obey the Law of Moses (Josh 1:7–8). King David said the same to Solomon (1 Kgs 2:3). A few centuries later, King Josiah became overwhelmed with grief when he realized how far Judah had gotten from the Law (2 Kgs 22:11–13). Still later, Jewish leaders lamented the disobedience that had brought exile upon God's people (Neh 9; cf. 2 Kgs 17). And after the millennium mentioned above, Malachi was exhorting his contemporaries, "Remember the law of my servant Moses, the statutes and rules that I commanded him at Horeb for all Israel" (Mal 4:4).

Turning to the New Testament, we find Jesus upholding the divine authority of the Old Testament writings (Matt 5:17–19; John 10:35). He also claimed that his own teaching carried this same authority (Matt 24:35; John 14:10, 24; cf. 1:16–18). Then prior to his ascension Christ told his original disciples not only to make other disciples but also to teach them "to observe all that I have commanded you" (Matt 28:20). In addition, he promised the apostles a powerful ministry

---

[1] Schnittjer, *Torah Story,* 457–58.

of the Holy Spirit that would enable them to convey Christ's words and works and to impart further revelation (John 14:26; 15:26–27; 16:12–15). Paul and a few others connected with the apostles enjoyed this unique role as well (e.g., 1 Cor 2:12–13; Gal 1:11–12).

As a result, the New Testament documents possess an authority parallel to the writings of the Old Testament prophets (Eph 2:20; 2 Pet 3:2; cf. Jude 17–18). And as with the Old Testament, this authority extends beyond the original recipients. For instance, Paul said that his letter to the Colossian church should be read to the Laodicean church (Col 4:16). This corresponds with the apostolic authority he claimed "in all the churches" (1 Cor 7:17; cf. 14:33, 37–38). Similarly, though Revelation's opening letters are addressed to particular local churches and deal with specific issues in those churches, each letter ends with a broader admonition: "He who has an ear, let him hear what the Spirit says to the churches" (2:7, 11, 17, 29; 3:6, 13, 22). Revelation's conclusion also uses universal language (22:7, 12, 14, 17–19).

The gospel call is for "all people everywhere" (Acts 17:30). So throughout its pages, the New Testament assumes that its teaching is normative for "all the nations" (Rom 1:5; 16:26) and especially for "we all" who have experienced the New Covenant, all believers in Jesus Christ (2 Cor 3:18). The New Testament records "the faith that was once delivered unto the saints" (Jude 3), whether first-century or twenty-first-century saints.

Application enables us to submit to this authority of Scripture even while filtering through its historical particularity. The process entails challenges and pitfalls but is feasible for at least three reasons.
- Though God has changed his methods from time to time, his character and values remain unchanging (Mal 3:6; Jas 1:17).
- All human beings are made in God's image (Gen 1:26–27; Jas 3:9), and all are sinners (Rom 3:10–23). Consequently, we can expect a significant degree of continuity in human experience despite historical and cultural differences.
- God's indwelling Spirit guides us as we seek the present relevance of his age-old Word (1 Cor 2:14; Eph 1:16–18).

Often the process of application is simple. It doesn't take much insight to move from Euodia and Syntyche (Phil 4:2) to a conflict you're having with a fellow church member. And when Paul appeals to the Corinthians to give to poor believers in Jerusalem (2 Cor 8–9), we readily transfer his teaching to our Sunday-morning offering. But whether easy or difficult, application is vital if we are going to *do* God's Word and not just hear it (Matt 7:24–27; Jas 1:22–25). In fact, the opening chapters of this book were an exercise in application: taking what God told various believers in Bible times and relating it to our own relationship with God and our own sanctification. The presupposition has been that God's Word to them indicates—by extension—God's will for us.

Examples in 2 Timothy

To illustrate further, I want to dwell on a biblical book whose historical background was rather narrow: 2 Timothy. As Paul anticipates his martyrdom, he writes this letter to encourage Timothy to carry on the apostle's gospel mission, particularly in the city of Ephesus. Given this setting, 2 Timothy contains detailed information that may seem irrelevant to us. We read of opposition to Paul from Phygellus and Hermogenes (1:15), Hymenaeus and Philetus (2:16–18), and Alexander (4:14–15). On the other hand, Onesiphorus is commended for supporting Paul (1:16–18). We find travel notes regarding Demas, Crescens, Titus, Luke, Mark, Erastus, and Trophimus (4:10–12, 19–20). Paul asks Timothy to visit him and bring the apostle's cloak and books (4:13). And the letter's closing includes some personal greetings (4:19, 21).

Yet the relevance of 2 Timothy extends beyond Paul's personal circumstances and Timothy's own ministry. "And what you have heard from me in the presence of many witnesses entrust to faithful men who will be able to teach others also" (2:2). Paul envisions that his instruction to Timothy will have an expanding influence over time. Furthermore, it's not difficult to detect universal truths taught by the historical particulars of the letter. From his experience of persecution, Paul explicitly generalizes: "Indeed, *all* who desire to live a godly life in Christ Jesus will be persecuted" (3:12, emphasis added). And Demas' reprehensible love for this present world (4:10) contrasts with the apostle and "*all* who have loved his [Christ's] appearing" (4:8, emphasis added).

Focusing on a Famous Text

We'll see this interaction between the particular and the universal as we study what is probably the most famous passage in 2 Timothy. It's arguably the most important passage on the role of Scripture in the Christian life. Second Timothy 3 concentrates on preparing Timothy to respond to false teachers. It climaxes with these memorable words (vv. 14–16):

> But as for you, continue in what you have learned and have firmly believed, knowing from whom you learned it and how from childhood you have been acquainted with the sacred writings, which are able to make you wise for salvation through faith in Christ Jesus. All Scripture is breathed out by God and profitable for teaching, for reproof, for correction, and for training in righteousness, that the man of God may be complete, equipped for every good work.

If you're familiar with this text, you may expect me to make the following three points about the Bible.

- The Bible is divine in origin. In verse 16 the expression "breathed out by God" emphasizes that Scripture is God's speech.
- The Bible is beneficial for conversion (v. 15), sanctification (v. 16), and effective service (v. 17). In fact, verse 16 lists four ministries of Scripture in sanctification: teaching, reproof, correction, and training in righteous living.
- The Bible is sufficient for the accomplishment of its sanctifying purposes. As verse 17 says, Scripture makes "the man of God . . . complete, equipped for *every* good work" (emphasis added).

The above propositions are foundational to orthodox Christianity, and I enthusiastically affirm them. Yet formulating these statements required making theological connections that amount to a kind of application. Take the word *Scripture* itself (v. 16). This term parallels "the sacred writings" that Timothy learned as a half-Jewish boy (v.15). Since the New Testament did not exist at the time of Timothy's childhood, "Scripture" and "the sacred writings" must refer to the Old Testament documents (a fact I get a lot of mileage out of since I'm an Old Testament professor). Nevertheless, my propositions referred to "the Bible," and I meant all sixty-six books of the Bible. How am I justified in including the New Testament?

Verse 15 provides part of the answer. It says that the Old Testament writings "are able to make you wise for salvation through faith in Christ Jesus." The Old Testament doesn't speak specifically about "salvation through faith in Christ Jesus." It prepared for the coming of the Messiah by revealing God's redemptive plan in a more general way. Once that plan came to fruition in the work of Jesus, however, the *ultimate goal* of the Old Testament became much clearer. Paul had taught Timothy this New Covenant perspective on the Old Testament,[2] and the apostles and their associates were in the process of codifying it in the New Testament books. Consequently, a close link exists between "Scripture" and the New Testament as the authorized "commentary" on the Old.[3]

With this in mind, note the word *all* in verse 16. The phrase *all Scripture* means "every part of Scripture" or "the entirety of Scripture." In either case, the breadth of this statement suggests that 2 Timothy 3:16 *applies* to any document that can rightfully be called "Scripture." Even before the end of the first century A.D., that title was beginning to be used for the New Testament writings (1 Tim 5:18; 2 Pet 3:16). So we naturally *conclude* that those writings are inspired and profitable as well as the Old Testament writings.[4]

---

[2] Compare verses 10 and 14 with Acts 16:1–5; 18:5; 1 Cor 4:17; 16:10; 1 Thess 3:2; and 1 Tim 1:2–11.

[3] For similar explanations, see Guthrie, *Pastoral Epistles,* 163–64; Knight, *Pastoral Epistles,* 447–48; Mounce, *Pastoral Epistles,* 561–65.

[4] Warfield, *Inspiration and Authority,* 163–65.

Our practical use of 2 Timothy 3:14–17 also depends upon application. This becomes clear as we look again at verse 17. Here Paul states the purpose of Scripture's ministries: "That the man of God may be complete, equipped for every good work." The expression *the man of God* indicates Paul's focus in this passage. This title was commonly used for prophets in the Old Testament (e.g., Deut 33:1; 1 Sam 9:6; 2 Kgs 1:9). In another passage on Timothy's pastoral example and ministry, Paul had called Timothy "man of God" (1 Tim 6:11). So it appears that when the apostle speaks of the sanctifying and equipping influence of Scripture in 2 Timothy 3, he is talking specifically about its influence in the life of Timothy as a divinely appointed leader/preacher in Ephesus.

But is 2 Timothy 3:16–17 true for Timothy only? One reason to answer no is that, in light of 2 Timothy 2:2, the phrase *the man of God* naturally *extends* to other men who hold ministries *analogous* to Timothy's ministry. Yet the relevance of this text doesn't stop there. The next chapter begins with a sobering mandate for Timothy: "Preach the word" (4:2). Here "the word" refers to the Scripture that has been under discussion: the Old Testament viewed in the light of the coming of the Messiah and, *by extension,* New Testament additions to the canon.

In proclaiming this revelation, Timothy must "reprove, rebuke, and exhort, with complete patience and teaching" (v. 2). These terms correspond roughly with the four ministries of Scripture in 2 Timothy 3:16. In other words, what Timothy himself experiences from God's Word he must bring to bear on the lives of the people of Ephesus. This preaching is itself an exercise in application. In addition, it leads us to *infer* that 3:16 isn't restricted to Timothy as "the man of God." Instead Scripture also teaches, reproves, corrects, and trains the believers to whom he is ministering in Ephesus.

Since we are New Covenant Christians, our spiritual situation *parallels* that of the Ephesian believers. Therefore we *deduce* that the Bible works in our lives in the same ways it did in their lives. As William Mounce says, "Scripture comes from God and is true; therefore it provides the content and direction necessary for Timothy, Christian leaders, and *by implication* all Christians to be fully equipped, enabled to do every good work."[5]

Look back at my comments on 2 Timothy 3:14–17 and notice some words and phrases that I italicized for emphasis: *ultimate goal, conclude, extends, analogous, by extension, infer, parallels, deduce,* and *by implication.* This is the language of application. It reflects a process of logically "connecting the dots" not only within the context of the passage and between the passage and other passages but also between the original recipients of Scripture and our own lives. In meditating on 2 Timothy 3:14–17, a seasoned Bible-reading Christian would likely have come to the same conclusions I argued for, though he may not have thought through them so explicitly. Yet overtly laying out the process helps to establish the point of this chapter: application is indispensable if we are to benefit from biblical writings.

So we had to do application even to say that the Bible teaches, rebukes, corrects, and trains us. And we have to do application if we're going to experience these ministries from other parts of Scripture.

One More Passage

Before moving on from 2 Timothy, I want to draw attention to one other text related to application. At the beginning of chapter 2, Paul is exhorting Timothy to persevere in the ministry. In verses 4–7 he gives a series of analogies:

> Share in suffering as a good soldier of Christ Jesus. No soldier gets entangled in civilian pursuits, since his aim is to please the one who enlisted him. An athlete is not crowned unless he competes according to the rules. It is the hard-working farmer who ought to have the first share of the crops. Think over what I say, for the Lord will give you understanding in everything.

The analogies come from the military (vv. 3-4), athletic (v. 5), and farming realms (v. 6), and each one communicates a different idea or ideas. Perhaps, like me, Timothy didn't have much experience with

---

[5] Mounce, *Pastoral Epistles,* 570–71 (emphasis added).

any of these areas of life. Whatever the case, Paul apparently did not expect Timothy to grasp immediately the connections between the illustrations and his ministry. I say that because in verse 7 the apostle continues, "Think over what I say, for the Lord will give you understanding in everything."

Here Paul is calling Timothy to application, to figuring out the specific relevance of the illustrations for his life and ministry. And he presents two factors vital to application: *meditation* ("think over what I say") coupled with divine *illumination* ("for the Lord will give you understanding in everything"). Even as the original recipient of this letter, Timothy had to sort through culturally oriented elements in order to arrive at God's message for his life.

More broadly, regarding this passage my colleague Randy Leedy has written,

> If I may put it this way, this passage says more than it says. Paul makes simple statements about a soldier, an athlete, and a farmer. But when he goes on to say, "Think about this, and may the Lord help you understand," he makes clear that he means to communicate more than he actually says. Of course he could have gone on to explain exactly what he had in mind, but he did not. He left it up to Timothy first, and every reader since then, to infer not only the correct interpretation of these statements but also their application to his or her own life. He is not simply allowing Timothy to infer such application; his presentation requires it.[6]

We'll see this dynamic recurring as we go on to examine other features of biblical revelation.

Implicit Genres

Through what types of literature did God choose to reveal himself? We might have expected that he would prefer straightforward theological essays. We do find something like theological essays in many portions of the New Testament Epistles. Romans 3:21–26 employs highly precise

---

[6] Leedy, *Love Not,* 93; cf. Mounce, *Pastoral Epistles,* 510–11.

terminology arranged in tight logic in order to articulate the doctrine of justification by faith. And Hebrews 8 provides a detailed exposition of Christ's ministry as the mediator of the New Covenant.

Likewise, clear-cut prohibitions and commands might seem to be the most effective means to teach ethics. Who can argue with the directness of "You shall not steal" (Exod 20:15; Rom 13:9)? Who could miss the relevance of 1 Thessalonians 4:3: "For this is the will of God, your sanctification: that you abstain from sexual immorality?"

Nevertheless, such forms of communication don't characterize the entirety, or even the majority, of the Bible. The Lord has filled his Word with a rich variety of genres, and often these genres do not directly indicate how the reader is supposed to respond to what he is reading. In fact, some genres may not even state their basic thesis in so many words. Frequently the reader—original or later—must infer the theological/ethical themes and then relate those to his particular situation. Even when such an exercise is more spontaneous than systematic, it remains necessary to the sanctifying work of Scripture.

The prominent example here is the narrative genre in its various forms, which accounts for nearly forty percent of the content of the Bible. At times narrative passages and books specify their theme and even their application. The Gospel of John does: "Now Jesus did many other signs in the presence of the disciples, which are not written in this book; but these are written so that you may believe that Jesus is the Christ, the Son of God, and that by believing you may have life in his name" (John 20:30–31). In addition, the Gospels may verbalize the point of a parable: "And he told them a parable to the effect that they ought always to pray and not lose heart" (Luke 18:1).

Most often, however, profiting from biblical narratives requires a good deal of inductive reasoning. Regarding the book of Acts, the theme of witnessing to Christ clearly applies to all generations of Christians (1:8). But does the author also intend to teach ministry methods that ought to be duplicated by God's people? For instance, to what degree are Paul's missionary strategies a model for us? Is a contemporary missionary supposed to evangelize in the local synagogue before approaching Gentiles? Should he typically work in one city for a few weeks or months and then move on to another location?

Questions such as these abound as we turn to Old Testament narratives. What should we learn from Genesis 14, where Abram and his servants carry out a military attack in order to rescue Abram's nephew Lot? Or take the book of Ruth. Is the point of this beautiful story simply that people should take care of their widowed mothers-in-law? And does Ruth's night-time proposal (Ruth 3) serve as a pattern for how marriages today should be initiated? Few would respond positively, yet some have argued that Abraham provides a model in the way he acquired a wife for Isaac (Gen 24). Is this conclusion legitimate?

Within narrative we will find other genres such as administrative lists. The middle chapters of Joshua sound like this (19:1–3):

> The second lot came out for Simeon, for the tribe of the people of Simeon, according to their clans, and their inheritance was in the midst of the inheritance of the people of Judah. And they had for their inheritance Beersheba, Sheba, Moladah, Hazar-shual, Balah, Ezem.

How do such details contribute to our sanctification?

Consider 1 Chronicles as well. Chapters 23–26 comprise a catalog of officials that David organized for Solomon's temple: Levites, priests, musicians, gatekeepers, and treasurers. Given that a physical temple isn't part of God's plan for the church today, what is the significance of all this material for us? Speaking of 1 Chronicles, the book begins with nine chapters of genealogy, yet another genre. What spiritual benefit can we derive from these lengthy rolls of hard-to-pronounce names? The text doesn't directly tell us. And within the genealogies, how should we respond to Jabez's famous prayer (1 Chron 4:9–10)?

Here are some other types of biblical literature that communicate their relevance implicitly: royal psalms (e.g., Pss 20–21), love songs (especially the Song of Solomon), prophetic visions (e.g., Ezek 40–48), and oracles against ancient nations (e.g., Jer 46–51). In bringing up these examples, my goal isn't to overwhelm you with Bible difficulties.

On the contrary, my burden is that by the end of this book you'll be encouraged and practically helped in your application efforts. But first we need to be thoroughly persuaded of the inseparable connection between Scripture's sanctifying ministry and the process of application. The Bible's implicit genres make this connection apparent.

General Instruction

Thankfully, as noted above, some biblical genres communicate explicitly what God requires people to believe and do. Even with these genres, however, matters may not be as simple as they at first appear. For instance, much of the Bible's instruction is rather general in nature. For this type of instruction to affect the reader in an appreciable way, he must move beyond the bare statement of the text and identify concrete expressions of that statement in his life.

Think about the Ten Commandments. What does honoring one's parents (Exod 20:12) actually look like? That question has many answers, and they depend significantly on the age of the children as well as the age of the parents. For younger children, honor includes obeying commands issued by the parents. That's the application Paul makes in Ephesians 6:1–3, to readers in a setting much different from that of the Israelites who first received the Ten Commandments.

As children grow older, they ought to realize that honor is shown in additional ways. When they speak about their parents, for example, they should speak as positively as they honestly can. They should also avoid foolish behavior that would embarrass their family—including behavior their parents haven't thought to put off-limits. Adult children can show honor by seeking their parents' counsel for major decisions. Even birthday cards and phone calls are means of living out the fifth commandment. And as parents age, honoring them includes ensuring that they are provided for materially. That, in fact, seems to have been the original focus of "honor" in Exodus 20:12.[7]

---

[7] Stuart, *Exodus,* 461–62.

Admittedly, a full discussion of honor for parents requires more detail. Some of the applications above could be further supported with direct biblical statements (e.g., 1 Tim 5:8). Additionally, many entail a discretionary element. Up to what age and what circumstances is obedience required? How often should adult children communicate with their parents? What kind of physical care should they provide for elderly parents? Later I'll discuss the role of judgment calls such as these. But here I'm arguing simply that without application the fifth commandment will have little or no effect.

Earlier I quoted the eighth commandment, "You shall not steal" (Exod 20:15; Rom 13:9). Presumably, no one would rationalize petty shoplifting based on the fact that this command does not mention an object for the verb *steal*. Yet common sense would also tell us that stealing encompasses more than physically carrying away someone else's possessions. Think of embezzlement, tax evasion, copyright infringement, software piracy, and identity theft. These are contemporary forms of stealing that are ruled out by the broad ancient prohibition. At least in cases of this nature, "unless applications are as authoritative as the explicit teachings of Scripture . . . then scriptural authority becomes a dead letter."[8]

In this connection, it seems that Yahweh was guarding against minimalistic approaches to his law when he elaborated on the tenth commandment. "You shall not covet your neighbor's house; you shall not covet your neighbor's wife, or his male servant, or his female servant, or his ox, or his donkey, *or anything* that is your neighbor's" (Exod 20:17, emphasis added).

We can also go to the book of Proverbs for examples of broad categories that must be filled out with real-life particulars. "Whoever troubles his own household will inherit the wind" (11:29a). "The wisest of women builds her house, but folly with her own hands tears it down" (14:1). There would be many ways in which one could build up or tear

---

[8] Frame, *Knowledge of God*, 84.

down one's house, and the reader is left to ponder what some of those ways would be. Likewise, oppressing and being generous to the poor can take various forms (14:31).

Generic teaching abounds in the New Testament Epistles. Multiple passages present ideals that may not be difficult to define but that are nevertheless abstract and require specification. Here are a few examples:

> But the fruit of the Spirit is love, joy, peace, patience, kindness, goodness, faithfulness, gentleness, self-control; against such things there is no law. (Gal 5:22–23)

> With all humility and gentleness, with patience, bearing with one another in love, eager to maintain the unity of the Spirit in the bond of peace. (Eph 4:2–3)

> Older men are to be sober-minded, dignified, self-controlled, sound in faith, in love, and in steadfastness. (Titus 2:2)

> But the wisdom from above is first pure, then peaceable, gentle, open to reason, full of mercy and good fruits, impartial and sincere. And a harvest of righteousness is sown in peace by those who make peace. (Jas 3:17–18)

In each case above, the reader must determine whether particular attitudes, responses, and behaviors in his own life reflect the ethical vision of the text. Typically this isn't a complicated process, but it still requires going beyond the simple wording of the text.

Let me illustrate by discussing Paul's directive to husbands: "Husbands, love your wives, as Christ loved the church and gave himself up for her" (Eph 5:25). This is a moving and challenging statement, but I am left asking, "*How* do I display sacrificial Christ-like love? What exactly should I *do* to love my wife in this way?"

In reading the next two verses, I find that the purpose of Christ's love is to sanctify the church. From this I infer that loving my wife includes promoting her sanctification. Practically, this would take various forms. I should exemplify for her the pursuit of holiness. I ought to ensure she has regular opportunity for Bible reading and prayer.

Maybe I need to help at home more to free up her time for this. I should also engage my wife in conversation about Christ and about her spiritual struggles and victories, providing encouragement and counsel as needed. And I should make sure we regularly attend a healthy church where she can be taught the Scriptures and develop edifying relationships.

In what other ways can I show Christ-like love to my wife? First Corinthians 13 comes to mind. Even though this passage was written to guide the Corinthian church in the use of spiritual gifts, its description of love takes the form of broad characteristics that naturally *apply* to any relationship, including the marriage relationship.

Yet that very breadth creates questions. First Corinthians 13:4 says that love is kind, but whether a specific behavior constitutes an act of kindness can depend on various personally oriented factors. My wife enjoys peanut butter, but maybe someone else's wife is allergic to it. Some wives are delighted when their husbands do the dishes. In other homes and cultures, that may actually be offensive because it could be perceived as encroaching on what the wife desires to do as an act of kindness.

As I sort through all this, I'm reminded of Peter's instruction: "Likewise, husbands, live with your wives in an understanding way" (1 Pet 3:7a). In this verse the phrase *in an understanding way* is also broad:

> The "knowledge" Peter intends here may include any knowledge that would be beneficial to the husband-wife relationship: knowledge of God's purposes and principles for marriage; knowledge of the wife's desires, goals, and frustrations; knowledge of her strengths and weaknesses in the physical, emotional and spiritual realms; *etc.*[9]

What this means is that in order to love her I must study my wife and her particularities. Through conversation and through observation I learn what she needs, what she enjoys, and what most helps her. Apart from this subjective process, I cannot fully love my wife as Christ loved the church, and so I cannot adequately obey Ephesians 5:25.

---

[9] Grudem, *1 Peter,* 143. Compare Clowney, *1 Peter,* 133–34.

Subjectively oriented analysis is especially necessary with epistolary imperatives that are so general as to be open-ended.

> But put on the Lord Jesus Christ, and make no provision for the flesh, to gratify its desires. (Rom 13:14)

> So, whether you eat or drink, or whatever you do, do all to the glory of God. (1 Cor 10:31)

> So then, as we have opportunity, let us do good to everyone, and especially to those who are of the household of faith. (Gal 6:10)

> And whatever you do, in word or deed, do everything in the name of the Lord Jesus, giving thanks to God the Father through him. (Col 3:17)

> Beloved, I urge you as sojourners and exiles to abstain from the passions of the flesh, which wage war against your soul. Keep your conduct among the Gentiles honorable, so that when they speak against you as evildoers, they may see your good deeds and glorify God on the day of visitation. (1 Pet 2:11–12)

Again the reader is expected to make life connections not specified in the text. Again that's the only way the text will have a significant effect.

Paradigmatic Instruction

As we deal with the challenges of general instruction, we might prefer passages that give highly specific guidance. Such passages raise other issues, however. On the one hand, their narrow scope might limit their relevance. On the other hand, we have to ask whether the particulars are also designed to teach something broader.

The Old Testament Law is the major case in point. When we read the Pentateuch, we might get the impression that Yahweh legislated every minute aspect of the Israelites' lives. This is far from the truth. Given the wide range of topics covered, what stands out is the selectivity and conciseness of the Pentateuch. Here we have not only the historical origins of Israel but also its national covenant (much like a constitution) and the entire body of God's laws for Israel's worship, government, military, judicial system, and social life. By way of contrast, think of the bookshelves at an attorney's office. The Pentateuch is nowhere near the length of the legal codes and case studies that modern lawyers have to analyze. Yahweh chose not to give Israel this much detail. Instead, in keeping with ancient Near Eastern legal custom, he provided enough specifics in order to establish patterns that the Israelites could relate to any number of situations not discussed in the law.

The term *paradigmatic* refers to this quality of Old Testament laws. I want to feature the paradigm concept as we'll be drawing on it throughout our study. The paradigmatic character of the Law represents a counterpoint to the story about Zelophehad's daughters that opened this chapter. Sometimes Yahweh did give new laws for new situations. But for the most part—especially once Moses was off the scene—God expected Israel to ascertain his will about new situations by reasoning from what he had already stated about parallel situations.

Different types of laws functioned paradigmatically. Scholars commonly distinguish between apodictic and casuistic laws. Apodictic laws are absolute imperatives, whether positive commands or prohibitions. We've already reflected on some of these; the Ten Commandments stand as the classic examples. As we've seen, such general commands entail many practical expressions. Yet some apodictic laws are more specific than the Decalogue. This specificity doesn't necessarily restrict their purview, however. It may well establish a paradigm that applies to comparable matters.

Leviticus 19:14 says, "You shall not curse the deaf or put a stumbling block before the blind, but you shall fear your God: I am the LORD." I'm not aware of a law that prohibited the Israelites from mocking the mentally impaired. But surely Leviticus 19:14 spoke to that issue. It demonstrated Yahweh's concern to protect anyone who was unable to perceive threats to his person and could not adequately defend himself. It taught Israel to reflect God's concern by treating such people respectfully not abusively.[10]

---

[10] Ross, *Holiness to the LORD*, 361; Rooker, *Leviticus*, 257.

Casuistic laws also established paradigms. These dealt with particular cases in an "if-then" format. Here's an example: "If you meet your enemy's ox or his donkey going astray, you shall bring it back to him" (Exod 23:4). Would an Israelite be "off the hook" if he came across his enemy's horse or camel? Interestingly, Deuteronomy 22:1 gives a similar law regarding "your brother's ox or his sheep." But verse 3 adds, "And you shall do the same with his donkey or with his garment, or with *any lost thing* of your brother's, which he loses and you find; you may not ignore it" (emphasis added). This expansion argues that the Exodus passage would apply to any animal or thing lost by an enemy, warding off a "letter of the law" reading.

Most often, casuistic laws had to do with legal penalties: if a certain offense was committed, then a certain punishment followed. Douglas Stuart illustrates that the Israelites were to understand these laws paradigmatically as well:

> No Israelite could say: "The law says I must make restitution for stole oxen or sheep [Exod 22:1], but I stole your goat. I don't have to pay you back," or "The law says that anyone who attacks his father or mother must be put to death [Exod 21:15], but I attacked my grandmother, so I shouldn't be punished," or "The law says that certain penalties apply for hitting someone with a fist or a stone [Exod 21:18], but I kicked my neighbor with my foot and hit him with a piece of wood, so I shouldn't be punished." Such arguments would have insulted the intelligence of all concerned and made no impact on those rendering judgments.[11]

Clearly, Old Testament laws taught patterns that were to be extrapolated to similar cases not stated in the text. This was one of the ways in which Scripture exercised authority over Israel. In later chapters we'll consider further the relevance of Old Testament laws for New Testament believers, but for now here is Stuart's thought-provoking conclusion: "If a reasonable number of comprehensive and comprehensible laws . . . are provided to a people as paradigms for proper living,

---

[11] Stuart, *Exodus,* 443.

there is no excuse for that people to claim ignorance of how to behave or to claim innocence when their sins are found out."[12]

Some New Testament passages explicitly function in a paradigmatic way. In introducing the Disciples' Prayer, Jesus told his followers to pray "like this" (Matt 6:9), or "in this way" (NASB). We don't have to use the exact words of the prayer every time we approach God. Instead the requests in the Disciples' Prayer indicate *priorities* that should characterize our prayers, priorities that can be expressed in a variety of ways. On another occasion Jesus introduced a different version of the Disciples' Prayer with "When you pray, say . . ." (Luke 11:2). So it's appropriate to repeat the words of the prayer. However, the fact that the Gospels contain two versions of the Disciples' Prayer indicates that Jesus's emphasis is on the themes not the phraseology of the prayer.[13]

Paul also teaches paradigmatically. In Galatians 5:19–21 he gives a lengthy list of the works of the flesh. Some are fairly narrow (e.g., witchcraft, v. 20), while others are broad (e.g., uncleanness, v. 19). After listing these sinful attitudes and actions, the apostle adds, "And things like these" (v. 21). In the same verse he says, "Those who do such things will not inherit the kingdom of God." Then after cataloging the fruit of the Spirit, verse 23 comments, "Against such things there is no law." This "like" and "such" wording indicates that Paul's lists are not exhaustive. Instead they represent the *kinds* of things that the flesh and the Spirit produce.[14] The apostle assumes that, based on the examples he gives, the reader will go on to identify other vices and virtues.

Galatians 5 is not the only passage that works this way. Romans also employs "such" language in enumerating sins (1:32; 2:2–3). So does Hebrews 13:16, when discussing acts of sacrificial service. First Timothy

---

[12] Ibid.

[13] Bock, *Luke, Volume 2,* 1050–51.

[14] This is a standard observation made by commentators. See, for example, Fung, *Galatians,* 260, 273; Moo, *Galatians,* 362, 366; Schreiner, *Galatians,* 348.

1 uses different terminology but is more emphatic. In verses 9–10 Paul lists various categories of law-breakers such as murderers and liars. Then he writes, "And whatever else is contrary to sound doctrine" (v. 10). This statement shows that "Paul not only *allows,* but *expects* the reader, as he encounters various circumstances in life, to expand the list to include items not mentioned."[15]

In addition to Old Testament laws and passages that explicitly indicate a paradigm, should we read other passages paradigmatically? Once more I'll defer a full answer until later chapters, but I'll appeal to common sense for the moment. It's unlikely that someone would say these precise words to a young person (Prov 1:11–14):

> Come with us, let us lie in wait for blood; let us ambush the innocent without reason; like Sheol let us swallow them alive, and whole, like those who go down to the pit; we shall find all precious goods, we shall fill our houses with plunder; throw in your lot among us; we will all have one purse.

Yet these words do reflect the selfish, violent *attitude* that characterizes those who should be avoided (vv. 15–19). Likewise, Proverbs 7 graphically depicts how a "forbidden woman" seduces a young man. The reader intuitively recognizes that he may not face every last detail in this account but that the passage reflects the *kinds* of temptations he will encounter.

Think again of the teachings of Jesus. In warning against sinful anger, he said, "Whoever says to his brother, 'You good-for-nothing,' shall be guilty before the supreme court; and whoever says, 'You fool,' shall be guilty enough to go into the fiery hell" (Matt 5:22, NASB). Should we suppose that "good-for-nothing" and "fool" are the only words that can communicate sinful anger? Or are these terms illustrative of a whole raft of hurtful epithets? Also in the Sermon on the Mount, Jesus urged his followers not to worry about whether they will have sufficient food, drink, and clothing (Matt 6:25–34). Do our Lord's

---

[15] Leedy, *Love Not,* 92.

heartwarming words not speak to other matters about which we are tempted to worry?

The Epistles provide us with more examples. Ephesians 5:18 says, "Do not get drunk with wine." Would this text not naturally relate to other intoxicating substances? James 1:27 teaches that a major component of "pure and undefiled" religion is "to visit orphans and widows in their affliction." Are these the only types of suffering people to whom we should show compassion? Surely such passages "say more than they say."

Conclusion

Our applications can end up undermining the authority of Scripture, and later chapters will warn against that danger. But here I've argued that rightly done application is actually *the way* the Bible exercises authority over us. We've observed this in the time-bound and timeless character of God's Word, its implicit genres, and its general and paradigmatic instruction. The very nature of Scripture demonstrates that application is an obligation not an option.

Chapter 5

The Scope of Sanctification

What we've concluded from the nature of Scripture correlates with the scope of sanctification. The comprehensiveness of sanctification requires moving beyond the biblical text and engaging in application. Without application we simply won't be able to display the image of God that we were created and redeemed to display.

The Heart

Whether in the Old or New Testament, God's plan for conforming his people to his image has always focused on the heart. Scriptural terms for the heart typically refer not to the physical organ that pumps blood but to the inner person, the immaterial core that drives our lives. "As in water face reflects face, so the heart of man reflects the man" (Prov 27:19). This verse uses "the heart" for the inner person generally. More commonly, heart terminology refers to specific aspects or functions of the inner person, whether the mind (e.g., Deut 4:9), the emotions (e.g., 1 Kgs 21:7), the will (e.g., 2 Cor 9:7), or even the conscience (e.g., 1 Sam 24:5).

The heart is the source of our actions and must therefore be carefully guarded (Prov 4:23; Matt 12:34–35; Mark 7:14–23). Indeed, the Bible's two most important commands—loving God and loving neighbor—are fundamentally affairs of the heart (Matt 22:34-40). So is saving faith (10:9–10). Before conversion the heart is corrupt, hardened against God, and selfish (Jer 17:9; Eph 4:17–19). But through regeneration God gives us a new heart, including a capacity and an inclination to please him (Deut 30:6; Ezek 36:26–27; Rom 2:29; 6:17).

Jesus taught, "Where your treasure is, there your heart will be also" (Matt 6:21). What we value and desire reveals the condition of our hearts and determines our actions. Even with a new heart, because of the flesh we continue to experience ungodly desires (Gal 5:17; Jas 4:1–3). So throughout our progressive sanctification the Lord calls us to a pure heart (1 Tim 1:5; 1 Pet 1:22) and works within us to that end (Eph 3:14–21; 1 Thess 3:13). True growth happens in our hearts, as desire for God and his glory increasingly displaces desire for sin—what the Scottish preacher Thomas Chalmers (1780–1847) memorably called "the expulsive power of a new affection."[1]

But how do we go about dealing with our hearts? For one, we should assess what is going on in our inner person. One writer suggests "X-ray questions" that help expose the state of our hearts. Here are some:

- *What do you love? Hate? . . .*
- *What do you seek, aim for, and pursue? What are your goals and expectations? . . .*
- *Where do you bank your hopes? . . .*
- *What do you fear? What do you not want? What do you tend to worry about? . . .*
- *Where do you find refuge, safety, comfort, escape, pleasure, security? . . .*
- *Whom must you please? Whose opinion of you counts? From whom do you desire approval and fear rejection? . . .*
- *What do you think about most often? What preoccupies or obsesses you? In the morning, to what does your mind drift instinctively?*[2]

Examining our hearts is an exercise in application. As we ponder such questions in the light of Scripture, God brings us to repentance and renewal. A healthy measure of self-evaluation contributes to our growth.[3]

---

[1] See the sermon by this title in *Works of Thomas Chalmers,* 381–88.

[2] Powlison, *Seeing with New Eyes,* 129–43 (emphasis original).

[3] See, for example, Ps 119:59; Lam 3:40; Hag 1:5–7; 1 Cor 11:27–31; 2 Cor 13:5–6; Gal 6:3–4; Jas 1:22–25.

This biblical focus on the heart means that we must not view our use of Scripture as a mechanical process. In a sense the Bible serves as our manual for life. Sanctification, however, is not about following neat steps such as you would find in the instructions for assembling a cabinet: "Attach panel A to panel B as pictured, insert cam screw 3 into predrilled hole Q, then turn screw 180 degrees." Actually, growth in holiness can be a rather messy ordeal. In addition to studying the Bible's teaching, we have to evaluate our own thoughts, motives, and desires in light of that teaching. Thankfully, the indwelling Holy Spirit guides us. But my point here is that application is indispensable if we're going to experience heart-sanctification.

Discernment

The priority of the heart doesn't imply that external behavior is insignificant. As evident from many passages I've referenced so far, God's work of sanctification transforms our internal dispositions *and* our external actions. In fact, sanctification is all-encompassing: God intends to make us like Christ in every detail of our lives (e.g., 1 Cor 10:31; Col 3:17). We have seen that in order to make progress toward this goal we need to draw inferences from Scripture. We have also seen that we must assess extra-biblical issues on the basis of biblical teaching. Several passages deal specifically with this duty of assessment. They teach that sanctification requires a skill in application called *discernment.*

Making Distinctions

Several biblical terms contribute to the biblical concept of discernment. In the Old Testament, the key Hebrew words are the verb *bîn* and the related nouns *bînâh* and *tebûnâh.* They overlap with other Hebrew words in the category of "understanding." Examples include terms denoting insight or prudence (noun *sekel,* verb *sākal*) and wisdom or skill in decision-making (noun *khokmâh,* verb *khākam,* adjective *khākām*).

Nevertheless, the *bîn* word group is associated with the aspect of discriminating or making distinctions between things. Solomon's prayer is a classic case: "Give your servant therefore an understanding mind to govern your people, that I may discern [*bîn*] between good and evil, for who is able to govern this your great people?" (1 Kgs 3:9). Here the idea of distinctions is reinforced by the fact that the Hebrew preposition translated "between" is *bên*, which also belongs to the *bîn* word group.[4] Because Solomon had asked for "discernment [*bîn*] to understand justice," God promised to give the king "a wise [*khākām*] and discerning [*bîn*] heart" (vv. 11–12, NASB). Solomon soon had an opportunity to put it to use: he deftly identified which of two women claiming a baby was the true mother (vv. 16–28).

Naturally, definitions of discernment often center on the idea of making distinctions. Jay Adams says discernment is "*the divinely given ability to distinguish God's thoughts and ways from all others.*"[5] Tim Challies expands: "*The skill of understanding and applying God's Word with the purpose of separating truth from error and right from wrong.*"[6]

This emphasis on distinctions is sometimes reflected in the New Testament verb *diakrinō* and its related noun *diakrisis*.[7] The key passage here is Hebrews 5:11–14:

> About this [the priesthood of Christ] we have much to say, and it is hard to explain, since you have become dull of hearing. For though by this time you ought to be teachers, you need someone to teach you again the basic principles of the oracles of God. You need milk, not solid food, for everyone who lives on milk is unskilled in the word of righteousness, since he is a child. But solid food is for the mature, for those who have their powers of discernment trained by constant practice to distinguish [*diakrisis*] good from evil.

The writer expresses disappointment with the spiritual immaturity of the Hebrew Christians to whom he was writing. He asserts that they have become sluggish in hearing (v. 11). He says that they need to

---

[4] See *HALOT*, 1:122–23.

[5] Adams, *Call for Discernment*, 49 (emphasis original).

[6] Challies, *Spiritual Discernment*, 61 (emphasis original).

[7] See BDAG, 231.

relearn the "milk" or "basic principles" of God's Word, calling them infants (vv. 12–13). Regardless of the specific content of "the word of righteousness" (v. 13),[8] their lack of skill with it includes a failure to use what they had been taught.

A breakdown in application has arrested the growth of the Hebrew Christians and has kept them from developing the discernment described in verse 14. This verse teaches key truths about discernment.

- Discernment involves distinguishing between "good and evil." This seems to be a general statement that relates to both doctrine and conduct.[9]
- Discernment results from spiritual maturity.
- More specifically, discernment comes from exercising one's sensibilities. The term translated "trained by constant practice" is *gymnazō,* the source of the English term *gymnasium.* It speaks of exercise and discipline. Sanctification requires the development of our moral faculties through practice with real-life issues.

Testing and Approving

We'll come to similar conclusions as we see another way in which the Bible describes discernment. In Ephesians 5:8 Paul exhorts us to "walk as children of light," which verse 9 defines as reflecting the moral goodness of our God. Then verse 10 explains how to do this: by "trying to learn what is pleasing to the Lord" (NASB). The Greek participle translated "trying to learn" is from the verb *dokimazō,* which means "to put to the test." It was used for the examination of an item such as an alleged precious metal to determine whether it was genuine. If the item passed the test, *dokimazō* carried the idea of "approve" (e.g., 1 Pet 1:7).[10] With this term, Ephesians 5:10 urges us to evaluate carefully each option before us in order to determine which one(s) would bring pleasure to God.

---

[8] See Lane, *Hebrews 1–8,* 137–39.

[9] Ellingworth, *Hebrews,* 309–10.

[10] See BDAG, 255-56.

This isn't mere Bible study or obedience to clear-cut commandments. As Harold Hoehner points out, God's statements in Scripture do not need our approval. Instead the testing evaluates the moral quality of extra-biblical matters on the basis of pertinent biblical instruction.

> It is to test the will of God for every aspect of life and to approve what would be pleasing to him. The Word of God is a guide for this purpose. However, certain situations in life are not directly addressed in the Scriptures. In such cases, believers need to find principles from the Scriptures whereby they might be able to make choices that will please the Lord. Although not mentioned here, as the Scriptures are consulted the Holy Spirit enlightens and enables believers to discern what is pleasing to the Lord.[11]

Ephesians 5 elaborates on the need for discernment. Verse 15 says, "Look carefully then how you walk, not as unwise but as wise." The adverb translated "carefully" (*akribōs*) refers to accuracy. Herod used it when he told the wise men to search "diligently" for the newborn Christ (Matt 2:8). Luke used it for the thoroughness of his research into the life of Jesus (Luke 1:3). Most strikingly, Paul employed the superlative form of the related adjective *akribēs* to describe the Pharisees as "the strictest party" of Judaism (Acts 26:5). The Pharisees had plenty of problems in matters of application, and we'll discuss those later. But we can't view their concern for details of conduct as problematic in itself since Ephesians 5:15 calls Christians to that very concern. Charles Hodge said that "look carefully then how you walk" means "to walk strictly by rule, so as not to deviate by a hair's breadth."[12] I'm reminded of the English pastor Richard Rogers (ca. 1550–1618). Like other early Puritans, he was mocked as a "precisian" because of his conscientious attention to details of Christian doctrine and lifestyle. Once someone asked him why he was so precise, and Rogers answered, "*I serve a precise God.*"[13]

---

[11] Hoehner, *Ephesians,* 676–77.

[12] Hodge, *Ephesians,* 218.

[13] Cited in Packer, *Quest for Godliness,* 114 (emphasis original).

As he concludes this section of Ephesians, Paul connects precise living with discernment: "Therefore do not be foolish, but understand what the will of the Lord is" (5:17). Here again, the apostle isn't telling us simply to read our Bibles. He is charging us to "figure out" God's will by bringing biblical truth to bear on whatever issue we face, whether or not it is explicitly discussed in Scripture.

Some Other Pauline Texts

In other passages penned by Paul, the Spirit underscores the need for discernment. Dealing with prophecies in first-century church meetings, the apostle writes, "But test [*dokimazō*] everything; hold fast what is good. Abstain from every form of evil" (1 Thess 5:21–22). And Romans 12:2 says that as our way of thinking is renewed, discernment is a key effect: "Do not be conformed to this world, but be transformed by the renewal of your mind, that by testing you may discern [*dokimazō*] what is the will of God, what is good and acceptable and perfect." Such passages lead Frank Thielman to write,

> This [discernment] approach to ethics seems to have been a studied aspect of Paul's theological convictions. Although he certainly handed on to those under his pastoral care a set body of ethical teaching . . . he also intentionally left room for believers to make decisions by using their own renewed thinking.[14]

Paul's prayer for the believers at Philippi also highlights the role of discernment in sanctification.

> And it is my prayer that your love may abound more and more, with knowledge and all discernment, so that you may approve what is excellent, and so be pure and blameless for the day of Christ, filled with the fruit of righteousness that comes through Jesus Christ, to the glory and praise of God.

Paul prays for the Philippians to have greater love, but he distinguishes love from mere emotion or sentimentality. He ties Christian love to four expressions related to discernment. First, the Greek word

---

[14] Thielman, *Ephesians*, 341.

for "knowledge" (*epignōsis,* v. 9) seems to refer to a depth of knowledge —personal knowledge of God and/or spiritual/moral knowledge gained by experience.[15]

Second, the term translated "discernment" (*aisthēsis,* v. 9) occurs only here in the New Testament. But it shares the same root with the word translated "powers" or "senses" (NASB) in Hebrews 5:14 (*aisthētērion*). The Greek translation of Proverbs regularly uses *aisthēsis* for practically oriented knowledge or insight (e.g., 5:2). It comes into English in the word *aesthesia* (the ability to feel or perceive) and its better-known opposite, *anesthesia.* Note also the comprehensiveness of the perception Paul requests: "all discernment" or "every kind of insight" (NET©).

Third, knowledgeable, discerning love will enable Christians to "test so as to approve" (*dokimazō*) "what is excellent" (v. 10).[16] The last phrase describes that which is superior to other things, as in Matthew 6:26: "Look at the birds of the air: they neither sow nor reap nor gather into barns, and yet your heavenly Father feeds them. Are you not *of more value* than they?" (emphasis added). In Philippians 1:10 the nuance may be "things that are essential" versus things that are indifferent (*adiaphora*), or "things that truly matter" versus things that are of little or no value.[17] Some see this idea as an anticipation of Paul's later statement that he abandoned all his credentials and achievements for "the surpassing worth of knowing Christ" (3:8).[18]

In any case, "that you may approve what is excellent" has broad relevance for Christian living. The phrase indicates the need to choose

---

[15] Melick, *Philippians,* 64–65.

[16] This translates a participle of the verb *diapherō* that occurs also in Romans 2:18 with reference to the Jews: "And know his [God's] will and approve *what is excellent,* because you are instructed from the law" (emphasis added).

[17] BDAG, 239.

[18] See Thielman, *Philippians,* 41.

not only the good over the evil but also the best over what is merely acceptable. Carson has some excellent comments on this excellence:

> There are countless decisions in life where it is not a question of making a straightforward decision between right and wrong. What you need is extraordinary discernment that helps you perceive how things differ, and then make the best possible choice. . . .
>
> The pursuit of such excellence does not turn on transparent distinctions between right and wrong. It turns, rather, on delicate choices that reflect one's entire value system, one's entire set of priorities, one's heart and mind. That is why Paul prays that the love of the Philippians might abound more and more in knowledge and depth of insight: he wants their hearts and minds to become profoundly Christian, for otherwise they will not discern what is best.[19]

And as Paul ends his prayer, he reveals the purpose for discernment: it will cause us to abound with God-honoring fruit when we stand before the Lord (vv. 10b–11). That expectation will surely motivate the heart of the believer to choose what is best!

A Few More Illustrations

While some passages state the need for discernment, others illustrate that need in discussing particular choices that God's people must make. Not surprisingly, using Solomon's writings requires evaluating specific situations to determine the best course of action. "A word fitly spoken is like apples of gold in a setting of silver" (Prov 25:11). "When words are many, transgression is not lacking, but whoever restrains his lips is prudent" (10:19). It takes discernment to know when to speak and when to remain quiet. "Faithful are the wounds of a friend" (27:6a). "Good sense makes one slow to anger, and it is his glory to overlook an offense" (19:11). Discernment helps us decide when to rebuke a friend and when to spare rebuke.[20]

---

[19] Carson, *Praying with Paul,* 106, 108.

[20] Another example might be Proverbs 26:4–5: "Answer not a fool according to his folly, lest you be like him yourself. Answer a fool according to his folly, lest he be wise in his own eyes." Challies concludes that discernment

We'll look at just one example from the New Testament, one that grows out of Paul's prayer in Philippians 1. In closing this epistle, the apostle writes, "Finally, brothers, whatever is true, whatever is honorable, whatever is just, whatever is pure, whatever is lovely, whatever is commendable, if there is any excellence, if there is anything worthy of praise, think about these things" (4:8). Parallel to other passages I've cited, the repeated "whatever" encompasses all manner of specifics not identified in the text.

Yet we need to look more closely at the actual criteria Paul gives for evaluating our thoughts. Some are fairly simple: you would probably not find it too difficult to determine whether your thoughts are "true," "just," or "pure." The other terms are not as straightforward, however. A lexicon or commentary can provide some help in defining these. For instance, the Greek word translated "honorable" (*semnos*) points to that which commands respect as opposed to that which is base. And "whatever is lovely [*prosphilēs*]" speaks of things that inspire love or are characterized by a wholesome attractiveness.[21] Such definitions are helpful, yet they remain broad.

Here we're facing a tension. On the one hand, Paul assumes that these standards represent objective realities. On the other hand, they are not arrived at simply by referencing clear-cut stipulations. They

---

shows us when to answer a fool and when not to answer him (*Spiritual Discernment,* 57). Following the Greek translation of the Old Testament, however, Waltke argues that the Hebrew preposition *kĕ*, "according to," has a different meaning in each verse. Thus verse 4 says one should not answer a fool *in kind with* or *in agreement with* his folly. But verse 5 says one should answer a fool *as* his folly *deserves,* i.e., one should counter his folly with wisdom (*Proverbs: Chapters 15–31,* 348–50). "Both proverbs are absolutes and applicable at the same time, contrary to the opinion of many commentators, who think they are relative to the situation. To be sure, there is a time to be silent and a time to speak (Eccl. 4:5) [meaning 3:7], but one must always, not only in certain situations, answer a fool to destabilize him, but, always, not sometimes, without becoming like him" (349).

[21] See Melick, *Philippians,* 150–51.

entail value judgments significantly informed by experience in life and culture. Apart from discernment that has been cultivated by the Holy Spirit through interaction between Scripture and life experience, Philippians 4:8 cannot ultimately be obeyed.

To illustrate further the necessity of discernment for sanctification, I leave you with some practical questions posed by Carson.

> What do you do with your time? How many hours a week do you spend with your children? Have you spent any time in the past two months witnessing to someone about the gospel? How much time have you spent watching television or in other forms of personal relaxation? Are you committed, in your use of time, to what is best?
>
> What have you read in the past six months? If you have found time for newspapers or news magazines, a couple of whodunits, a novel or two or perhaps a trade journal, have you also found time for reading a commentary or some other Christian literature that will help you understand the Bible or improve your spiritual discipline or broaden your horizons? Are you committed, in your reading habits, to what is best?[22]

After asking many more such questions, Carson rightly concludes that the best choices in such areas "are the kinds of choices that cannot be made on the basis of mere law. They spring from a heart transformed by God's grace."[23]

Conclusion

Sanctification is so intensive and so extensive that it necessitates the discipline of application. This fact could be discouraging in light of the difficulties we often face in application. We might wish God had included more detail in his Word so that we wouldn't have to think so hard. We might also wish that sanctification were more like following fool-proof steps. While I can relate to such desires, I am convinced they are misguided.

---

[22] Carson, *Praying with Paul,* 108.

[23] Ibid., 109.

Think of how tedious the Bible would be if God had set out to cover every contingency we might face in life. Earlier I spoke of cabinet-assembling instructions. Here's another illustration:

> Because life is not stagnant, no book could give a single command for every possible situation. Not only would such a work be highly un-wieldy, it would also be incredibly boring, resembling an auto-parts catalogue rather than our Bibles (e.g., Cloning sheep: Book 3, section A, part 1, law 3,034,578: You shall not monkey with the genomes of animals.) Thankfully, God had another plan.[24]

More importantly, in light of Hebrews 5:14, consider the stunted growth that would result from such an approach. As an educator, I'm regularly reminded to teach students "higher order thinking skills" not just facts. In particular, I should keep in mind Bloom's taxonomy. In its revised form, this model identifies six categories of cognitive learning that move from simple to complex: Remember, Understand, Apply, Analyze, Evaluate, and Create.[25] As I design curriculum, teach, and assess student learning, I need to concentrate on the latter categories. The goal is not for students to regurgitate information. It is to teach them how to think and how to use what they are learning in real life. This will most contribute to their maturity and long-term success.

Similarly, spiritual growth doesn't come by rote obedience. Christ-likeness isn't robotic compliance with a list of commands. Instead God enables us to develop a genuinely personal relationship with himself. He calls on us to nurture heart affections toward him and to internalize his values through meditation on Scripture. And he intends that we be actively engaged in discerning the relevance of his Word to our circumstances. This is how he moves us from childhood to maturity.

---

[24] Köstenberger and Patterson, *Invitation to Biblical Interpretation*, 786–77.

[25] See Bloom, *Taxonomy of Educational Objectives;* Anderson et al., *Taxonomy for Learning, Teaching, and Assessing.*

The Lord has also blessed us with multiple resources to teach us how to use his Word. The next part of our study will explore one of these resources.

Part III

Patterns
for Biblical Application

Chapter 6

Foundational Application Patterns

As I began to write this chapter, our church's administrative assistant was finishing up the annual pictorial directory. It's a tedious process. It involves making sure that each person's contact information is correct, not to mention all the birthdays and anniversaries. Even in a smaller church, that's a lot of numbers to keep straight! In addition, photographs have to be scheduled, taken, formatted, and inserted into what becomes a hefty electronic file that seems to have a mind of its own. Why go through all this hassle, especially with the pictures? The pictorial directory serves us in several ways, but newcomers find it especially useful. The directory helps them become familiar with the church folks by putting a face with a name.

We all understand the value of images, whether visual or verbal, to engage people and clarify ideas. It's why children's books abound with drawings and pictures. It's why designers enrich websites with graphics. And it's why teachers use object lessons and preachers use sermon illustrations. Our Creator also understands the benefits of analogies, and he has filled his Word with them.

In establishing the necessity of application, Part II shared many biblical illustrations related to the nature of Scripture and the scope of sanctification. Part III centers on illustrations of another sort: cases where biblical writers apply earlier biblical teaching. Yet these instances of application do more than illustrate. They provide divinely inspired *patterns* for our own application of God's Word.

Old Testament Precedent

We'll study these patterns inductively and gradually draw conclusions for our application of Scripture. First I'll cover a few examples from the Old Testament. Application belongs so much to the warp and woof of the Old Testament that we could easily overlook it. And the practice of the Old Testament writers established a precedent that would be followed extensively in the New Testament.

Applying the Torah

From Joshua forward, almost everything in the Old Testament could be described in some way as an application of the books of the Pentateuch, or the Torah—Israel's foundational covenant documents. First, the Historical Books assess the nation and her leaders on the basis of the Mosaic Law. Joshua, Judges, Samuel, and Kings, for instance, characteristically evaluate developments in Israel's history as consequences of the nation's obedience or disobedience to the mandates of Deuteronomy particularly.[1] To cite just one passage, 2 Kings 14 gives a mixed assessment of Amaziah, king of Judah. On the one hand, verse 4 says he did not remove the high places, which violated Deuteronomy 12's insistence on a single place of corporate worship for Israel. On the other hand, verse 6 says Amaziah did not kill the children of his father's assassins, quoting Deuteronomy 24:16 as the law that the king was obeying here.

As we move to the Poetical Books, we find more applications of Mosaic instruction. For instance, the Pentateuch's theology of Yahweh and his covenant with Israel undergirds the Psalms. Passages such as Psalms 1, 19, and 119 emphatically teach the transforming power of the Torah beyond the lives of its original recipients. So it's no wonder that

---

[1] Scholars often call these books the "Deuteronomistic History." This label is associated with liberal approaches to the Old Testament. Yet the basic idea of dependence on Deuteronomy remains compatible with an orthodox view of inspiration and belief in the Mosaic authorship of the Pentateuch. See Pratt, *He Gave Us Stories,* 285–94. In fact, the multitude of links between Deuteronomy and later books testifies to the divine unity of Scripture.

general concepts and specific statements from the Pentateuch are cited as relevant for the psalter's readers. Psalm 8 glories in man's dignified position as taught in Genesis 1's Creation account. In extolling God's goodness, Psalm 103:8 reflects Exodus 34:6: "The LORD is merciful and gracious, slow to anger and abounding in steadfast love."

Additionally, several historical psalms relate accounts from the Pentateuch (and the Historical Books) in order to draw practical lessons. Psalm 78 provides such a review so that later generations "should set their hope in God and not forget the works of God, but keep his commandments; and that they should not be like their fathers, a stubborn and rebellious generation, a generation whose heart was not steadfast, whose spirit was not faithful to God" (vv. 7–8).

Perhaps more than any other Old Testament section, the Prophetic Books overflow with applications of the Torah. Ezekiel 18 represents prophetic passages that explicitly cite Mosaic laws as binding on Israelites far removed from Moses's time. But the dependence goes deeper than such quotations. The Torah—particularly its covenant curses and blessings (Lev 26; Deut 28)—supplies the prophets' core message of judgment and restoration. Scholars have done much work to detail the connection between the Pentateuch and the Prophetic Books. Niehaus lists over forty "literary echoes" of the Torah in the nine chapters of Amos alone.[2] Garrett presents similar research on Hosea and concludes, "Hosea's critique of his generation is founded entirely upon the Pentateuch. . . . The interpretation of Hosea is impossible without reckoning with how he used the Torah as his canon."[3] Such evidence leads Fee and Stuart to call the prophets "covenant enforcement mediators," raised up by God to apply the Mosaic Law to their audiences and to announce the consequences of obeying and disobeying it.[4]

---

[2] Niehaus, "Amos," 322–23.

[3] Garrett, *Hosea, Joel,* 27–29.

[4] Fee and Stuart, *How to Read the Bible for All Its Worth,* 190–92.

Applying the Spirit of the Law

Applications of the Pentateuch involved more than technical compliance with precise commands. For instance, the book of Ruth portrays Boaz as a model Israelite who generously implements the ethics of the Law in the particular circumstances of his life. The Law told landowners to leave gleanings for the poor (Lev 19:9–10; 23:22; Deut 24:19). Boaz surpasses this requirement. He not only allows Ruth to glean in his field but also invites her to eat and drink with his workers (Ruth 2:8–14). Furthermore, he instructs his workers to drop stalks of grain on the ground intentionally for Ruth (vv. 15–16).

Boaz's character becomes more impressive as the story unfolds. By the end of the book of Ruth he takes upon himself two familial responsibilities outlined in the Pentateuch. First, in acquiring Elimelech's field (or the rights to use the field), Boaz plays the role of the kinsman-redeemer (Heb. *gō'ēl;* Lev 25:25–29). This guarantees economic stability for Naomi and Ruth. Second, Boaz applies the levirate law of Deuteronomy 25:5–10: if a man died without a son, his brother was to take the man's wife as his own in order to sire a son who would carry on the man's name.[5] Boaz wasn't Ruth's brother-in-law. Nor does the Old Testament stipulate that the kinsman-redeemer law and the levirate law had to be connected. But common-sense custom did connect the two: if Naomi and Ruth survived but had no descendant, their family name would ultimately die out, and their family property would be lost (Ruth 4:5).

Unlike the nearer kinsman, Boaz sacrificially steps in to solve all these problems (Ruth 4:6–13). He understands what we saw in chapter 4 of our study: that the Law is paradigmatic not exhaustive.

> The story of Ruth is the story of *khesed* [loving loyalty, often in a covenant context] motivating beyond the letter of law. The activities of the *gō'ēl* were not confined merely to those prescribed by the law, but the specific laws were pointers or guides showing in concrete fashion how *khesed* might operate within the family. . . . The story of Ruth is

---

[5] The term *levirate* comes from the Latin *levir,* brother-in-law.

therefore the story of the true *gōʾēl*, for it gives us a picture of *khesed* at work, capturing the spirit of the levirate law and operating in a manner consistent with the other activities of the *gōʾēl* on behalf of family members.[6]

Furthermore, Boaz's concern for the spirit of the law does not begin or end with himself; it is a reflection of Yahweh's covenant loyalty (cf. Ruth 1:8; 2:20; 3:10). And as an ancestor of David, Boaz foreshadows the ultimate covenant loyalty of the Messiah.[7] Boaz's applications advance the redemptive plan of God!

Applying Other Sections of the Old Testament

While the Old Testament emphasizes the application of Pentateuchal teaching, each new segment of books begins to be applied in later books. Among the Historical Books, much of Chronicles is an exercise in application, shaping accounts from Samuel and Kings to address the needs of post-exilic Jews as they work to restore the theocracy and its worship.[8] Toward the very end of the Old Testament timeframe, Nehemiah does something similar. He rebukes his contemporaries not only for violating the Pentateuch's commands about the Sabbath (Neh 13:17–18) but also for not learning from Israel's history (vv. 26–27):

> Did not Solomon king of Israel sin on account of such women? Among the many nations there was no king like him, and he was beloved by his God, and God made him king over all Israel. Nevertheless, foreign women made even him to sin. Shall we then listen to you and do all this great evil and act treacherously against our God by marrying foreign women?

---

[6] Leggett, *Levirate and Gōʾēl Institutions*, 249 (transliteration scheme adapted). Various expositors argue for this perspective of Boaz and his place in the book of Ruth, e.g., Block, *Judges, Ruth*, 715. For more on the key word *khesed*, see Baer and Gordon, "חסד," 211–18.

[7] See Ulrich, *From Famine to Fullness*, 103–39.

[8] See Pratt, *He Gave Us Stories*, 296–98.

In addition to the historical psalms, Psalms 89 and 132 represent a number of psalms that apply material from the Historical Books. These two prayers for deliverance appeal to the covenant promises Yahweh made to David about his dynasty (2 Sam 7). So application is not only about obeying commands and implementing ethical ideals. It includes nurturing one's faith on and praying in response to what God has said about his character and commitments.

The Prophetic Books contain various kinds of applications from sections other than the Pentateuch. Jonah's prayer from the fish's belly (Jonah 2) is rich with the language of the psalter.

> It is a good example of Hebrew psalm-poetry in which the poet drew upon the regular liturgical language common to the Book of Psalms and other poems in the Old Testament to fit the situation. It is a beautiful example of a believer who prayed biblically. Inevitably, those who know the Lord will not only speak to one another using biblical language (cf. Eph. 5:19-20) but also to God.[9]

Jeremiah 26:17–19 provides yet another type of example. Here some Jewish elders recall an earlier prophecy of Micah as an argument for heeding the warnings of Jeremiah. And later, Daniel responds to Jeremiah's prophecy of a seventy-year exile by praying for Yahweh to restore his people to their homeland (Dan 9:1–19; cf. Jer 25:11–12; 29:10). God's words are profoundly interconnected and far-reaching!

Christ's Applications in Matthew

While we could look at additional applications in the Old Testament, even more pertinent are the patterns in the New—specifically, New Testament applications of Old Testament texts. Here also I'll need to be highly selective. According to one count, the New Testament contains 295 Old Testament quotations.[10] I've chosen certain ones that seem especially helpful for our topic.

---

[9] Page, "Jonah," in Smith and Page, *Amos, Obadiah, Jonah,* 244–45.

[10] Roger Nicole, "New Testament Use of the Old Testament," in Henry, *Revelation and the Bible,* 137–38. Compare the index of quotations in

Admittedly, the New Testament's use of the Old can be difficult to analyze and highly controversial.[11] Scholars debate the degree to which we should take Jesus Christ, the God-Man, and the supernaturally influenced New Testament writers as models for our own use of the Bible. Here the thorniest issues relate to prophecy, typology, and fulfillment. While not entirely avoiding such matters, our discussion will concentrate on texts dealing with more basic theological and practical topics.[12] I trust you'll see that, regardless of difficulties, these passages do provide us patterns to follow as we seek to apply the Scriptures today. No, we won't be able to follow the patterns inerrantly. But then again, we can't do anything inerrantly! Our fallibility isn't an argument for inactivity but for God-reliant diligence.

In the remainder of this chapter we'll study several biblical applications in the Gospel of Matthew. The theme of this Gospel is that Jesus is the long-awaited Messianic King. This Jewish focus is evident in his frequent applications of the Old Testament. We'll examine a number of these from the mouth of our Lord himself.

Resisting Temptation

Matthew's account of Jesus's temptation abounds with Old Testament connections (4:1–11; cf. Mark 1:12–23; Luke 4:1–13). In general, the

---

Aland, *Greek New Testament,* 887–90. This figure does not include the hundreds or even thousands of Old Testament allusions.

[11] For an entry point into the discussion, see Berding and Lunde, *Three Views.* For a collection of articles arguing for various viewpoints, see Beale, *Right Doctrine from the Wrong Texts?* Especially helpful is Beale, *Handbook on the New Testament Use of the Old Testament,* which explains the method followed in *CNTUOT.* Recent years have seen an explosion of scholarly interest in this field of biblical "intertextuality." The results have been mixed. See, for example, Hays, Alkier, and Huizenga, *Reading the Bible Intertextually.*

[12] In dealing with these passages, I will not be discussing the textual source of their Old Testament quotations (Masoretic-type Hebrew text, Septuagint, etc.). For such questions, consult the relevant sections in *CNTUOT;* cf. Archer and Chirichigno, *Old Testament Quotations in the New Testament.*

passage alludes to Israel's wilderness experience. The nation spent forty years in the desert as punishment for their unbelief and disobedience. By contrast, after forty days and nights in the desert, Jesus displays complete faith and obedience in the face of Satan's attacks. Here Christ acts both as our righteous substitute (Gal 4:4–5) and as the ultimate example of the obedient, self-denying lifestyle to which he calls us as his disciples (Matt 16:24–25; 20:25–28). As our example, his use of the Old Testament to resist temptation models proper application of Scripture.

Satan first tells Jesus to use his power to turn stones into bread (Matt 4:3). Our Lord replies by quoting Deuteronomy 8:3, "Man shall not live by bread alone, but by every word that comes from the mouth of God" (Matt 4:4). In its original context this statement describes a lesson Yahweh taught Israel in the desert. He put them through periods of hunger and fed them with manna so that they would learn to prioritize obedience to his Word over the satisfaction of their physical needs.

Jesus sees a parallel between Israel's situation and his own: he needs to follow God's instructions as to how his bodily needs should be met, and obeying Satan is surely out of keeping with those instructions. As we'll see, our Lord's emphasis on divine instructions pervades his response to the other temptations. He takes Scripture as the *foundation* for all his decisions. He also uses it as a *filter* to assess the options before him. He would not, of course, violate anything God had stated. And in areas where there isn't a specific command, Jesus looks for reasonable parallels between Scripture and what he is facing.

Surprisingly, the second temptation quotes Scripture to argue that Jesus should jump from the pinnacle of the temple. Satan cites Psalm 91:11, "He will command his angels concerning you," and then verse 12, "On their hands they will bear you up, lest you strike your foot against a stone" (Matt 4:6). The devil's application of these verses suffers from two fallacies. First, while Psalm 91 does promise protection, many other passages teach that often it is God's will for his people to suffer— not the least Job, a book that Satan should have known especially well. No one passage or book may be taken as a total description of God's ways with his people; our applications need to be consistent with the whole counsel of God. But second, Satan was twisting Psalm 91 itself. This passage assumes that the dangers in view are faced as a believer walks the path of obedience to Yahweh, not as he does foolish, self-willed things. Verse 14 specifically ties God's deliverance to the psalmist's devotion: "Because he holds fast to me in love, I will deliver him; I will protect him, because he knows my name."

Jesus's response to Satan gets at this point. He quotes Deuteronomy 6:16, "You shall not put the Lord your God to the test" (Matt 4:7). In Deuteronomy this command continues, "As you tested him at Massah." "Massah" refers to a place where the Israelites complained because they had no water, as recorded in Exodus 17:1–7. So Jesus is applying a text that is itself making an application from an event recorded in earlier Scripture. At Massah the Israelites tested the Lord by demanding that he provide for them according to their dictates and refusing to trust him unless he complied. In Deuteronomy 6 Moses reminds the people of this incident in warning them not to test Yahweh, specifically by seeking help from pagan gods instead of depending on him and following his ways (vv. 10–15, 17–19).

By jumping off the temple, Jesus would also have been testing God, insisting that his Father act according to a selfish agenda instead of humbly following the Father's plan. The touching irony is that momentarily that plan would include the ministry of angels to Jesus (Matt 4:11), in keeping with the promise of Psalm 91. In any case, although the testings of God in Exodus, Deuteronomy, and Matthew differ in their particulars, they share the basic ideas of unbelief and presumption. Because of this unity of thought, Jesus takes the Old Testament passages as reflecting God's answer to Satan's second temptation.

The third temptation is the most blatant, calling on Jesus to worship the devil (Matt 4:9). Jesus's answer is the most straightforward, citing Deuteronomy 6:13: "You shall worship the Lord your God and him only shall you serve" (v. 10). This command had been given to the Israelites almost 1500 years earlier, prohibiting them from worshiping the gods of surrounding nations (Deut 6:14). But it also prohibits Jesus, the ultimate Israelite, from worshiping God's arch-enemy.

So how does Jesus respond to Satan's temptations? All three times he quotes a passage from the Old Testament. He assumes that each passage teaches a theological/ethical truth that transcends the time and circumstances of its original recipients. He relates that truth to his own circumstances. And he accepts this connection as indicating the Father's will for him. As Blomberg says, "Jesus is distilling the timeless spiritual or moral principle contained in the text of Deuteronomy and applying it to his temptation."[13]

The Spirit of the Law Revisited

Applications of the Old Testament permeate Jesus's Sermon on the Mount (Matt 5–7; cf. Luke 6:17–49). The most explicit appear in Matthew 5, beginning with these words: "Do not think that I have come to abolish the Law or the Prophets; I have not come to abolish them but to fulfill them" (v. 17). "The Law or the Prophets" reflects the Jews' way of describing their entire Bible as "the Law and the Prophets." So our Lord says he didn't come to abolish the Old Testament but to fulfill it. The term *fulfill* suggests the accomplishment of a prediction. Yet a great deal of the Old Testament doesn't fall into the category of predictive prophecy. In particular, how does Jesus fulfill the legal portions?

To answer this question, we first need to note that the Greek term translated "fulfill" (*plēroō*) essentially means to fill or make full. The New Testament uses the word for different kinds of filling, and the context determines which kind is in view.[14] The idea that seems to fit best in Matthew 5:17 is that of bringing something to *completion or full realization*. The Messiah and his work constitute the full realization of everything the Old Testament revealed about God and his ways.

---

[13] Craig L. Blomberg, "Matthew," in *CNTUOT,* 15. I found Blomberg's analysis especially helpful in writing this section.

[14] For a survey of the usage of *plēroō,* see BDAG, 827–29.

This takes several forms. Jesus Christ certainly brings about the accomplishment of specific predictions such as Isaiah's Immanuel prophecy (Isa 7:14, cited in Matt 1:22–23).[15] He also culminates divine patterns established by historical events such as the Exodus (Hos 11:1, cited in Matt 2:15).[16] But as it relates to the Old Testament's legal material, I believe Christ is saying that he fulfills it in that he teaches the *full intention or goal* of the Mosaic Law.[17] Our Lord begins to explain this in verses 18–20. Here he not only upholds the abiding authority of the Law but also calls his disciples to a righteousness that surpasses that of the legal experts and the Pharisees.

Six Case Studies

What this means becomes evident as Christ goes on to discuss six kinds of laws, expounding the ethical goal at which these laws were aiming. In the first two cases he identifies internal dispositions that were ultimately

---

[15] On Isaiah 7:14 as a prediction of the virginal conception of the Messiah, see Motyer, *Isaiah*, 84–86.

[16] On Matthew's use of Hosea 11:1, see Barrett, *Love Divine and Unfailing*, 169–77.

[17] For interpretations generally parallel to mine, see Bock and Simpson, *Jesus*, 207–16; Hagner, *Matthew 1–13*, 102–36; Nolland, *Matthew*, 215–71; Stott, *Sermon on the Mount*, 69–124; Turner, *Matthew*, 157–78. Alternatively, many hold that *plēroō* indicates that Christ personally brings about the eschatological realization of the Law. See, for example, Carson, "Matthew," 171–96; compare Blomberg, *Matthew*, 103–15; Poythress, *Shadow of Christ*, 263–69; 363–77. The idea here is that the Messiah himself fulfilled the Mosaic Law, and one result is that the Law as a whole is not directly binding on believers in this era. At the same time, "the law of Christ" for Christians (1 Cor 9:21) may transform, maintain, extend, or annul individual Mosaic laws. For an excellent presentation of this view and further documentation, see DeRouchie, *How to Understand and Apply the Old Testament*, 427–59. I find much to appreciate in this approach. My own approach likewise sees the coming of Christ as central to the issue of the Law today. Additionally, there is much overlap between the two approaches when it comes to the present relevance of individual laws. See further, Casillas, *The Law and the Christian*, and my comments about the Law in chapter 12 below.

being addressed by the Law's external prohibitions. He says that hostile anger, not just the act of murder, is sinful (vv. 21–26). Likewise, lust counts as a form of adultery (vv. 27–30). These truths should have been apparent to readers of the Old Testament. Leviticus 19 told the Israelites not to hate, take vengeance on, or bear a grudge against their countrymen (vv. 17–18). And the tenth commandment prohibited coveting the wife of one's neighbor (Exod 20:17). But our Lord brings these matters of the heart to the forefront.

The other case studies are more complex. In verses 31–32 Jesus allows divorce only in the case of sexually immoral activity. This seems to be more restrictive than the concession in Deuteronomy 24:1–4 and is definitely more restrictive than the use of that text by many Jewish teachers.[18] Matthew's parallel passage on divorce explains Christ's reasoning (19:1–12). God originally designed marriage to be a permanent union (vv. 4–6; cf. Gen 2:24), but the Law permitted divorce "because of your hardness of heart" (Matt 19:8). Jesus's position moves back toward the original divine ideal. Something like this is Christ's point in the fourth instance of how he fulfills the Law: oaths (5:33–37). Though assumed by the Law (Lev 19:12; Num 30:2; Deut 23:21, 23), such emphatic affirmations of one's trustworthiness are unnecessary if Jesus's disciples are unswervingly honest people.

Next Jesus quotes the law, "An eye for an eye and a tooth for a tooth" (Matt 5:38; cf. Exod 21:24; Lev 24:20; Deut 19:21). A judicial penalty had to correspond to the offense committed. While this law promoted the punishment of the guilty, it also limited that punishment to what was fair, thus curtailing vengeance. Christ fulfills this law by taking the restraint on vengeance a step further: there will be times when his

---

[18] In Deuteronomy 24:1 the phrase "some indecency" (lit. "nakedness of a thing") probably does not refer to adultery since the Pentateuch elsewhere requires the death penalty for adultery (Lev 20:10; Deut 22:22). For discussion of this matter and the Bible's broader teaching on divorce and remarriage, see Murray, *Divorce;* Strauss, *Remarriage after Divorce.* Compare Newheiser, *Marriage, Divorce, and Remarriage.*

followers should humbly suffer injustice (vv. 39–41). Positively, they should give to the needy, beyond the requirements of justice (v. 42).

Jesus's final sample begins this way: "You have heard that it was said, 'You shall love your neighbor and hate your enemy'" (Matt 5:43). The Law commanded love for one's neighbor (Lev 19:18) but nowhere commanded a corresponding hatred for one's enemy. In fact, a passage I mentioned in chapter 4 required compassion toward the animal of one's enemy (Exod 23:4-5). In other texts, however, Yahweh ordered Israel to execute his judgment on or otherwise oppose certain people groups that had incurred his righteous wrath (e.g., Deut 7; 23:3–6; cf. Ps 139:21–22). Perhaps from such passages some Jews inferred that they should hate their enemies generally.[19]

This would illustrate another way that Scripture can be *mis*applied: by overgeneralizing from narrow contexts while ignoring other biblical evidence (e.g., Deut 23:7–8; Prov 25:21–22). By contrast, Jesus tells his disciples to love their enemies actively (Matt 5:43–44). This would accomplish the Law's overriding concern that God's people imitate his unique character (vv. 45–48; cf. Lev 19:2; Deut 10:18–19).

Getting at the Essence

What is our Lord doing in Matthew 5:17–48? He is clarifying, emphasizing, and applying the internal virtue that the Mosaic Law was driving at. The essence of this virtue is God-like love, a love that motivates behavior that goes beyond the stated requirements of the Law (vv. 45–48; cf. 7:12). This parallels the pattern we saw in the life of Boaz.

It also parallels the viewpoint of some Jewish teachers. In documenting the oral tradition of the Rabbis, the Talmud refers to the concept of *lifnim mishurat hadin.*[20] This phrase means "beyond the line

---

[19] Craig L. Blomberg, "Matthew," in *CNTUOT,* 27.

[20] For a brief summary, see "Li-Fenim Mi-Shurat Ha-din," *New Encyclopedia of Judaism,* 478. For analysis of the evidence from the Talmud, see Newman, *Past Imperatives,* 17–44. I thank Craig Hartman of Shalom Ministries for drawing my attention to the concept of *lifnim mishurat hadin.*

of the law." It describes implementations of the spirit of the law that exceed its letter, particularly the foregoing of a legal right in order to show compassion to another party. Rabbinic scholars have compared Jesus's teaching to this strand of Jewish tradition, over against a tendency toward superficiality among the Pharisees.[21]

Our next section will begin dealing with our Lord's frequent criticism of the Pharisees for being unduly "strict." Yet in the Sermon on the Mount he issues a counterpoint: in many respects the Pharisees' standards are too *low*. They focus only on externals and technicalities while ignoring the internal and relational things that matter most to God (cf. Matt 23:23–24). Jesus calls his followers to live on a higher plane, internalizing the ethical objectives of the Law. This does not necessarily mean that a disciple will do less than what the Pharisees do. It will often mean that he will do *more* than what the Pharisees and the Law itself stipulate. That is our Lord's point in saying, "Unless your righteousness exceeds that of the scribes and Pharisees, you will never enter the kingdom of heaven" (5:20).

In fact, Christ indicates that in its toleration of certain practices the Mosaic Law itself did not completely embody God's ethical ideal. In some areas such as divorce it was a provisional statement. Jesus expresses fully what the Law, as an early expression in the progress of revelation, expressed partially.

---

[21] A key proponent is Sigal, *Halakhah*, 93–97. He has some extreme views, e.g., a sharp distinction between the Pharisees and the forerunners of Rabbinic Judaism. More importantly, one must exercise great caution with scholars who do not believe in the inspiration of the New Testament and the divine Messiahship of Jesus. Yet writers such as Sigal can provide helpful material on the Jewish milieu in which Jesus taught. For more comparisons between the Sermon on the Mount and various Jewish methods of application, see Flusser, *Judaism*, 102–25, 490–508. Due to space constraints, I will not be detailing further connections between the New Testament and Jewish methods of interpretation and application. On this issue, see Beale, *Handbook on the New Testament Use of the Old Testament*, 1–5, 46–48, 103–32.

Furthermore, Jesus's own teaching needs to be wisely applied. In dealing with the issue of lust, he speaks hyperbolically as he urges his followers to tear out an eye or cut off a hand that causes one to sin (Matt 5:28–29). Actually, blind and maimed people can still lust. Each disciple will need to figure out what it is that he may need to "amputate."[22]

Additionally, Jesus's prohibition of oaths doesn't seem to be absolute (vv. 34–37). After all, he allows himself to be put under oath in a legal setting (26:63). Paul also calls on God as his witness (e.g., Rom 1:9), and the writer of Hebrews views God's oath to Abraham as a good thing (6:13–17). Likewise, "turning the other cheek" (Matt 5:39) is not the only acceptable response to hostility. Sometimes even Jesus avoided his persecutors (Luke 4:29–30; John 8:59; 10:39). So did Paul (Acts 9:23–25).

Following our Lord's teaching involves not only comparing Scripture with Scripture but also identifying specific life situations to which it applies. Thankfully, as we saw in chapter 3, believers enjoy union with Christ and the power of the Holy Spirit so that we can increasingly live by the ideals of the Sermon on the Mount.

Sabbath Applications

Sabbath observance was a major bone of contention between the Pharisees and Jesus. In Matthew 12:1–8, the charge was that Jesus's disciples were disobeying the Law by picking heads of grain as they walked through some fields on the Sabbath (cf. Mark 2:23–28; Luke 6:1–5). No Old Testament law prohibited this, but the disciples' activity violated the rules that Jewish tradition had established as "fences" to avoid breaking God's command to refrain from work on the Sabbath (e.g., Exod 20:8–11). Jesus doesn't reply that building such fences is inherently inappropriate. Instead he argues for his own application.

First, Christ cites an event recorded in 1 Samuel 21:1–6 (Matt. 12:3–4). Here, as they flee from Saul, David and his men are starving,

---

[22] See Adams, *Temptation.*

and David asks Ahimelech the priest for some food. Ahimelech gives what he has available at the time—the sacred Bread of the Presence that the Law restricted to the priesthood (Lev. 24:5–9). From this incident Jesus infers that meeting human needs takes priority over matters of worship ritual. Consequently, his disciples should be permitted to pick some grain on the Sabbath.

Jesus's second argument addresses ritual issues more specifically. He reminds his opponents that the Law provides for priests to work in the temple on the Sabbath, by preparing and offering sacrifices (Matt 12:5; cf. Num 28:9–10). Then follows this bold assertion: "I tell you, something greater than the temple is here" (v. 6). This is a lesser-to-greater inference: if temple priests can work on the Sabbath, then the one who supersedes the temple can let his disciples "work" as well. This kind of logic was likely implicit in Jesus's initial argument: he is greater than David, so the needs of his followers take precedence over Sabbath scruples.[23]

Third, Christ quotes Hosea 6:6: "And if you had known what this means [lit. what is], 'I desire mercy, and not sacrifice,' you would not have condemned the guiltless" (Matt 12:7). In my view, the Greek term underlying "mercy" (*eleos*) would best be rendered "loyalty" or "loyal love" here.[24] That's because it is itself translating the Hebrew *khesed,* the word for loyal love that we noted in the book of Ruth. And by paralleling *khesed* with "the knowledge of God," Hosea 6:6 suggests that *khesed* here is loyalty to God. The verse teaches that a personal relationship with and commitment to God are more important than the liturgical duties he has prescribed.

How does this relate to the Sabbath controversy? Jesus's logic goes something like this:

- Loyal love for God is more important than ceremonial regulations (Hos 6:6).

---

[23] See Carson, "Matthew," 322–27; France, *Matthew,* 458–59.

[24] For a similar view, see Carson, "Matthew," 264–65, 326.

- Loyal love for God is reflected in love for others. (This truth is implicit in Hosea 6. Verses 8–9 specifically condemn certain Israelites for violent treatment of their countrymen.)
- Love for others would allow the disciples to pick and eat grain on the Sabbath.

To be sure, Jesus is rebuking the Pharisees for not showing "mercy." But his point is stronger than this: though the Pharisees observe the Sabbath fastidiously, their lack of love for the disciples shows that they don't genuinely love *God*. Using the same verse from Hosea, Jesus had similarly rebuked the Pharisees when they questioned his eating with tax collectors and sinners (Matt 9:13).

The final argument simply declares, "For the Son of man is lord of the sabbath" (Matt 12:8). Jesus asserts the prerogative to teach about the Sabbath authoritatively since he is the Messiah. And his teaching has been impressive indeed. In making his case, he has appealed to passages from throughout the Old Testament: the Pentateuch (Lev 24; Num 28), the Historical Books (1 Sam 21), and the Prophetic Books (Hos 6).

What does Jesus do with these passages? He uses deductive logic, reasoning from premises to conclusions. And he takes the conclusions as resolving the Sabbath debate. Given his divine identity, Christ expects the Pharisees to accept his applications as definitive. But he isn't saying that no one else should reason from Scripture in this way. Notice how our Lord introduces the first three arguments:
- "Have you not read what David did . . ." (Matt 12:3)
- "Or have you not read in the Law . . ." (v. 5)
- "And if ye had known what this means . . ." (v. 7)

These statements suggest that the Pharisees should be able to come to the same applications Jesus did. If they begin with the right premises and then reason correctly, they should arrive at our Lord's conclusions.

The third statement above is especially thought-provoking. It implies that the Pharisees' failure to apply Hosea 6:6 indicates that they do not truly *understand* the verse. Proper application is what proves that one properly understands Scripture. So Jesus's controversy with the Pharisees is not over *whether* to apply Scripture but over *how* to apply it.

111

Proving the Resurrection

In our final example from Matthew we'll see more emphasis on the use of logic to relate a passage to an issue beyond the explicit statement of that passage. Though this example doesn't center on a question of ethics, it contributes significantly to our discussion.

Matthew 21–23 records Jesus's final confrontations with the Jewish leadership, leading up to his arrest, trial, and crucifixion. This section contains multiple Old Testament applications, but I want to concentrate on the discussion Christ has with the Sadducees (22:23–33; cf. Mark 12:18–27; Luke 20:27–40). As the custodians of the high priesthood and the majority party in the Sanhedrin, the Sadducees had reason to fear Jesus's influence. Like the Pharisees, they attempt to trip him up theologically. Unlike the Pharisees and Jesus himself, the Sadducees denied the doctrine of the resurrection (Matt 22:23). They present our Lord with a scenario aimed at exposing this doctrine as absurd: at the resurrection, whose wife will a woman be if she had married seven men due to the Old Testament's levirate law (vv. 24–28)?

Christ answers with two rebuttals: "You are wrong, because you know neither the Scriptures nor the power of God" (v. 29). He then develops these thoughts in reverse order. As it relates to "the power of God," Jesus says that at the resurrection God will so transform humanity that marriage will no longer be a part of our experience (v. 30).

As it relates to "the Scriptures," Jesus cites Exodus 3:6: "Have you not read what was said to you by God: 'I am the God of Abraham, and the God of Isaac, and the God of Jacob'? He is not God of the dead, but of the living" (Matt 22:31b–32). Our Lord does well to use a text from Exodus since the Sadducees seem to have required that all doctrines be established from the Pentateuch.[25] Interestingly, Jesus holds that in Exodus 3:6 God was speaking to "you," the Sadducees, even though the verse records words that Yahweh addressed to Moses about

---

[25] See Ferguson, *Backgrounds of Early Christianity*, 486–87; Strauss, "Sadducees," 823–25.

a millennium and a half earlier. The difficulty is in explaining how Christ derives the doctrine of the resurrection from Exodus 3:6. Scholars debate over his logical progression.

Blomberg lists seven possible analyses and then suggests that Jesus employs an *ad hoc* or *ad hominem* argument, using logic accepted in that day though perhaps flawed from our perspective.[26] This view is problematic for two main reasons. First, throughout this section of Matthew Jesus establishes himself as the authoritative interpreter of the Old Testament, over against the obtuse Pharisees and Sadducees (see 21:12–17, 33–45; 22:34–45; 23:1–36). For Jesus to follow unsound logic would ultimately undermine his position. Second, Christ quotes Exodus 3:6 to defend his assertion that the Sadducees do not know the Scriptures (Matt 22:29). He is specifically claiming that his conclusion about the resurrection reflects accurately the teaching of Exodus 3:6.

How does the statement, "I am the God of Abraham, and the God of Isaac, and the God of Jacob" establish the resurrection? I find two explanations cogent. First, Jesus may be basing his argument on the present tense of "I am," which is implicit in the Hebrew and made explicit by Greek translations. For Yahweh to say that he is (not *was*) the God of the patriarchs centuries after their physical deaths implies that these men were still alive. In Jewish theology generally—unlike Greek dualism—the afterlife was physical not immaterial, so that the existence of an immortal spirit automatically established the resurrection.[27]

Alternatively, our Lord may be focusing on the covenantal character of Yahweh's statement in Exodus 3:6. His reasoning would go something like this:

---

[26] Craig L. Blomberg, "Matthew," in *CNTUOT*, 79. This differs from his earlier assessment: "Contemporary objections to Jesus's logic here perhaps reveal an unnecessary rigidity in our modern historical/grammatical hermeneutics rather than any fallacy with Jesus's interpretation" (*Matthew*, 334).

[27] See Morris, *Matthew*, 561; Turner, *Matthew*, 532; cf. Carson, "Matthew," 520.

Yahweh bound himself by covenant to Abraham, Isaac, and Jacob. Death is not going to annul that covenant. God made promises to the patriarchs that he did not entirely fulfil. These include physical promises, especially the land of Canaan (e.g., Gen 17:8; Exod 6:3). Yahweh will resurrect the patriarchs so that they can enjoy everything promised to them. He will remain unswervingly faithful to his word.[28]

Such logic parallels Abraham's own reasoning that God would resurrect Isaac after he had been sacrificed (Heb 11:17–19).

Christ's argument possibly combines the two lines of thought above. In any case, for our purposes what is striking is this: our Lord views ignorance of a biblical implication as tantamount to ignorance of Scripture itself—and as blameworthy (v. 29).

Conclusion

It may surprise you that an implication could have such weight. But the Old Testament's applications prepared us for this reality, and we have seen it repeatedly in the teachings of the Founder of our faith. We'll encounter it again as we move further into the New Testament. A rightly arrived-at implication from the Bible carries divine authority.

---

[28] See France, *Matthew*, 840–41; cf. Bock, *Luke, Volume 2*, 1624–29; Edwards, *Mark*, 368–69. Commentators do not typically bring out the connection with the land promises. On that point see Collins, "Scripture, Hermeneutics, and Theology," 245. I thank my colleague Layton Talbert for his help in refining my discussion of Matthew 22:23–33.

Chapter 7

Application Patterns in the Epistles

Our study brings us now to the Epistles. Since these letters address New Testament churches and believers so directly, they are especially beloved by Christians. We can expect that they will yield valuable patterns of biblical application. We'll be concentrating on four epistles that abound with examples: Romans, 1 and 2 Corinthians, and Hebrews.

Application in Romans

Paul does more in Romans than expound the doctrines of justification and sanctification (though he does not do less). Directed by the Spirit, the apostle is preparing the way for a visit to the Roman Christians—to minister to them and to garner their support for his mission to evangelize in Spain (1:9–15; 15:22–29). Since he hasn't visited their church before, Paul writes to introduce himself and his message. This includes demonstrating that his gospel is the fulfillment of God's redemptive plan anticipated in the Old Testament (1:2; 3:21; 16:25–27).

It also includes teaching how God's plan encompasses both Jews and Gentiles. The Jew-Gentile theme is central in chapters 9–11 but permeates the letter from beginning (1:5, 16) to end (15:8–13; 16:25–27). This theme is particularly needful in the Roman church, which is experiencing some division evidently among ethnic lines (14:1—15:13; see my discussion in chapter 10). Only through biblical unity could these brothers and sisters render to God the glory he deserves for his great salvation (15:5–13).[1] Given these emphases, Romans teems with applications of past revelation. The epistle contains around sixty quotations from the Old Testament, "more numerous and concentrated than any of Paul's other letters."[2] We'll probe a few of these.

Every Mouth Stopped

In arguing for the universal need for justification through Christ, Paul asserts the sinfulness and condemnation of all humanity before its Creator (Rom 1:18—3:20). Romans 3:9–20 climaxes this theme with a chain of a half-dozen quotations, "the lengthiest citation of Scripture in all of [Paul's] letters."[3] The following verses are quoted or adapted:

- Psalm 14:1–3 and/or Psalm 53:1–3 and/or Ecclesiastes 7:20 (Rom 3:10–12)
- Psalms 5:9; 140:3; 10:7 (Rom 3:13–14)
- Isaiah 59:7–8 (Rom 3:15–17)
- Psalm 36:1 (Rom 3:18)

The difficulty is that the context of each Old Testament passage makes a distinction between the righteous and the wicked. In fact, the wicked are those who persecute godly Israelites. Paul's irony in turning these passages on his fellow Jews is rhetorically effective, but how is it exegetically defensible? How can he use these verses to argue that all Jews as well as all Gentiles are sinners?[4]

Several factors help to explain Paul's application here. First, Romans 2:17–24 denies that Jewish people keep the Law as carefully as they claim. Paul's charge of hypocrisy is designed to convict the self-

---

[1] Ash concurs: "The purpose of Romans is the glory of God seen in a united missionary church humbled together under grace." *Teaching Romans, Volume 1,* 37; cf. Schreiner, *Romans,* 10–23.

[2] Mark A. Seifrid, "Romans," in *CNTUOT,* 607.

[3] Ibid., 616.

[4] Commentators tend not to answer this question in detail. For approaches similar to mine, see Ash, *Teaching Romans, Volume 1,* 127–27; Dunn, *Romans 1–8,* 144–60.

righteous. Their consciences should tell them that they are innately no different from the wicked in the Old Testament.

Second, Romans 2:25–29 states that a person—Jew or Gentile—becomes one of God's true people by experiencing "circumcision of the heart" (vv. 25–29). Such a radical change is necessary because, despite any spiritual privileges, by nature every human being is under the control of sin (3:9). This idea coheres with Paul's Old Testament texts. The Psalms passages do not restrict the wicked to Gentiles. Except for Psalm 10, all of them are attributed to David, who faced persecution from his own people as well as from outsiders. Furthermore, in Isaiah 59 the wicked are Israelites who have rebelled against Yahweh. Only a small remnant of them turns away from evil (v. 15). The end of the chapter promises a transformation in Israel. It will involve a Redeemer, repentance, and the work of the Holy Spirit (vv. 19–21). The need for supernatural intervention agrees with Paul's assessment that Old Testament descriptions of the wicked apply to unregenerate Jews.

Third, in all of Paul's proof texts the righteous are people marked by faith. The psalms cited are prayers for deliverance from oppression. Their atmosphere is characterized by confessions such as Psalm 5:7, "But I, through the abundance of your steadfast love, will enter your house. I will bow down toward your holy temple in the fear of you." This attitude fits perfectly with the teaching of Romans that God considers people righteous not because of their own performance but because they are trusting solely in his provision.

Romans 3:19–20 wraps up Paul's discussion of sin: the Law (here encompassing the entire Old Testament) establishes that both Jews and Gentiles are guilty before God and unable to justify themselves. Yet the Old Testament passages that Paul has just quoted do not make this point directly. They do support the point, however, through various connections and implications. Paul's argumentation may involve some subtlety, yet he considers it irrefutable.

By Faith Alone

In defending the doctrine of justification by faith, Romans 4 appeals to the experience of Abraham. Here again the Spirit guides Paul to use implicit as well as explicit biblical evidence. Paul's main text is Genesis 15:6: "Abraham [technically Abram at this point] believed God, and it was counted to him as righteousness" (Rom 4:3). Paul is following a Greek translation of the Old Testament that modifies the wording of Genesis. The point remains the same, however: God was crediting righteousness to Abram in response to his faith.[5]

Paul isn't arguing, however, that Abram was "saved" on the occasion recorded in Genesis 15. The patriarch's conversion to Yahweh took place when he left his homeland years earlier (cf. Gen 11:31—12:5; Josh 24:2–3; Acts 7:2–4). Yet Genesis 15 does mark a crucial moment in Abram's life, as he embraces God's promise to give him a physical descendant and innumerable offspring through him (vv. 1–5). The Lord goes on to expand his original promises and formalize them by making a covenant with Abram (vv. 7–21).

Transitioning between these two developments, Genesis 15:6 emphasizes that the patriarch's relationship to God was essentially a matter of trusting him. Paul takes this as supporting his teaching that man enjoys a righteous standing before God not through his own merit but by receiving righteousness as a gift (Rom 4:4–5). Douglas Moo calls this use of Genesis 15:6 a "theological application," deriving a principle from an incident in one man's life and relating it to God's broader way of salvation.[6]

Romans 4:6–8 references Psalm 32:1–2 as confirmation. Here, having confessed his sin, David rejoices in the blessing of forgiveness. David did not earn forgiveness; he simply asked for it with a repentant heart. As a matter of grace, God did not credit David's sin to him. In a

---

[5] For detail on the wording of Romans 4:3, see Hodge, *Romans,* 105–12; Moo, *Romans,* 261–63.

[6] Ibid., 263.

parallel way, Paul reasons, God credits righteousness to believers as a matter of grace.

Romans 4:9–12 takes up the issue of circumcision. Paul points out the simple historical fact that God was recognizing Abram as righteous (Gen 15) *before* he commanded the patriarch to be circumcised (Gen 17). From the information given in Genesis, we know that at least fourteen years separated these two events (12:4; 16:16; 17:1). However long the gap, Paul infers from it that circumcision isn't necessary for justification. More specifically, he says that the sequence of Abraham's experiences was designed to make him a spiritual father to all believers, whether Gentile (uncircumcised) or Jewish (circumcised). This advances Romans' emphasis on the unity of all Christians. It also shows that the details of biblical history can have great relevance beyond their immediate concerns.

Beginning with verse 13, the remainder of Romans 4 develops the theme that God's promise to Abraham came not through the Mosaic Law but through faith (cf. Gal 3:6–29). Eventually Paul returns to Genesis 15:6 and ends the chapter with these comments:

> But the words "it was counted to him' *were not written for his sake alone, but for ours also.* It will be counted to us who believe in him who raised from the dead Jesus our Lord, who was delivered up for our trespasses and raised for our justification. (Rom.4:23–25, emphasis added)

This has been the assumption throughout Romans 4: that the Old Testament speaks to people far removed from its original context. And Paul has shown a key way in which it speaks: patterns in the history of redemption from which we infer theological truths that govern our relationship with God.

Love and Unity

In discussing the Christian's interpersonal relationships, Romans often develops its teaching with Old Testament material. Take Romans 12:19: "Beloved, never avenge yourselves, but leave it to the wrath of God, for it is written, 'Vengeance is mine, I will repay, says the Lord.'"

As an argument for waiting on the Lord to deal with one's opponents, this verse cites a line from the Song of Moses (Deut 32:35). In its original context the statement promises that God will judge Israel's enemies. Paul unhesitatingly applies it to those who oppose New Covenant believers (whether those believers are Jew or Gentile). Interestingly, Hebrews 10:30 applies Deuteronomy 32:35 to professing believers who turn away from Christ. So the same principle governs different groups and different issues.

As Paul concludes Romans 12, he urges not simply non-retaliation but positive kindness toward personal antagonists. To make this point he cites Proverbs 25:21–22: "If your enemy is hungry, feed him; if he is thirsty, give him something to drink; for by so doing you will heap burning coals on his head" (Rom 12:20).[7] The Hebrew proverb mentions giving bread and water specifically. Paul, evidently following a Greek rendering, generalizes the statement to food and drink. And surely the Holy Spirit intends us to generalize even further: "Understand as included under the words *meat* [bread] and *drink,* all acts of kindness. Whatsoever then may be thine ability, in whatever business thy enemy may want either thy wealth, or thy counsel, or thy efforts, thou oughtest to help him."[8]

Paul's ethic sounds much like Jesus's teaching, and that is especially the case in Romans 13. Our Lord had taught that the essence of the Law is love (Matt 7:12; 22:34–40). In Romans 13:8–10 Paul writes,

> Owe no one anything, except to love each other, for the one who loves another has fulfilled [*plēroō*] the law. For the commandments, 'You shall not commit adultery, You shall not murder, You shall not steal, You shall not covet,' and any other commandment, are summed up in this word: 'You shall love your neighbor as yourself [Lev 19:18].'

---

[7] The image of fiery coals likely refers to moving an enemy to shame and repentance by treating him graciously. See Waltke, *Proverbs: Chapters 15–31,* 330–32; Moo, *Romans,* 787–89.

[8] Calvin, *Romans,* 475.

Love does no wrong to a neighbor; therefore love is the fulfilling [*plērōma*] of the law.

Paul references most of the socially oriented commands from the Decalogue and assumes that they continue to indicate God's will. However, the apostle emphasizes not the commands themselves but their moral essence: love. If believers devote themselves to loving others, they will end up "fulfilling" the Law (cf. Gal 5:13–14). This language should sound familiar as it parallels something we studied in our last chapter: Jesus's statement that he came to fulfill the Law in the sense of teaching its ultimate goal (Matt 5:17–20).

Accordingly, I understand Paul to say that as we love others we will accomplish (by the enabling of the Spirit, Rom 8:4) the ethical objective that the Law's commands are driving at.[9] This suggests a two-sided concept that we will encounter again: the Mosaic Law continues to provide guidance to Christians, but we should focus primarily on the ethical ideals that motivate its commands.

Romans 14:1—15:13 explains what love should look like in the Roman church specifically. In chapter 10 we'll survey the broader teaching on Christian liberty in this section of the epistle. Here I want to highlight only the Old Testament application Paul makes at the beginning of Romans 15. Verses 1–2 make an appeal: "We who are strong have an obligation to bear with the failings of the weak, and not to please ourselves. Let each of us please his neighbor for his good, to build him up." Verse 3 provides the model and motivation for living this way: "For Christ did not please himself, but as it is written, 'The reproaches of those who reproached you fell on me.'"

Paul is quoting from Psalm 69, a godly Israelite's prayer for deliverance from his enemies. The New Testament indicates that this psalm finds its climactic expression in Jesus Christ, the ideal Israelite.

---

[9] For similar explanations, see Murray, *Romans,* 2:158–64; Schreiner, *Romans,* 690–95.

John 2:17 sees in Psalm 69:9a Christ's zeal for God's house. And Romans 15:3 sees in Psalm 69:9b Christ's willingness to suffer, on the Cross, reproach that was ultimately directed against the Father.[10] The Savior's self-sacrificing attitude should move the "strong" in Rome to set aside their personal desires and restrict their liberties out of concern for the "weak."

Paul may intend more specific connections with Psalm 69. Maybe the "strong" will end up suffering reproach from outsiders because of their ministry to the "weak." And perhaps Paul wants the "strong" to relate the remainder of Psalm 69 to their case: like the psalmist and Christ, they will be vindicated in the end.[11]

In a sweeping assertion, Paul goes on to give his rationale for directing an obscure Old Testament text to the situation in Rome: "For whatever was written in former days was written for our instruction, that through endurance and through the encouragement of the Scriptures we might have hope" (Rom 15:4). This programmatic statement could almost serve as a summary of our whole book. It teaches that the entire Old Testament ("whatever"), though first addressed to people of the Old Covenant era, was nevertheless designed by God to teach and encourage those living in the New Covenant era ("our," "we"). And once again Paul has illustrated how this ministry of the Old Testament takes place: through a process of inference and comparison.

Furthermore, it does not seem to bother the apostle that so much time and so many theological and cultural factors separate New Covenant people from Old Covenant people. On this point George

---

[10] The New Testament references Psalm 69 several other times. The sour wine given to Jesus at the Cross reflects Psalm 69:21 (Matt 27:34, 48; Mark 15:23, 36; Luke 23:36; John 19:29). Christ sees Psalm 69:4 in his experience as well: "They hated me without a cause" (John 15:25). Acts 1:20 applies Psalm 69:25 to Judas. And Romans 11:9–10 applies Psalm 69:22–23 to unbelieving Israelites.

[11] Mark A. Seifrid, "Romans," in *CNTUOT,* 686.

Knight's comments provide a fitting wrap-up to our samplings in Romans:

> What is so remarkable and instructive about Paul's use of the Scriptures in his understanding that they directly instruct us is that he writes almost as if there were no gap at all between the Scriptures written centuries or years before and "us" for whom they are written. He presupposes that the analogies and similarities are so that the gap is not only easily bridged, but intended by God to be bridged: he had us in mind when they were written.[12]

Application in 1 and 2 Corinthians

Paul's eighteen months of ministry in Corinth had been immensely fruitful (Acts 18:1–18). But before long the church he planted found itself beleaguered by internal problems as well as opposition to the apostle himself. The two canonical letters Paul writes to the Corinthian church are highly situational, addressing specific controversies unsettling that assembly. Yet this divinely inspired correspondence bears a universal character. In fact, several times Paul deals with Corinthian issues by applying highly situational texts from the Old Testament. These applications are especially noteworthy since the church at Corinth seems to have been composed largely of Gentiles.[13] We'll look at three key examples.

The Ox and the Preacher

First Corinthians 8:1—11:1 tackles the topic of food that has been offered to idols. We'll revisit this passage in chapter 10 because, like Romans 14:1—15:13, it's often cited in discussions of Christian liberty. For our present emphasis on Old Testament applications, I'll concentrate on parts of 1 Corinthians 9 and 10.

---

[12] George W. Knight III, "Written for Our Instruction," in Pipa and Wortman, *Written for Our Instruction,* 62. Compare Brian S. Rosner, "'Written for Us'" in Satterthwaite and Wright, *Pathway,* 98–105.

[13] See Fee, *First Epistle to the Corinthians,* 3–4.

In 1 Corinthians 9 the Holy Spirit guides Paul to present himself as an example of the self-denial the Corinthians need to develop. Though he has a right to receive financial remuneration as a preacher, Paul generally declines it so as to avoid any hindrance to the influence of the gospel.

The first half of 1 Corinthians 9 defends Paul's right to be compensated by the people to whom he ministers. Five arguments support this right:

- Paul's position as an apostle (vv. 1–6)
- Common sense: the fact that other kinds of workers benefit from their occupations (v. 7)
- The Mosaic Law, specifically the command not to muzzle an ox while it is threshing grain (1 Cor 9:8–12; Deu 25:4)
- The practice of priests (v. 13), who eat from the sacrifices they offer (e.g., Lev 6:16–18, 26)
- The commandment of the Lord (1 Cor 9:14), evidently a reference to Jesus's statement that "the laborer deserves his wages" (Luke 10:7; cf. Matt 10:10; 1 Tim 5:18).

All of these have relevance for our topic as they all involve some use of logic to arrive at a position regarding Christian practice. But I'll elaborate on the third argument, the command regarding the ox.

In a context emphasizing humane treatment of people, Deuteronomy 25:4 called for such treatment of animals. It required that oxen not be kept from eating grain they were helping to harvest. Paul quotes this law and then asks, "Is it for oxen that God is concerned?" (1 Cor 9:9b). The apostle isn't denying the original, contextual meaning of the law or God's concern for animals. As suggested by the next verse, he is dealing with the relevance of the law to the question at hand: "Does he not certainly speak for our sake? It was written for our sake, because the plowman should plow in hope and the thresher thresh in hope of sharing in the crop."[14]

---

[14] The ESV provides the better rendering of the Greek word *pantōs:* "certainly" instead of "altogether" (KJV, NASB). See BDAG, 755.

In other words, what should the Corinthian Christians "get out of" Deuteronomy 25:4? In a metropolis such as Corinth, presumably many of them would not be farmers, so they might conclude that this law has no bearing on them. Yet Paul insists that the Old Testament verse "was written for our sake." Moses would not have been aware of Paul or the Corinthians when he penned Deuteronomy 25:4. Yet the verse was written for them in the sense that the Holy Spirit, the ultimate Author of the verse, intended for them to apply it to their circumstances.

Paul's application may follow the lesser-to-greater logic commonly used by Jewish teachers: if God's people were to compensate animals that helped meet their physical needs, how much more should they compensate men who helped meet their spiritual needs? More generally, Paul recognizes a concept I introduced in chapter 4: the paradigmatic nature of the Old Testament Law.

> In keeping with the entire ancient Near East, Paul well understood the paradigmatic, analogical character of law. By their very nature the laws, which are limited in number, do not intend to touch all circumstances; hence they regularly function as paradigms for application in all sorts of human circumstances. It should be noted at this point that Paul does not speak to what the law *originally meant,* which tends to be our concern. He is concerned with what it *means,* in terms of its *application* to their present situation. There is a sense in which he clearly keeps the original intent; he simply changes the application.[15]

To understand the paradigm in Deuteronomy 24:5, we need to ask what ultimately motivated this law. The book of Deuteronomy roots Israel's humanitarianism in the character of Yahweh. He is a God of justice and love, and he calls on his people to display these qualities in all their dealings (e.g., 10:18–19; 24:17–22; 25:13–16). This is why the Israelites should let their oxen eat some grain. It is also why churches should pay their preachers. Though these behaviors differ, they both express the unchanging nature of God.

---

[15] Fee, *First Epistle to the Corinthians,* 450–51. Compare Thiselton, *First Epistle to the Corinthians,* 685–88.

Deuteronomy 25:4 doesn't say anything about compensating ministers. Yet Paul argues that the verse "says more than it says." he expects the Corinthians to accept his application as authoritative because it reflects accurately a general theological/ethical pattern taught by Deuteronomy 25:4's particulars. And this application is not for the Corinthian church only. The apostle argues identically in 1 Timothy 5:17–18, confirming that Deuteronomy 25:4 establishes ministerial remuneration in churches generally. The verse functions paradigmatically under the New Covenant as it did under the Old Covenant. And given the evidence mounting in our study, we have every reason to think that God designed all Scripture to work this way.

Lessons from the Wilderness

In 1 Corinthians 10 Paul forcefully urges the Corinthians not to participate in feasts held at pagan temples. As part of this warning against idolatry, verses 1–13 apply to the Corinthian Christians several incidents from the early history of Israel. The Israelites had enjoyed miraculous displays of the presence of God: the guiding cloud, the parting of the Red Sea, and the provision of food and drink in the desert (vv. 1–4).[16] "Nevertheless," Paul writes, "with most of them God was not pleased, for they were overthrown in the wilderness" (v. 5).

The apostle isn't merely recounting history, however. He refers to the Israelites as "our fathers" (v. 1), even though many of his readers are Gentiles. Like the Israelites, the Corinthians enjoyed great spiritual privileges (cf. vv. 16–17). Yet they also suffered from the same sinful proclivities that afflicted God's ancient people. Regarding Israel's failures, verse 6 says, "Now these things took place as examples for us, that we might not desire evil as they did."

The Greek word translated "examples" is *tupos,* from which English derives *type* and *typology.* Here, however, *tupos* doesn't carry the narrow meaning of a pictorial prediction. It seems a stretch to say that

---

[16] Some of the language in these verses is difficult. See Fee, *First Epistle to the Corinthians,* 487–96; Thiselton, *First Epistle to the Corinthians,* 717–30.

the Israelites' sin foreshadowed the Corinthians' sin. Instead Israel's experiences function as a *pattern:* a "paradigmatic model" or even a "formative model."[17] They serve as a warning of the *kinds* of temptations the Corinthians face (cf. v. 13) and of the consequences of succumbing to such temptations.

Paul lists four specific ways in which the Israelites sinned and for which they were judged.

- Idolatry, specifically in the form of pagan feasting (1 Cor 10:7; cf. Exod 32:6)
- Sexual immorality in the context of idolatry (1 Cor 10:8; cf. Num 25:1–9)
- Testing God (1 Cor 10:9; cf. Num 21:4–6; Ps 78:18)
- Complaining (1 Cor 10:10; cf. Num 11:1 and other passages in Numbers)

The apostle tells the Corinthians that they stand in danger of these same sins and their corresponding punishments. He climaxes the list with this statement: "Now these things happened to them as an example [*tupikōs*, related to *tupos*], but they were written down for our instruction, on whom the end of the ages has come" (1 Cor 10:11).

This sounds much like Romans 15:4, but the final phrase is distinctive: "on whom the end of the ages has come." According to this description, New Covenant Christians live in the final phase of God's program for the ages. Because we are living in the Messianic "last days" (cf. Heb 1:1–2), we have the most revelation available to us and the most redemptive history behind us. Observing the fulfillment of so much Scripture, we can see most clearly God's purposes and ways.

More specifically, we have the best vantage point to understand the paradigms taught by Old Testament narratives and to discern their many applications. God planned for us to enjoy this privilege and to make full use of it. It is in this sense that the Lord wrote Israel's history "for our admonition." This teaching about the Old Testament has implications for our use of the New Testament as well.

---

[17] Ibid., 731-32.

> Since this principle [of the far-reaching intent of Scripture] is applied to the Old Testament Scriptures written long before the end of the ages had come, how much more is it applicable to . . . the New Testament Scriptures written in the period in which we today, and they who originally received it, both live. Since the ethical instruction bridges the significant gap between the Old and New Testaments and applies to us, certainly where there is no gap of religious moment between us and the New Testament church, we should expect an even more direct application of the New Testament teaching to ourselves.[18]

Come out from among Them

Second Corinthians is largely a defense of Paul's apostolic ministry. This became necessary because of the growing influence of unorthodox teachers who were maligning and undermining him in the Corinthian church. The apostle's response becomes the sharpest in chapters 10–13, where he describes his detractors as "false apostles," "deceitful workmen," and disguised "servants" of Satan (11:13–15). The epistle calls the Corinthians to realign themselves with Paul, their spiritual father, and distance themselves from the false teachers (e.g., vv. 2–4).

In this vein, in chapter 6 Paul pleads with the Corinthians to widen their hearts toward him (vv. 11–13). A little later he repeats: "Make room in your hearts for us" (7:2). Sandwiched in between these appeals is the well-known prohibition, "Do not be unequally yoked with unbelievers" (6:14). Paul's point seems to be that the Corinthians must not associate with the false apostles.[19]

The apostle's arguments for this separation culminate with a striking series of Old Testament quotations. He asks, "What agreement

---

[18] Geroge W. Knight III, "Written for Our Instruction," in Pipa and Wortman, *Written for Our Instruction,* 63.

[19] See Hafeman, *2 Corinthians,* 277–304; compare Schreiner, *Paul,* 98–99. More commonly, this passage is seen as a call not to engage in compromising alliances with unbelievers generally or pagan idolaters specifically. See, for example, Garland, *2 Corinthians,* 330–33. These aspects of separation are legitimate *applications* of Paul's teaching, but they do not appear to be the topics under discussion in the context of 2 Corinthians 6:14—7:1.

has the temple of God with idols?" (6:16a). He then presents a quotation from Leviticus 26:11–12 and/or Ezekiel 37:27: "For we are the temple of the living God; as God said, 'I will make my dwelling among them and walk among them, and I will be their God, and they shall be my people'" (2 Cor 6:16b). In Leviticus 26 these words promise the climactic blessing of God's covenant with Israel. In Ezekiel 37 they promise Israel's end-times enjoyment of this blessing. Yet Paul claims that they describe the church's present identity as the dwelling of God.

The succeeding quotations develop a practical ramification of this incomparable identity. Second Corinthians 6:17a draws from Isaiah 52:11: "Therefore go out from their midst, and be separate from them, says the Lord, and touch no unclean thing." In Isaiah these commands may allude to Israel's deliverance from the Babylonian exile but probably point to the nation's end-times restoration to Yahweh. When the Lord works this "new exodus" on behalf of the Israelites, he expects them to leave behind anything that would defile them spiritually.[20] Paul relates this concept to the Corinthians' need to separate from false teachers.

Then he quotes a line from a Greek translation of Ezekiel 20:34, "Then I will welcome you" (2 Cor. 6:17b). Ezekiel is predicting that Yahweh will re-gather Israel in order to purge and reestablish the nation. Paul uses this prediction to speak of the renewed fellowship with God that the Corinthians would enjoy when they reject the false apostles.

Second Corinthians 6:18 further describes this blessing: "And I will be a father to you, and you shall be sons and daughters to me, says the Lord Almighty." This is an expansion of 2 Samuel 7:14, a key element in the Davidic Covenant. Here Yahweh commits himself to a special Father-son relationship with David's descendants, the divinely chosen human rulers over Israel. Paul uses Yahweh's promise to speak of the family relationship between God and the Corinthian believers, including female believers ("daughters").

---

[20] See Motyer, *Isaiah*, 420–22; Oswalt, *Isaiah, Chapters 40–66*, 371–73.

We might think that the apostle is simply borrowing Old Testament phraseology to strengthen his rhetoric, without intending to connect the Corinthians with promises and commands Yahweh gave to Israel. Or perhaps Paul is making a general analogy between Israel and the Corinthian church. In actuality, his presentation goes beyond rhetoric and analogy. He introduces the first quotation as a proof: "For we are the temple of the living God; as God said . . . ." (2 Cor 6:16b).

Then as the apostle looks back on all his quotations, he makes this surprising declaration: "*Since we have these promises, beloved,* let us cleanse ourselves from every defilement of body and spirit, bringing holiness to completion in the fear of God" (7:1, emphasis added). Paul claims that in some meaningful sense God's promises to Israel—and their practical implications—belong to the Corinthian Christians, and by extension to all believers in this age.

How can this be? I would reject the idea that the church has replaced Israel or that Israel has forever forfeited the blessings God promised to the nation (see Rom 9–11).[21] However, in 2 Corinthians 3 Paul presents himself as a minister of the New Covenant, teaching that the spiritual blessings of that covenant are available to believers in this age (Jew or Gentile).[22] Furthermore, believers are united to Christ, the ultimate Descendant of Abraham (Gal 3:6–29). This means that there is a great deal of application for the church to derive from Israel's Scriptures. In particular, the spiritual realities that form the core of God's relationship with Israel belong to the church as well (cf. Eph 2:11–22).

Second Corinthians 6:14—7:1 helps us by illustrating the kinds of spiritual realities we share with Israel: the privilege of being God's special people and the resulting obligation to separate from error.

---

[21] See Vlach, *Has the Church Replaced Israel?* Compare Bock and Glaser, *The People, the Land, and the Future of Israel;* Campbell and Townsend, *Case for Premillennialism;* McDermott, *New Christian Zionism.*

[22] See Decker, "Church's Relationship," 290–305, 431–56.

This section does not address the question of the fate of the OT "people of God"; it simply affirms in a natural way that the followers of Christ are now also the people of God, even if they are of "Gentile" origin. The OT quotations address them now; God is their father as well; they too are now God's people.[23]

God's ancient Word addressing us now—that's the essence of application!

Application in Hebrews

Our final category of patterns comes from Hebrews. This book is directed to professing Jewish Christians who are tempted to abandon Christ and return to Judaism, especially due to the pressure of persecution. The writer expounds the theme that the person and work of Jesus are superior to every aspect of Old Testament revelation. This superiority of Christ should compel the readers to endure in their commitment to him. He is worthy of all their faith, ministry, and even suffering.

In one sense Hebrews is pointing its readers away from the Old Testament. Yet ironically it applies all manner of Old Testament texts and themes to the situation of those readers. Nor should these applications be restricted to the book's original Jewish audience. A central aspect of Christ's superiority is his role as the Mediator of the New Covenant (Heb 8:7–13). As we've just seen, Gentile believers today share in the spiritual blessings of this covenant. Consequently, all Christians have much to learn from the content and method of the applications of Scripture in Hebrews.

Strive to Rest

Hebrews 3:1–6 describes the superiority of Christ over Moses, and then a lengthy passage challenges readers to continue trusting Christ (3:7—4:13). The challenge is based on an Old Testament text related to Moses's ministry. Interestingly, this text itself constitutes an application of

---

[23] Peter Balla, "2 Corinthians," in *CNTUOT,* 773.

earlier Scripture. It is Psalm 95:7b–11, where David warned his contemporaries not to harden their hearts against Yahweh as the Exodus generation had done (cf. Num 14:20–35; 20:1–14). The writer of Hebrews uses Psalm 95 to speak to the struggles of his own contemporaries (cf. 1 Cor 10:1–13).

Hebrews 3:7–19 develops the negative element of warning. The quotation from Psalm 95 is introduced as follows: "Therefore, as the Holy Spirit says" (Heb 3:7a). This wording indicates not only that the Spirit is the ultimate Author of the psalm but also that he continues to speak through the passage centuries after David penned it. Following his quotation (Heb 3:7-11), the writer draws attention to the word *today* in the statement, "Today, if you hear his voice, do not harden your hearts as in the rebellion" (Ps 95:7b–8a; Heb 3:15). Here again, "today" emphasizes that the psalm is presently speaking to the readers of Hebrews. In addition, it suggests that their window of opportunity to respond is limited. If they turn away from Christ, they would suffer devastation like the Israelites of Moses's time.

Hebrews 4:1–11 turns to the positive element of promise. Here the writer fastens on the key term *rest* (Ps 95:11). He takes this word as pointing to the bliss of a restored relationship with God, the result of his redemptive plan. More specifically, "rest" is the ultimate consummation of that relationship—an eternal Sabbath, including the cessation of earthly labor. It may also encompass the partial enjoyment of that relationship in the present life.[24]

Because the "rest" in Psalm 95 was associated with Israel's possession of the Promised Land of Canaan, however, further explanation is needed. The writer references God's own rest after the Creation week (Gen 2:2) and connects it with the rest mentioned in Psalm 95 (Heb 4:4–5). His basic argument is that rest in the Old Testament wasn't essentially a physical locale; God himself enjoyed rest long before Moses

---

[24] See George H. Guthrie, "Hebrews," in *CNTUOT,* 958–60; Lane, *Hebrews 1–8,* 98–102.

132

and Israel were around. Furthermore, Psalm 95 was written centuries after the conquest of Canaan under Joshua. If rest were strictly the Promised Land, the psalm would not have continued to speak of the possibility of rest in David's time (Heb 4:6–10).

William Lane summarizes: "The theology of rest developed in 4:1–11 takes account of the pattern of archetype (God's primal rest, v 4), type (the settlement of the land under Joshua, v 8), and antitype (the [eternal] Sabbath celebration of the consummation, v 9)."[25] Based on this theology, the writer of Hebrews urges, "Let us therefore strive to enter that rest, so that no one may fall by the same sort of disobedience" (v. 11). These paradoxical words mean that in order to arrive at eternal bliss readers need to persevere in trusting and following Christ now.

Looking back on the use of Psalm 95, Hebrews 4:12–13 makes some exquisite yet sobering comments:

> For the word of God is living and active, sharper than any two-edged sword, piercing to the division of soul and of spirit, of joints and of marrow, and discerning the thoughts and intentions of the heart. And no creature is hidden from his sight, but all are naked and exposed to the eyes of him to whom we must give account.

Since it is God's Word, the Bible is a living Book! Though written millennia ago, it has the ability to penetrate our inner person, exposing our unbelief and moving us to repentance and change. And it accomplishes this work through application, through the kinds of analogies and correlations that the writer of Hebrews has just unfolded.

More Motivations to Endure

Once the doctrinal body of Hebrews comes to a close at 10:18, the remainder of the book is highly exhortational and motivational. Among the multiple Old Testament applications here, most prominent is chapter 11, the celebrated "Hall of Faith." In a sweeping review of Old Testament history, the writer underscores the necessity and centrality of

---

[25] Ibid., 104.

faith for a relationship with God. He takes for granted that the bio-graphical material recorded in the Old Testament exemplifies spiritual truths that hold for God's people in all ages.

These spiritual truths are as varied as they are practical. Some are explicitly mentioned in the Old Testament contexts; others are in-ferred. Note the themes that Hebrews 11 associates with faith:

- Worship (Abel, v. 4)
- Divine reward (Enoch, vv. 5–6)
- A righteous standing (Noah, v. 7)
- Obedience (Abraham, v. 8)
- Pilgrim living (the patriarchs, vv. 9–10, 13–16)
- The fulfillment of divine promises (Sarah, vv. 11–12; Isaac, Ja-cob, and Joseph, vv. 20–22)
- Testing (Abraham, vv. 17–19)
- Persecution (Moses and his parents, vv. 23–27; various un-named individuals, vv. 35b–38)
- Mighty deliverances and victories (Israel at the Exodus, vv. 28–29; Israel at Jericho, v. 30; Rahab, v. 31; various named and unnamed individuals, vv. 32–35a).

The writer wraps up his survey with these intriguing remarks: "And all these, though commended through their faith, did not receive what was promised, since God had provided something better for us, that apart from us they should not be made perfect" (vv. 39–40). New Covenant Christians form part of the "final installment" of redemptive history. In God's providence we are involved in the conclusion of the story of faith. The themes of that story come to heightened expression in our lives.

Hebrews 12 goes on to call Old Testament believers "a cloud of witnesses" (v. 1). The idea probably isn't that they are spectators watching us. Rather, having lived lives of faith, they bear witness to the fact that such a life is worth living and can indeed be lived regardless of the world's hostility. Their experience testifies to the trustworthiness of the God in whom they trusted. Consequently, their example encourages

New Covenant believers to stay the course for Christ.[26] In fact, the climactic "witness" is Jesus himself (vv. 2–4), whose faith endured the ultimate trial and issued in the ultimate victory.

Hebrews 12:5–11 introduces the thought that the readers' difficult circumstances are at least partially due to divine discipline. Here the writer quotes Proverbs 3:11–12: "My son, do not regard lightly the discipline of the Lord, nor be weary when reproved by him. For the Lord disciplines the one he loves, and chastises every son whom he receives" (Heb 12:5b–6). Originally these words were addressed to a specific son by his father. Yet the writer of Hebrews prefaces the passage by contemporizing and personalizing it to his readers: "And have you forgotten the exhortation that addresses you as sons?" (v. 5a). Then he applies it to them more specifically, arguing that God's discipline is a sign of their sonship and designed for their growth in holiness (vv. 7–11).

Hebrews 12 contains other Old Testament applications such as the warning not to follow Esau's example of disparaging his privileges (vv. 16–17). But as we close I want to touch on Hebrews 13. Here the writer briefly addresses several practical issues, including the problem of covetousness. "Keep your life free from love of money, and be content with what you have" (v. 5a). Why can a Christian live with a spirit of contentment? The Old Testament has the answer! "For he has said, 'I will never leave you nor forsake you'" (v. 5b).

This promise occurs in various forms in several passages. The Lord spoke in these terms to Jacob when he was traveling to Mesopotamia (Gen 28:15). Moses relayed the promise to Israel and Joshua with regard to the conquest of Canaan (Deut 31:6, 8). Then Yahweh Himself assured Joshua of his presence (Josh 1:5). Much later, David applied the promise to Solomon in encouraging him about building the temple (1 Chron 28:20). Finally, the writer of Hebrews directs it to New Covenant Christians as a motivation for contentment. The one promise covers believers in multiple eras and addresses a variety of circumstances.

---

[26] Bruce, *Hebrews,* 333.

And how should Christians respond to this promise? Again the Old Testament answers: "So we can confidently say, 'The Lord is my helper; I will not fear; what can man do to me?'" (Heb 13:6). Taken from Psalm 118:6, this statement expresses the psalmist's certainty of divine help as he faced overwhelming opposition. But the verse also expresses the settled faith that the readers of Hebrews should have in the Lord. Psalm 118 goes on to recount a divinely wrought decisive victory. That the New Testament sees the psalm's pattern culminating in the experience of the Messiah makes it all the more relevant to New Covenant believers.[27]

Conclusion

We could study many more samples of biblical application within the Bible itself. The New Testament brings into the church the Old Testament law that two or three witnesses are required to establish an accusation (Matt 18:16; 2 Cor 13:1; 1 Tim 5:19). James uses the life of Abraham to prove that faith without works is dead (Jas 2:21–26). And like the writer of Hebrews, James encourages endurance by appealing to the examples of Old Testament characters (5:10–11; cf. 16–17). Peter teaches that Old Testament predictive prophecy is *more* for New Covenant believers than for the original Old Testament audience, since we live after the coming of the promised Messiah (1 Pet 1:10–12). Peter also teaches that the church's position and calling parallel those of Israel (2:4–10).

Without citing additional passages, we can safely summarize the big ideas that have been emerging from our biblical patterns.

- The relevance and authority of Scripture transcends time and circumstances. This is true of both Testaments of the Bible and every genre in those Testaments.

---

[27] Ps 118:22–23 is cited in Matt 21:42; Mark 12:10–11; Luke 20:17; Acts 4:11; 1 Pet 2:7. Ps 118:25–26 is cited in Matt 21:9; 23:39; Mark 11:9–10; Luke 13:35; 19:38; John 12:13.

- Scripture's timeless authority flows from God's immutable character and the spiritual continuity of his people in all ages (specifically through the New Covenant today).
- Scripture functions paradigmatically. Its specifics teach universal truths that speak to issues beyond the scope of the issues originally addressed. Another way of saying this is that God expects us to pursue in our setting the ultimate purpose(s) he had in mind when he communicated a text to its first audience. In this regard, we must prioritize the spirit of Scripture over its letter.
- Identifying and applying Scripture's universal truths requires the use of deduction, analogy, and other exercises in logic.[28]
- The authority of applications depends upon the accuracy of the exegesis and the logic behind them.
- Misapplication is a real possibility to be guarded against.

All of these factors argue that, based on the Bible's patterns, we should develop a careful method for applying Scripture. Our discussion is heading in that direction. First, however, I need to respond to some objections to the practice of application.

---

[28] Reflecting on the same kind of New Testament theologizing that I've considered in chapters 6 and 7, Reymond writes: "The apostolic model of exposition of, reflection upon, and deduction from Scripture supports our engagement in the theological enterprise. If we are to help our generation understand the Scriptures, we too must deduce and arrange conclusions from what we have gained from our exegetical labors in Scripture and be ready to 'dialogue' with men. Engagement in and the result of this task is theology." *Systematic Theology*, xxx.

Part IV

Objections
to Biblical Application

Chapter 8

The Sufficiency of Scripture

Biblical application often faces skepticism and resistance. In many cases the fault lies with those who make applications, and our previous chapter began to point out errors in this regard. Those who resist application tend to concentrate on two theological concepts: the doctrine of the sufficiency of Scripture and the problem of legalism.

As we explore these themes in the next three chapters, I'll be quoting multiple writers, especially for purposes of definition. On the other hand, my approach will not be to critique individual authors who challenge some aspect of biblical application. The space required for substantial and nuanced critique would distract from the focus of this book. In a sense the entire book constitutes my critique. Here in Part IV I am largely responding to trends I've encountered through years of growing up in conservative Christianity, ministering to others, and observing online discussions. It's especially in such popular-level venues that one encounters objections to application.

The concept of *sola Scriptura*—Scripture alone—constituted the foundation of the Protestant Reformation. Scholars refer to it as the Reformation's "formal principle." Over against Roman Catholicism's elevation of tradition as co-authoritative with Scripture, the Reformers held that the Bible is the only final norm for faith and practice.[1]

---

[1] See "Sola scriptura," in Muller, *Dictionary,* 284; Anthony N. S. Lane, "*Sola Scriptura?* Making Sense of a Post-Reformation Slogan," in Satterthwaite and Wright, *Pathway,* 297–327.

A key aspect of *sola Scriptura* is the doctrine of the sufficiency of Scripture: the Bible constitutes all the verbal divine revelation needed to know and please God. We'll analyze this doctrine in this chapter because it has been increasingly pitted against the practice of biblical application. Are we not adding to God's Word by claiming that human deductions from Scripture can be authoritative? A related question stems from the nature of man: given our fallibility, how can we put stock in our conclusions? Are we not also denying the Bible's sufficiency when we use extra-biblical information in applying Scripture? Is God's Word enough, or isn't it? All the biblical argumentation in Parts II and III helps to answer such questions, but more needs to be said.

Preliminary Considerations

While these kinds of objections may reflect a high view of Scripture, they also reflect several misperceptions.[2] To begin with, they fail to appreciate what happens throughout the entire process of interpretation. The interpretation of Scripture requires extra-biblical information. We define words on the basis of our knowledge of human life and language. We identify geographical and historical referents. We read with sensitivity to the characteristics of each genre. Of course, to have a Bible at all we rely heavily on the research and conclusions of textual critics and translators. Using such extra-biblical resources does not entail "adding" to Scripture. These tools help us to interpret the Bible, and in principle there should be no objection to using similar tools to relate biblical teaching to contemporary life.

The same must be said about the use of logic. The simplest reading of any biblical passage depends on the use of logic, following an author's flow of thought by making connections among his statements. Similarly, the deductive logic commonly used in application does not add to the author's words. If done correctly—a major condition that we'll examine later—it simply identifies what's implicit in the text.

---

[2] My discussion in this section follows Frame, *Word of God*, 220–38.

In the classic syllogism "All men are mortal; Socrates is a man; there-fore Socrates is mortal," the conclusion doesn't tell you anything you couldn't find out from the premises themselves. What the syllogism does is to make the implicit content explicit. Logic is a hermeneutical [interpretive] tool, a device for bringing out meaning that is already there in the text. So (a) the "content of Scripture" includes all the logical implications of Scripture, (b) the logical implications of Scrip-ture have the same authority as Scripture, and (c) logical deductions from Scripture do not add anything to Scripture.[3]

Furthermore, as in every act of communication, human fallibil-ity is a painful reality at every stage of biblical interpretation. This should cause us to follow a careful methodology and to remain humbly open to correction. It should also encourage us to appreciate the contributions of scholars and fellow-believers. Most of all, it should move us to plead with God to open our eyes to his truth (Ps 119:18). But the possibility of error does not deter us from seeking to understand Scripture the best that we can. Nor does it inherently undermine biblical application.

The Basis of Sufficiency

With this background in mind, we can consider more closely the doc-trine of the sufficiency of Scripture. First, we should recognize that formulating this doctrine involves application-oriented logic. Several texts warn readers not to add to or take away from God's words (Deut 4:2; 12:32; Prov 30:5–6; Rev 22:18–19). This surely *implies* that God has given his people all the words he wants us to have and that we should be content with them (cf. Deut 29:29).

Yet this statement needs to be qualified. In Psalm 19:7 David describes God's Word with the Hebrew adjective *tâmîm,* meaning per-fect, complete, or blameless. The psalm extols the Scriptures with other

---

[3] Ibid., 222. Cf. Frame, *Knowledge of God,* 242–301; Paul Helm, "The Role of Logic in Biblical Interpretation," in Radmacher and Preus, *Hermeneu-tics,* 839–58, with responses by Mark M. Hanna (859–70) and John H. Gerstner (871–78).

glowing terms and also depicts its life-changing ministry in the life of the believer. In fact, verse 14 uses the verb *tâmam*, related to *tâmîm*, to express the effect of God's work through Scripture: "Then I shall be blameless." The complete Word makes the psalmist complete.

A dilemma arises, however. This passage is talking about "the Law of the LORD," or "the Torah of Yahweh" (v. 7). Since the Pentateuch was likely the only written revelation available to David, this phrase evidently refers to the Mosaic Law or to the Pentateuch as a whole.[4] God would add much more to his Word over time. In fact, this very psalm was adding to the canon. So how could Scripture be sufficient for David?

We have to *conclude* that the revelation each generation received was sufficient for its time but that God chose to reveal himself further to later generations, giving them enough for their circumstances. We can and should use Psalm 19 as a proof text for the sufficiency of all Scripture, but we do so by *extending* its statements to books of the Bible that didn't even exist when the psalm was written.[5]

In chapter 4 we came to a parallel *conclusion* regarding 2 Timothy 3:14–17. There Paul asserts the sufficiency of the Old Testament for Timothy's conversion, sanctification, and service. But the context and other passages *imply* that this sufficiency *extends* to the New Testament documents in production in the first century and also *applies* to every New Covenant believer.

We're left with the question of whether we should expect God to keep adding to Scripture in our day. The New Testament *implies* a negative answer. John 1:18 states that Jesus Christ came in order to make the Father known. Similarly, Hebrews 1:1–3 says that, as the divine Son, Christ reveals God with a clarity and a finality that distinguishes him from all past spokesmen for God. Such verses strongly

---

[4] Lane, *Psalms 1–89*, 98; Ross, *Psalms: Volume 1*, 478.

[5] Ibid.

suggest that once Christ accomplished his redemptive work and explained it through his initial disciples, no further revelation is needed.[6]

It should be apparent that when we say, "Scripture alone!" we're not ruling out human logic altogether, nor are we limiting God's truth to the bare text of Scripture. Indeed, the doctrine of the sufficiency of Scripture itself relies upon logical inferences.[7]

The Definition of Sufficiency

What I've just said corresponds with the standard Protestant understanding of the Bible's sufficiency. I want to defend this by sharing material by theologians from a variety of denominational traditions.

Martin Luther

The role of logic makes an appearance in one of the earliest and most famous statements of *sola Scriptura*. In defending his views before the Diet of Worms, Martin Luther (1483–1546) said,

---

[6] Of course, the argument for a closed canon involves additional considerations. See, for example, Kruger, *Canon Revisited,* 260–87.

[7] Sometimes 1 Corinthians 4:6 is used as a proof text for the sufficiency of Scripture. Paul writes, "I have applied all these things to myself and Apollos for your benefit, brothers, that you may learn by us not to go beyond what is written, that none of you may be puffed up in favor of one against another." Yet expositors debate the phrase, "that you may learn by us not to go beyond what is written." As many as seven interpretations have been proposed. See Thiselton, *First Epistle to the Corinthians,* 351–56. Blomberg says, "Given the uncertain meaning of verse 6a, one must beware of drawing any overly dogmatic applications from this half-verse" (*1 Corinthians,* 94). Paul may be referring to biblical sufficiency but, as argued above, this does not exclude deductions from Scripture. There are right ways to "go beyond" Scripture as well as wrong ways. In fact, Paul's more likely meaning *supports* the role of deductions. "What is written" seems to point back to six Old Testament quotations in 1 Corinthians 1–3. Paul uses these in urging the Corinthians not to boast about and divide over their favorite spiritual leaders. Then he tells them not to "go beyond" Scripture, probably meaning that they should not *disobey* the Old Testament as he has *applied* it to them. See Ciampa and Rosner, *First Letter to the Corinthians,* 175–77; Garland, *1 Corinthians,* 131–36.

Unless I am convinced by the testimony of the Scriptures or by clear reason (for I do not trust either in the pope or in councils alone, since it is well known that they have often erred and contradicted themselves), I am bound by the Scriptures I have quoted and my conscience is captive to the Word of God. I cannot and I will not retract anything, since it is neither safe nor right to go against conscience.[8]

Here the Reformer affirms that only Scripture binds his conscience. He also denies the authority of men to fabricate doctrines. Yet he allows for the role of "clear [or, evident] reason." Anglican J. I. Packer explains:

Luther's reference to "evident reason" as a source of conviction does not cut across the principle of Scripture *only,* for "reason" here means precisely "logical inference from biblical principles." Luther rejected the idea that fallen man's rational reflection could be a source of religious truth apart from the Bible, and when he envisaged reason trying to pronounce on divine things independently of Scripture he called it "the devil's whore." This is his distinction between the *magisterial* use of reason, which he condemns as a damnable expression of human pride, and the *ministerial* use of it, which he treats as right and necessary. None of the Reformers were irrationalists![9]

The Westminster Confession

In the century after Luther, the English Puritans formulated the classic Protestant statement on the Bible's sufficiency. Section 1.6 of the Westminster Confession of Faith (1646) says,

The whole counsel of God, concerning all things necessary for his own glory, man's salvation, faith and life, is either expressly set down in Scripture, or by good and necessary consequence may be deduced from Scripture: unto which nothing at any time is to be added, whether by new revelations of the Spirit, or traditions of men. Nevertheless, we acknowledge the inward illumination of the Spirit of God

---

[8] Luther, "Luther at the Diet of Worms, 1521," in *Luther's Works, Volume 32,* 112.

[9] J. I. Packer, "'Sola Scriptura,'" in Montgomery, *God's Inerrant Word,* 44.

to be necessary for the saving understanding of such things as are revealed in the word; and that there are some circumstances concerning the worship of God, and government of the Church, common to human actions and societies, which are to be ordered by the light of nature, and Christian prudence, according to the general rules of the word, which are always to be observed.[10]

Centuries later, this statement remains impressive for its carefulness and balance. First, sufficiency relates to "the whole counsel of God, concerning all things necessary for his own glory, man's salvation, faith and life." Here it's important to note that the whole Confession begins by recognizing that God has revealed himself through means other than Scripture. "The light of nature and the works of creation and providence do so far manifest the goodness, wisdom, and power of God, as to leave men unexcusable."[11] Theologians refer to this as "general revelation."

The reality of general revelation indicates that when the Confession speaks of the sufficiency of Scripture, it means that the Bible is all the *verbal* divine revelation we need in order to be reconciled to God and live for his glory.[12] This does not mean that Scripture contains all the *information* we need in every area of life. The Bible doesn't tell a Christian everything he needs to know in order to drive a car, get a college degree, grow his small business, or remodel his house. In fact, Scripture doesn't even tell him everything he needs to know in order to serve in his local church. If it did, I wouldn't need to be researching nursery policy manuals for the church that I pastor! The Bible does, however, give us everything God has verbally revealed to us to direct us in every area of life.[13]

---

[10] Section 1.1, in Carruthers, *Westminster Confession of Faith*, 22–23, citing Ps 19:1–3; Rom 1:19–20, 32; 2:1, 14–15.

[11] Ibid., 19.

[12] Warfield, *Westminster Assembly*, 224.

[13] Frame, *Word of God*, 221.

Thus the doctrine of sufficiency excludes other alleged sources of verbal revelation. The Confession disallows any additions to Scripture, "whether by new revelations of the Spirit, or traditions of men." This phrase rejects both the claim of some radicals that they had received revelation and the claim of Rome that extra-biblical traditions can be equally authoritative with the Bible.

On the other hand, the Confession clarifies *how* the Scriptures exercise their sufficient authority. God's words for our faith and practice encompass what "is either expressly set down in Scripture, or by good and necessary consequence may be deduced from Scripture." "Good and necessary consequence" refers to logical deductions from Scripture. The Confession views these as authoritative because they bring out what is implicit in the Bible.[14]

The adjectives "good and necessary" provide crucial qualifications regarding deductions from Scripture.

> For any argument to be sound, it must meet two specific criteria, namely, (1) the premises must be true and (2) the conclusion must follow necessarily from the premises ("deductive validity"). True premises make an argument "good," while deductive validity makes its conclusion "necessary."[15]

Part V of our study will return to these matters. But for the moment another qualification is in order: the Confession regards logic as a tool not an authority.

> This is not, of course, to make reason the ground of the authority of inferred doctrines and duties. Reason is the instrument of discovery of all doctrines and duties, whether "expressly set down in Scripture"

---

[14] For detailed study of this expression, see McGraw, *By Good and Necessary Consequence;* Richard A. Muller, "Either Expressly Set Down . . . or by Good and Necessary Consequence," in Muller and Ward, *Scripture and Worship,* 59–82; Warfield, *Westminster Assembly,* 224–32; C. J. Williams, "Good and Necessary Consequence in the Westminster Confession," in Selvaggio, *Faith Once Delivered,* 171–90.

[15] Ibid., 179.

or "by good and necessary consequence deduced from Scripture": but their authority, when once discovered, is derived from God, who reveals and prescribes them in Scripture, either by literal assertion or by necessary implication.[16]

Seventeenth-century theologians defended "good and necessary consequence," in part, on the same basis our previous two chapters used: the New Testament's use of the Old Testament. George Gillespie (1613–1648), a Scottish commissioner to the Westminster Assembly, highlighted the authority of deduction in Christ's argument for the resurrection against the Sadducees (Matt. 22:31–33).[17] So did the Swiss-Italian theologian Francis Turretin (1623–1687). He emphasized that Jesus didn't predicate his argument on his own divine infallibility since the Sadducees did not accept his deity. Instead our Lord silenced his opponents through logical extrapolation from Scripture.[18]

In 1689 the Westminster Confession was revised to produce the London Baptist Confession. Interestingly, the expression "or by good and necessary consequence may be deduced from Scripture" was changed to "or necessarily contained in Scripture."[19] This seems to be an even stronger statement about accurate deductions: they are viewed as being *in* Scripture, as part of Scripture.[20]

While denying new revelations of the Spirit, the Westminster Confession acknowledges the need for "the inward illumination of the Spirit of God." The Bible is sufficient, but its truth cannot be adequately accessed apart from the personal ministry of its Author (1 Cor 2:6–16). This is especially the case in the area of application.

---

[16] Warfield, *Westminster Assembly,* 226.

[17] Gillespie, *Treatise of Miscellany Questions,* 240.

[18] Turretin, *Elenctic Theology,* 1:39.

[19] Section 1.6, cited in Waldron, *Modern Exposition,* 26.

[20] Ibid., 42–43; McGraw, *By Good and Necessary Consequence,* 51–52, n. 10.

Finally, the Confession speaks of "some circumstances concerning the worship of God, and government of the Church, common to human actions and societies, which are to be ordered by the light of nature, and Christian prudence." Here is an important caveat: some questions of church life (and personal life, for that matter) cannot be resolved entirely by the Bible's express statements or deductions from Scripture. I suppose that nursery policies fall in this category.

Thankfully, we have two resources available to help with such matters. First is "the light of nature." We shouldn't equate this category exactly with "general revelation" because general revelation deals specifically with the existence of God and basic truths regarding his character (cf. Rom 1:19–20).[21] Yet we can learn about any number of topics by observing the nature of things as God has made them. The church father Augustine (354–430) was onto a legitimate if complex point when he argued for the idea that all truth is God's truth.[22]

Second, "Christian prudence" is what the Bible calls "discernment," and I explained this in chapter 5 from passages such as Hebrews 5:14, Ephesians 5:10, and Philippians 1:9–11. We need to note, though, that even with these more subjectively oriented factors, the Bible continues to exercise authority: it dictates "general rules . . . which are always to be observed."

Recent Theologians

Many theologians have echoed Westminster's definition of the sufficiency of Scripture. For further clarification, I'll share a few quotations from recent authors. First, Baptists Dockery and Nelson write,

> The believer is not lacking adequate revelation since the inspired Bible itself provides all the revelation necessary for knowing and living as

---

[21] I thank my colleague Jim Berg for helping me to appreciate this distinction. Cf. McCune, *Systematic Theology, Volume 1,* 40–43, 171–83.

[22] See Augustine, "On Christian Doctrine," Book II, Chapter 18, in Schaff, *Nicene and Post-Nicene Fathers,* 544–45.

God intends. The doctrine of sufficiency does not indicate that scriptural revelation is exhaustive, or that it contains all knowledge about the subjects taught therein, but the Bible is sufficient such that further revelation is not necessary beyond the scope of Scripture for faithfully living the Christian life.[23]

The context indicates that here "revelation" is referring to special, verbal revelation. Earlier Dockery and Nelson say this: "Divine truth exists outside special revelation; but it is consistent with and supplemental to, not a substitute for, special revelation. General revelation is consistent with special revelation yet distinct from it."[24] In the same volume Russell Moore writes, "Biblical wisdom . . . includes not just 'common sense' decision-making but also a consideration of the wisdom through which God designed the natural order to exercise dominion stewardship over the creation." Furthermore, the Reformation principle of *sola Scriptura* "does not evaporate insights from general revelation. But it maintains that special revelation provides the sole, final authority for all human thought."[25]

John Frame, a Presbyterian, elaborates extensively on the Westminster Confession's statement on the Bible's sufficiency. His basic definition is as follows: "Scripture contains all the divine words needed for any aspect of human life."[26] But Frame goes on to distinguish two kinds of sufficiency. *General* sufficiency is "the principle that any point of redemptive history, the revelation given at that time is sufficient."[27] *Particular* sufficiency is "the sufficiency of the present canon to present Christ and all his resources. God himself will not add to the work of

---

[23] David S. Dockery and David P. Nelson, "Special Revelation," in Akin, *Theology for the Church*, 163.

[24] Ibid., 119.

[25] Russell D. Moore, "Natural Revelation," in ibid., 109, 111.

[26] Frame, *Word of God*, 220.

[27] Ibid., 226.

Christ, and so we should not expect him to add to the message of Christ."[28]

These further remarks by Frame are especially relevant for the purposes of this book:

> So we may formulate the sufficiency of Scripture for ethics as follows: Scripture is sufficient to provide all the ultimate norms, all the normative premises, that we need to make any ethical decision. Scripture contains all the words of God that we need for any area of life, and all ultimate norms come from divine words.[29]

The Outworking of Sufficiency

Application takes the Bible's sufficient norms and relates them to the varied issues of life. In fact, far from contravening the Bible's sufficiency, application is essential to it. Chapter 4 demonstrated that for various reasons application is the only way the Bible can exercise its authority over our lives. Similarly, application is the only way the Bible can be sufficient for our lives. This is because of a basic challenge that prompted this book: Scripture does not deal explicitly with many of the questions we face. We can appreciate how sufficiency works by thinking through some examples. The first two are called "doctrines," but even these may be considered applications because they teach us what we should believe as Christians.

The Personality of the Holy Spirit

What should we believe about the identity of the Holy Spirit? The Bible never calls him a person, and Jehovah's Witnesses argue that the Spirit is merely a force emanating from God. Christian theology arrives at the personality of the Spirit through various deductions from Scripture. Several passages list the Spirit in parallel with the Father and the Son,

---

[28] Ibid., 228.

[29] Ibid., 231. For further discussion of the sufficiency of Scripture, see Barrett, *God's Word Alone;* Pipa and Wortman, *Written for Our Instruction;* Weeks, *Sufficiency of Scripture;* and White, *Scripture Alone.* Compare Vanhoozer, *Biblical Authority after Babel,* 109–46.

suggesting that all three are Persons (e.g., Matt 28:19; 2 Cor 13:14). A syllogism adds to the argument:

- *Major premise:* All who possess a mind, a will, and emotions are persons. (This is a common-sense observation; it seems to reflect the structure of humanity as created by God.)
- *Minor premise:* The Holy Spirit possesses a mind (1 Cor 2:10–11), a will (1 Cor 12:11), and emotions (Eph 4:30).
- *Conclusion:* Therefore, the Holy Spirit is a person.

Likewise, the Spirit performs various personal actions: teaching (John 14:26; 16:13), convicting (John 16:8), commanding (Acts 13:2, 4), and interceding (Rom 8:26–27). Additionally, human beings can sin against the Spirit. He can be resisted (Acts 7:51), blasphemed (Matt 12:31–32), lied to (Acts 5:3), tested (Acts 5:9), quenched (1 Thess 5:19), grieved (Eph 4:30), and insulted (Heb 10:29). Such arguments, based on biblical implication coupled with human experience, lead us to conclude that the Holy Spirit is a person not an impersonal influence or force.[30]

The Trinity

The doctrine of the Spirit's personality overlaps with our second example, the Tri-unity of the Godhead. The words *Tri-unity* and *Trinity* do not occur in Scripture. Nevertheless, the Bible clearly teaches the truths that these terms bring together. Here are the basic truths, with a few of the relevant texts:

- There is only one God (Deut 6:4; Isa 45:5–6; 1 Tim 2:5).
- The Father, the Son, and the Holy Spirit are each God (1 Cor 8:6; John 1:1; Acts 5:3–4).
- The Father, the Son, and the Holy Spirit are distinct from each other (Matt 27:46; John 14:26; 15:26).

The question is how all these propositions can be true at the same time. Borrowing categories from philosophy, we infer that God is one in *essence* but exists as three *persons.* This conclusion, though ultimately a mystery, accounts for all the biblical data. The doctrine of the

---

[30] For further discussion, see Ferguson, *Holy Spirit,* 15–33.

Trinity is a "good and necessary consequence" from what the Bible states regarding the Godhead.[31]

Abortion

Moving to matters of ethics, consider the horrific problem of medically induced abortion.[32] No verse states that abortion is wrong. However, the following syllogism establishes its sinfulness.

- *Major premise:* Murdering human persons is sinful (Gen 9:5–6; Exod 20:13; Rom 3:9).
- *Minor premise:* Unborn human babies are human persons.
- *Conclusion:* Therefore, murdering unborn human babies is sinful.

The minor premise is crucial, yet it isn't explicitly stated in Scripture either. We could argue that it's evident from "the light of nature." If not at conception at what other point would human personhood begin?

More importantly, we infer the human personality of unborn babies from biblical data such as the following.

- David was a sinner from the time of his conception (Ps 51:5).
- God tenderly cared for David as he shaped him in his mother's womb (Ps 139:13–16).
- John experienced joy while in Elizabeth's womb (Luke 1:44).

Christians have long opposed the evil of abortion on the basis of such inferences. Let's continue doing so![33]

Racism

Let's also resist the evil of racism. Here again, however, we do not have a verse that commands, "Thou shalt not be a racist." What we have is a series of biblical teachings that drive us to this conclusion.

- All human beings are equally created in God's image (Gen 1:26–28; Jas 3:9), having descended from one man (Acts 17:26).

---

[31] For further discussion, see Sanders, *Deep Things*.

[32] In explaining *sola Scriptura*, Aniol also uses abortion as an example (*Worship in Song*, 17–19).

[33] For further discussion, see Best, *Fearfully and Wonderfully Made*.

- After love for God, our second greatest duty is to love our neighbor as ourselves (Matt 22:34–40). There is no limitation on this duty based on ethnicity, skin color, or any other factor. Indeed, when teaching on love, Jesus indirectly challenged a form of ethnic prejudice in his day (Luke 10:25–37, the Good Samaritan parable).
- In Christ all believers have been reconciled to God. On the same spiritual footing, we have also been united to each other in one body, irrespective of ethnic or cultural differences. Consequently, we are to love our fellow Christians fervently despite these differences (Gal 3:27–28; Eph 2:11–22; Col 3:9–15).
- God's redemptive plan includes the eternal unity of people from diverse origins (Rev 5:9–10; 7:9–10).
- Both Testaments prohibit discrimination that is motivated by socio-economic differences (e.g., Deut 24:27–18; Jas 2:1–13; cf. Prov 17:5; 22:2). We have every reason to extend this prohibition to discrimination on the basis of "race."

Given all these factors, how can it be maintained that God is pleased when we view or treat another human being as inferior because his skin color or ethnicity is different from ours? We don't need a pointed command in order to know our Lord's will. Once again, through application a non-exhaustive Bible functions as our sufficient norm for faith and practice.[34]

Conclusion

Far from precluding application, the doctrine of the sufficiency of Scripture actually motivates application. This has become clear from the biblical basis for sufficiency, the historic definition of sufficiency, and the outworking of sufficiency in commonly accepted applications. Again, the argument of this chapter can be abused, and later discussion will help guard against such abuses. But if we constrict the meaning of biblical sufficiency out of fear of abuse, we will end up seriously limiting

---

[34] For further discussion, see Hays, *From Every People and Nation.*

the authority and value of Scripture. Here's another way to put it: the Bible is enough, but we need to make sure that we are doing enough with the Bible.[35]

---

[35] Adapted from Leedy, *Love Not,* 91.

Chapter 9

The Problem of Legalism

The earnest effort to apply biblical teaching is sometimes labeled "legalism." In addressing this issue, we face an immediate problem: what does "legalism" mean? Robert Spinney recounts an experience he had as a professor at a conservative Christian college. He was teaching about the Puritans, and it became apparent that his students were not too fond of this group. When Spinney pressed his students for an explanation, they opined that the Puritans were "legalistic." The students could not, however, provide a definition of that term. "Finally, one student haltingly said, 'Well, they [the Puritans] were just like, um, so concerned with obeying God all the time.'"[1]

As an admirer of the Puritans, I get frustrated when these spiritual giants are misunderstood and maligned. More importantly, it should alarm us all when being "concerned with obeying God all the time" is viewed as something negative. In addition, especially as we discuss theology we need to consider carefully how we are defining our terms. Here Spinney's conclusion reflects my own experience:

> *Legalism* is a word that we Christians throw around with reckless abandon. It seems like every churchgoer can use the word *legalistic* with zest. Yet when I ask Christians to define the concept, I invariably get mumbled and imprecise answers. If you asked ten Christians to define *legalism*, you would likely receive ten different definitions.[2]

---

[1] Spinney, *Are You Legalistic?*, 2.

[2] Ibid., 2-3.

The purist (Puritan?) in me wants to insist on defining *legalism* in only one way. While that would make matters simpler, it seems unrealistic at this point in church history. Word meanings change over time. The meaning of a word at a particular time is determined by its usage at that time. Yet each speaker or writer must at least clarify what he means when he uses a term, especially when he uses it to critique someone else's beliefs or practices. In this chapter I'll discuss what appear to be the three most common senses of legalism. Whether or not "legalism" is the best term for all these ideas, they constitute genuine concerns that must be addressed in relation to the topic of biblical application.

Justification by Self Effort

First and fundamentally, legalism is the notion that, to one degree or another, human works merit a righteous standing before God. In *The Oxford English Dictionary,* the first entry for "Legalism" reads, "Applied reproachfully to the principles of those who are accused of adhering to the Law as opposed to the Gospel; the doctrine of justification by works, or teaching which savours of that doctrine."[3] Jaeggli agrees: "Historically the term *legalism* has been used to describe the idea that a person can obtain salvation through fastidious adherence to a particular code of law, whether Mosaic or manmade."[4] According to Packer, the "first fault" of legalism "is that it skews motive and purpose, seeing good deeds as essentially ways to earn more of God's favor than one has at the moment."[5]

Scripture records multiple examples of legalism in this sense. In contrasting the prayers of the Pharisee and the publican, Jesus indicated that a major problem among the Pharisees was their proud dependence on their own works (Luke 18:9–14). The Apostle Paul's pre-conversion life stands as another case in point (Phil 3:2–11). And he generalizes regarding his fellows Jews: "For, being ignorant of the righteousness of

---

[3] "Legalism," *OED,* 8:804.

[4] Jaeggli, *Love, Liberty, and Christian Conscience,* 5.

[5] Packer, *Concise Theology,* 175.

God, and seeking to establish their own, they did not submit to God's righteousness" (Rom 10:3). Sadly, such legalism began to afflict the church as early as Acts 15. In the Epistle to the Galatians especially, Paul intensely countered the legalism of the "Judaizers" as false teaching of the most dangerous order (see especially 1:8–9).

If someone actually is a legalist in the first sense, he isn't a Christian at all, "because by works of the law no one will be justified" (Gal 2:16b). Legalism may, however, continue to have a subtle influence on the Christian. Remember that the dictionary includes as legalism "teaching which savours of" justification by works. An ambiguous concept, this can be difficult to identify in one's own thinking or in someone else's theology. Yet in focusing on our duty to apply God's Word to the details of our lives, it is certainly possible to lose sight of the graciousness of salvation.

For instance, while knowing that he has been justified by faith, a Christian may live with a vague sense that he *stays* justified by his own works. Spinney's definition encompasses this possibility: *"Legalism is an attitude (or motive) that leads people to try to establish, maintain, or improve a righteous standing before God by their own activities."*[6]

Accepting the Complexities

This is a complex matter since disobedience does, in fact, have an impact on the Christian's relationship with God. Our sin grieves the Holy Spirit (Eph 4:30). It causes us to lose the joy of our salvation (Ps 32:3–34; 51:12). A lack of spiritual growth decreases our assurance that we are genuine believers (2 Pet 1:5–11). The Lord may not grant our petitions (Ps 66:18; 1 Pet 3:7). And as our Father, he may choose to discipline us (Heb 12:4–11). These realities demonstrate that sin remains a serious matter for the Christian. So it's not legalistic to avoid sin at all costs (Matt 5:29–30; 2 Tim 2:22) or to confess it with a broken heart (Ps 51; 1 John 1:9).

---

[6] Spinney, *Are You Legalistic?,* 12 (emphasis original).

We also need to take into account Jesus's teaching in the Upper Room Discourse. Starting in John 14:15, our Lord ties together the disciples' love for him, their obedience to his commands, and their experience of the Holy Spirit's post-ascension New Covenant ministry. In this context he makes the following statements (vv. 21, 23):

> Whoever has my commandments and keeps them, he it is who loves me. And he who loves me will be loved by my Father, and I will love him and manifest myself to him. . . . If anyone loves me, he will keep my word, and my Father will love him, and we will come to him and make our home with him.

These words refer to the historical situation of the disciples in the first century. If they would persevere in following and obeying Christ, they would enter into a deeper level of intimacy with the Godhead through the new ministry of the Spirit. Of course, they did not persevere perfectly. But except for Judas, by God's grace they all eventually renewed their commitment to Christ after his resurrection. Consequently, they experienced the fulfillment of Jesus's prediction when the Spirit came on the Day of Pentecost (Acts 2).

Yet as argued by many expositors, John 14 applies in principle to Jesus's disciples of all times. The passage cannot mean that our obedience merits God's saving love or produces our righteous standing before Him. That would be legalism indeed! The Apostle John would balk at such a conclusion. After all, he emphasizes that God alone initiates our salvation (1:13; 6:37, 44, 65). He also emphasizes that God is the one who preserves us in eternal life (10:28–29).

This doesn't mean, however, that our obedience to the Lord has no effect on our experiential relationship with him. As D. A. Carson comments,

> The believer's growth in the knowledge of God and in the experience of the Holy Spirit turns at least in part on his love for Christ and obedience to him. . . . We must not think that we may somehow win the Father's love and Jesus's love by being obedient and loving. We cannot wrest God's love from him by our obedience. . . . But once a

person has become a follower of Jesus, he must understand that such a relationship is characterized by faith, love, and obedience, and that within this framework he experiences God's love in a special way.[7]

Elsewhere Carson distinguishes five ways in which Scripture speaks of the love of God:

- *The peculiar love of the Father for the Son, and of the Son for the Father* [e.g., John 3:35]. . . .
- *God's providential love over all that he has made* [e.g., Matt 5:44–48]. . . .
- *God's salvific stance toward his fallen world* [e.g., John 3:16]. . . .
- *God's particular, effective, selecting love toward his elect* [e.g., Eph 5:25]. . . .
- *Finally, God's love is sometimes said to be directed toward his own people in a provisional or conditioned way—conditioned that is, on obedience.*[8]

It is the last dimension of love that Jesus is discussing in John 14. He returns to it in John 15: "As the Father has loved me, so have I loved you. Abide in my love. *If you keep my commandments, you will abide in my love,* just as I have kept my Father's commandments and abide in his love" (vv. 9–10, emphasis added). Likewise, Jude writes: "But you, beloved, building yourselves up in your most holy faith and praying in the Holy Spirit, *keep yourselves in the love of God,* waiting for the mercy of our Lord Jesus Christ that leads to eternal life" (vv. 20–21, emphasis added). In terms of obtaining and securing the salvation of his people, God's love is gloriously unconditional. Yet the experiential aspect of God's love involves a certain conditionality.

Carson illustrates this distinction with the dynamics of parenting. There's a sense in which a good father loves his child in the same way all the time. His heart continues devoted to the child. In all circumstances the father remains caring toward the child and committed to his

---

[7] Carson, *Farewell Discourse,* 59, 61. For further detail, see Carson, *John,* 498–505. Compare Bruce, *John,* 301–4; Kruse, *John,* 303–10.

[8] Carson, *Difficult Doctrine,* 16–19 (emphasis original).

well-being. Yet love involves other dimensions such as a sense of closeness and an emotional enjoyment of the relationship. Positively, a father's affection for his child grows as they share bonding experiences. But negatively, a father rightly manifests displeasure toward a disobedient child—even strong displeasure in the case of aggravated disobedience.[9] While this shouldn't cause him to be less devoted to his child, it does have a significant impact on the way his love expresses itself and on his level of intimacy with the child. The application to our relationship with God is searching:

> God's discipline of his children means that he may turn upon us with the divine equivalent of the "wrath" of a parent on a wayward teenager. Indeed, to cite the cliché "God's love is unconditional" to a Christian who is drifting toward sin may convey the wrong impression and do a lot of damage. Such Christians need to be told that they will remain in God's love only if they do what he says. Obviously, then, it is pastorally important to know what passages and themes to apply to which people at any given time.[10]

Carson chooses carefully his words regarding "wrath." He is *not* speaking of God's wrath in the sense of the legal penalty for our sins, eternal punishment in the lake of fire. The believer stands forever free from this condemnation (Rom 8:1). Yet our very joy over this gracious deliverance becomes a motive to avoid displeasing our Lord and disturbing our communion with him.

Dealing with the Tensions

Maintaining our justification and our obedience in their proper relationship is one of the great challenges of Christian living. At various periods of history, the church has wrestled with the extreme of legalism and the extreme of antinomianism, the diminishing or rejection of the

---

[9] Ibid., 19–20.

[10] Ibid., 24.

role of God's law in the life of the believer.[11] How can we avoid these extremes?

First and fundamentally, we take into account the entirety of the Bible's teaching on our relationship with God. It's tempting to disregard one element of scriptural teaching out of concern for another. This is a perennial danger in theology and one that we need to be warned about regularly. We must base our approach to the Christian life on "the *whole* counsel of God" (Acts 20:27, emphasis added).

Second, we distinguish carefully between our daily experience with God and our ultimate, legal standing before him. The former fluctuates depending on various factors, including our obedience. The latter cannot change—for better or for worse—because it is based on the perfect performance of Jesus Christ (Rom 3:21–26; 5:18–19; 8:1, 31–39).

For another family analogy, consider marriage. Kind interactions and romantic getaways deepen a marriage, but they don't make a couple any more married in the eyes of the government. Nor does our loving obedience to Christ make us any more justified in God's sight. Conversely, harsh words and selfish actions create a rift between a husband and wife, cooling affection and making for an unhappy home. As serious as such offenses are, however, they do not legally end the marriage. Likewise, our disobedience disrupts our fellowship with God without altering our legal status.

Third, we keep our obedience in its proper, gracious context. We remind ourselves regularly that our obedience is the *result*—not the basis—of the righteous standing we enjoy as a gift from the hand of a loving, self-sacrificing God (Rom 12:1; 2 Cor 5:14–15). I began this book by emphasizing this soul-relieving truth, and recalling it now is critical as we move further into our study.

---

[11] *Antinomianism* reflects the Greek terms *anti*, "against," and *nomos*, "law." For a brief summary of different kinds of antinomianism, see Packer, *Concise Theology*, 178–80. For historical discussion, see Ferguson, *Whole Christ*; Jones, *Antinomianism*; Kevan, *Grace of Law*.

More broadly, as Sinclair Ferguson argues, understanding and enjoying the grace of God in our union with Christ is the cure for both legalism and antinomianism. Legalism—especially in the first sense—views God as unwilling to bless us until we obey. Antinomianism views obedience to God's law as antithetical to our happiness. Both reflect the satanic lie that duped Eve in Eden: that God doesn't truly love us and therefore can't be trusted. "The gospel is designed to deliver us from this lie. For it reveals that behind and manifested in the coming of Christ and his death for us is the love of a Father who gives us everything he has: first his son to die for us and then his Spirit to live within us."[12]

Sanctification by Self-Effort

This brings us to the second sense of "legalism." Sometimes the term is used to describe an overemphasis on the Christian's role in sanctification. Referring to Oxford's first definition, Robert Reymond says that "an ethical position might 'savor' of legalism if it failed to give adequate attention to union with Christ as the ethical dynamic of the Christian life (see Rom. 6:1–14) and to the enabling work of the Holy Spirit in sanctification."[13] We may also categorize this as a manifestation of legalism according to Oxford's second definition: "A disposition to exalt the importance of law or formulated rule in any department of action."[14] The term *moralism* can communicate much the same: "The practice of a natural system of morality; religion consisting of or reduced to merely moral practice; morality not spiritualized."[15]

Johnson distinguishes between the legalism of the Judaizers and the legalism of the Pharisees. Though the latter overlaps with my third definition below, it also relates to our present discussion. According to Johnson, the legalism of the Pharisees is

---

[12] Ferguson, *Whole Christ,* 69.

[13] Reymond, *Systematic Theology,* 771.

[14] "Legalism," *OED,* 8:804.

[15] "Moralism" (entry 2), *OED,* 9:1070.

the tendency to measure spirituality by a list of manmade rules. At the root of Pharisaical legalism is a belief that holiness is achieved by legal means—living one's life by rigorous rules and restrictions: 'Do not handle, do not taste, Do not touch' (Colossians 2:20–22). This type of legalism doesn't necessarily destroy the doctrine of justification like the legalism of the Judaizers. But it does significant damage to the doctrine of sanctification, and it is certainly appropriate to call it what it is: *legalism.* It is a sinful misapplication of law, an attempt to make law do the work that only grace can do.[16]

The distinction between the Pharisees and the Judaizers should not be pressed because, as noted above, the Pharisees did tend to view their obedience as meritorious. Johnson raises a real problem, however. Our pursuit of holiness can easily degenerate into a self-reliant and therefore defeating experience.

Johnson aptly points to Colossians for a warning of the futility of will-power and asceticism. Positively, Colossians tells us that we are complete in Christ (2:10), possessing all the resources needed for spiritual growth. This is what Reymond is emphasizing when he refers to union with Christ and the enabling of the Spirit. Our discussion of sanctification in chapter 3 highlighted these very truths. God's grace is the source of our progress in Christ-likeness. If we forget this, we can expect failure no matter how well founded our biblical applications may be.

Yet once again we're facing a tension, as Reymond and Johnson would agree. Immediately after warning the Colossians about "legalism," Paul urges them to seek heavenly things and put to death specific sins (3:1–17). So union with Christ does not make effort unnecessary. It empowers us for effective effort. Forgetting this leads to failure just as much as self-reliance. Sometimes we may need to pray as Pastor Scotty Smith suggests. Reflecting on Jesus's rebuke of the Pharisees in Mark 7, a passage we'll consider shortly, Smith offers "A Prayer for Gospel Pharisees and Scribes." It includes requests such as these:

---

[16] Phil Johnson, "Real Love and Real Liberty," in Kistler, *Law and Liberty,* 164.

Forgive us when we call ourselves "recovering Pharisees" or "recovering legalists" when in actuality, we're not really recovering from anything. . . .

Forgive us for being just as arrogant about grace theology as we were obnoxious about legalistic theology.

Forgive us when we don't use our freedom to serve one another in love, but rather use it to put our consciences to sleep.

Forgive us when our love for the gospel does not translate into a love for holiness, world evangelism, and caring for widows and orphans.

Forgive us for having a PhD in the indicatives of the gospel yet failing so miserably when it comes to the imperatives of the gospel.[17]

We avoid pendulum swings with sanctification-legalism the same way we do with justification-legalism: by accepting *everything* the Bible says on the topic, not just a portion. As I explained in chapter 3, Philippians 2:12–13 summarizes the Bible's teaching on how we progress in sanctification: God energizes us to work.

Motivation for Sanctification

A subset of sanctification-legalism relates to the question of motivation for pursuing holiness. We can err in various directions here. On the one hand, a distorted view of gratitude leads us to think that by our good deeds we're somehow paying Christ back for his saving work. On the other hand, gratitude for God's grace, especially in justification, can be so emphasized as to disregard other motives or suggest they are legalistic.

In responding to this tendency, perhaps "balance" is not the best way to express our goal. Instead we aim at maintaining the same proportion that Scripture does. Tabulating precisely the Bible's motivations for obedience goes beyond the scope of this book. Yet it would seem that a believing, adoring response to God's gracious salvation—past, present, and future—dominates those motivations.[18] It should

---

[17] Smith, *Everyday Prayers,* 56.

[18] See, for example, Rom 12:1–2; 2 Cor 5:14–15; Eph 4:1; Phil 1:27; Col 3:1–4; 1 Thess 2:12; Titus 2:11–14; 1 Pet 1:18–19.

therefore dominate Christian thinking and preaching. "We love because he first loved us" (1 John 4:19). This dynamic forms the overall context of our obedience.

Within that context, however, the Bible speaks with a richness that resists simplification and reductionism. Various writers have drawn attention to this. Frame identifies three scriptural reasons for doing good works: the history of redemption (e.g., John 13:34), the authority of God's commands (e.g., Matt 5:19), and the presence of the Spirit (e.g., Gal 5:16–17).[19] Grudem lays out extensive New Testament evidence for obeying God out of a desire to please him (e.g., 1 Thess 4:1).[20] And DeYoung lists forty biblical motivations for obedience—everything from following Christ's example (Eph 5:2) to fearing the Lord (2 Cor 5:11a) to avoiding the devil's snares (Eph 4:26-27).[21] In isolation such incentives can become legalistic. But under the umbrella of grace they inspire the regenerate heart.

One of the best treatments of this subject is by (surprise!) a Puritan. Countering antinomians of his day, Westminster divine Samuel Bolton (1606–1654) expounded the nature of Christian freedom and the place of obedience in the believer's life. He enumerated nine differences between "legal obedience" and "evangelical obedience." For instance, legal obedience is a burden, obeying merely out of duty. But evangelical obedience is a delight, obeying out of a relationship with God and as a means of fostering communion with him.[22]

Given our flesh and the many pressures of life, we can certainly grow cold and revert to a legally oriented obedience. As we renew our focus on Christ and God's grace through him, our hearts are warmed

---

[19] Frame, *Christian Life,* 29–31.

[20] Wayne Grudem, "Pleasing God," in Storms and Taylor, *For the Fame,* 272–92.

[21] DeYoung, *Hole in Our Holiness,* 56–60. For a complementary study, see Powlison, *How Does Sanctification Work?*

[22] Bolton, *True Bounds,* 140–44.

again and again. We develop the perspective needed to appreciate rightly our Lord's varied motivations. We come to experience more of 1 John 5:3, "For this is the love of God, that we keep his commandments. And his commandments are not burdensome." In fact, our duty increasingly becomes our delight.[23]

Imposing Human Standards

The third definition of legalism may be the most common today: imposing on others a manmade standard of conduct as though it were a divine requirement. This often includes the idea of judging the spirituality of others on the basis of such standards. In his classification of legalists, Daniel Doriani speaks of those who "love the law so much they create new laws, laws not found in Scripture, and require submission to them."[24] Swavely says that "when used in connection with sanctification (the Christian life after coming to salvation), the term [*legalism*] usually has something to do with man-made traditions added to the Bible."[25] Sam Storms concurs: "*Legalism is the tendency to regard as divine law things that God has neither required nor forbidden in Scripture, and the corresponding inclination to look with suspicion on others for their failure or refusal to conform.*"[26]

---

[23] Ferguson, *Whole Christ*, 157.

[24] Doriani proposes a four-tier classification of legalists: "Class-one legalists are autosoterists [self-saviors]; they declare what one must do in order to *obtain* God's favor or salvation. The rich young ruler was a class-one legalist. Class-two legalists declare what good deeds or spiritual disciplines one must perform to *retain* God's favor and salvation. Class-three legalists love the law so much they create new laws, laws not found in Scripture, and require submission to them. The Pharisees, who built fences around the law, were class-three legalists. Class-four legalists avoid these gross errors, but they so accentuate obedience to the law of God that other ideas shrivel up." *Putting the Truth to Work*, 279.

[25] Swavely, *Who Are You to Judge?*, 51.

[26] Storms, *Tough Topics*, 311 (emphasis original).

Avoiding Pharisaism

With this definition, Jesus's rebuke of Pharisaic tradition comes into focus. The connection between legalism and the Pharisees is so close that "legalism" and "Pharisaism" are sometimes used synonymously. Our study has touched on the Pharisees several times, but I've reserved for this chapter the key incident in Mark 7 (cf. Matt 15:1–20). Here the Pharisees and the scribes challenge Jesus because his disciples were eating without following the Jews' hand-washing ritual (Mark 7:1–5).

Our Lord responds with a crushing denunciation that applies to the Pharisees an Old Testament passage, Isaiah 29:13: "This people honors me with their lips, but their heart is far from me; in vain do they worship me, teaching as doctrines the commandments of men" (Mark 7:6–7). Extending to verse 23, Jesus's comments epitomize his rebuke of the Pharisees throughout the Gospels. We may summarize his teaching in four propositions.

First, in developing applications we must constantly guard against hypocrisy (Mark 7:6). Jesus describes the Pharisees with a theatrical term that means "play-actor." He expands on this in the woes of Matthew 23, excoriating the Pharisees for an internal rottenness that was masked by punctilious external observances. It is a frightening prospect that our lips may overflow with expressions of devotion to God while our hearts are far from him. As we apply the Bible to life, we must first apply it to our own hearts, regularly evaluating our motives and repenting of any self-seeking that the Spirit exposes.

Second, application that is not truly rooted in Scripture is not binding on God's people (Mark 7:7). In the Old Testament the only case that requires ceremonial hand-washing for laypeople is contact with bodily discharge (Lev 15:11). The other hand-washing commands are directed to priests involved in tabernacle/temple service (Exod 30:18–19; 40:12; Lev 22:1–6). Yet without compelling biblical deduction, oral tradition set forth detailed hand-washing regulations for Jews generally.

The original intent was noble: since in a sense all Israelites were priests (Exod 19:6), ritual purity in all of life was viewed as desirable.

But the regulations themselves were so far removed from Scripture as to have no authority.[27] Jesus identifies them as "commandments of men" that were being taught as though they were divine "doctrines" (Mark 7:7). We face the same danger in application. For our biblical inferences to carry force, we must be able to show that they are "good and necessary," a topic to which we'll return in Part V. And we need to moderate our dogmatism based on the strength of the argumentation that underlies each application.

Third, an application of one biblical teaching must never circumvent another biblical teaching (Mark 7:8–13). The Pharisees did more than impose dubious applications on people. Jesus says that these men *replaced* God's Word with their ideas. "You have a fine way of rejecting the commandment of God in order to establish your tradition!" (v. 9).

As an example, our Lord cites the tradition of "Corban." This term means "gift" and refers to something given or devoted to God, following the precedent of Leviticus 27:28 and Numbers 18:14. In the time of Christ an individual could will his assets to the temple yet retain personal use of them during his lifetime. Since the assets had been given to God, they could not be given to anyone else. In particular, they could not be used to support the donor's parents in their old age. This was a convenient way to get around the obligation to honor one's parents—with the blessing of one's religious leaders.[28] And Jesus says that the Pharisees did "many such things" (Mark 7:13). Before we become too indignant at the Pharisees' corruption, we ought to ask: do any of our biblical applications serve to salve our consciences concerning the violation of some divine directive?

---

[27] Edwards, *Mark,* 205–6; Garland, *Mark,* 277–82; Lane, *Mark,* 245–47. For the fully developed hand-washing tradition, see the tractate *Yadaim,* in Danby, *Mishnah,* 778–85.

[28] Edwards, *Mark,* 210–11. For the fully developed Corban tradition (renamed "Konam"), see the tractate *Nedarim,* in Danby, *Mishnah,* 264–80.

Fourth, our biblical applications must prioritize God's concern for the heart (Mark 7:14-23). Returning to the hand-washing issue, Jesus teaches that uncleanness derives from the inner person not from what enters the body. The Pharisees' legalism is closely associated with *externalism,* an overemphasis on external conduct coupled with an underemphasis on internal devotion and character. Jesus addresses this problem in Matthew 23 when he says that the scribes and Pharisees "have neglected the weightier matters of the law: justice and mercy and faithfulness" (v. 23). As we saw in chapter 6, this is the sense in which our righteousness must exceed the righteousness of the scribes and Pharisees (Matt 5:20). They were experts at extrapolating the letter of law. With a heart of love for God and neighbor (Matt 22:34–40), Jesus's disciples major on extrapolating the spirit of the law.[29]

The forcefulness and frequency of our Lord's rebuke of Jewish casuistry gives us pause as we deduce applications. We are sinners like the Pharisees. We remain susceptible to the problems that plagued them, and we need to be warned regularly about these problems.

Yet Jesus's words should not be taken as a blanket rejection of application or tradition.[30] In its entirety, Matthew 23:23 says, "Woe to

---

[29] This way of stating the matter was suggested to me by some comments in Keener, *Matthew,* 350.

[30] In this connection, it's difficult to interpret Jesus's words in Matthew 23:2–3, "The scribes and the Pharisees sit on Moses's seat, so practice and observe whatever they tell you—but not what they do. For they preach, but do not practice." Some think Christ is speaking sarcastically. There are good arguments for this view, including the word "whatever" and the negative assessment of Pharisaic teaching in the very next verse: "They tie up heavy burdens, hard to bear, and lay them on people's shoulders, but they themselves are not willing to move them with their finger." See Carson, "Matthew," 530–33; France, *Matthew,* 859–60. On the other hand, Jesus's statement may center on the Greek particle *oun* ("so") that connects "the scribes and the Pharisees sit on Moses's seat" with "practice and observe whatever they tell you." That is, people should heed the Pharisees to the extent that their teaching accurately reflects Moses. See Blomberg, *Matthew,* 340–41; Turner, *Matthew,* 545–46. Adopting this

you, scribes and Pharisees, hypocrites! For you tithe mint and dill and cumin, and have neglected the weightier matters of the law: justice and mercy and faithfulness. These you ought to have done, without neglecting the others." Note the final phrase, "without neglecting the others." This statement indicates that our Lord wanted the Jews to apply the Old Testament agricultural tithing laws to their smallest herbs (Lev 27:30; Deut 14:22–23). He was rebuking the Pharisees' gross imbalance and hypocrisy not their attention to detail. "It is not that tithing herbs is unimportant but that justice, mercy, and faithfulness are *more* important. This is not a hierarchical ethic but an incisive teaching that prioritizes the central values supporting the specific legal obligation."[31]

In addition, remember all the evidence we considered in Part III: multiple times Jesus and the New Testament writers used logic to arrive at conclusions that were not directly stated in the Old Testament. In reproving the Pharisees, Christ cannot be saying that we shouldn't apply the Bible. He is challenging us about *how* and *how not* to apply it. Though we could call Pharisaic application legalistic, rightly done application is Christ-like.

Conclusion

I take seriously the charge that biblical application can be done legalistically. Our application enterprise must remain alert to this danger. First, however, we need to understand what legalism is. This chapter has argued that the term may mean justification by self-effort, sanctification by self-effort, or the imposition of human standards as though they were divine. These issues are complex, and our next chapter will only introduce more complexity. None of this changes the thrust of our study, however. Well-reasoned, gospel-driven application remains imperative.

---

view, Bock and Simpson say, "Jesus did not engage in a wholesale rejection of what the law taught (cf. Matt. 5:17) or even what the leadership claimed to teach about following the law" (*Jesus*, 434).

[31] Turner, *Matthew*, 556.

Chapter 10

Christian Liberty

Our previous chapter identified three definitions of legalism, and the third of these was the imposition of manmade requirements as though they were God's. A more specific way of saying this is that legalism can take the form of violating Christian liberty. Two passages demand our attention here: Romans 14:1—15:13 and 1 Corinthians 8:1—11:1. You would do well to read each of these texts carefully before reading my corresponding discussions below.

To use these passages responsibly, we need to look closely at their original setting and context. I trust the following survey will help in this regard. At the outset, let's recognize that the Apostle Paul is dealing here with highly specific issues troubling two first-century local churches. The use of these texts to deal with contemporary debates—including the use of them to argue for specific freedoms—*is* an exercise in application. This fact should keep us from the position that expectations not specifically stated in Scripture necessarily violate Christian liberty. We are *all* "going beyond" these very passages in determining how to practice Christian liberty today.

1 Corinthians 8:1—11:1

We'll study the 1 Corinthians passage first since it was written first.[1] Here Paul addresses the matter of eating food that had been offered to idols, focusing primarily on feasts that were held within the precincts of

---

[1] Paul wrote 1 Corinthians around A.D. 55, whereas Romans dates to around A.D. 57. See Carson and Moo, *Introduction,* 393–94, 447–48.

pagan temples. Modern western Christians have difficulty understanding the degree to which image-worship and idolatrous associations pervade many cultures of the world. When first-century Gentiles embraced Christ, they struggled over how to respond to the practices of their former lifestyle. These included civic and social events that were held within pagan temple precincts. Festive meals on these occasions had idolatrous overtones since they involved eating portions of food that had recently been offered up to idols in a nearby place of worship. Yet to refrain from such events could result in social ostracism or worse.

In 1 Corinthians 8:1—11:1 Paul is dealing with this issue and related issues among the Corinthian Christians. He assumes that his original readers understand the precise shape of the debate in their church, so he doesn't provide much background information. Scholars disagree on some of the particulars of the background, and their viewpoints affect how they interpret portions of the passage. Without getting embroiled in these details, I'll attempt to outline Paul's flow of thought.[2]

Exposition

The apostle's main objective throughout is to prohibit idolatry, specifically in the form of participation in idolatrous feasts. He states this flatly in chapter 10, but he begins the discussion in a less direct way. In chapter 8 he acknowledges that idols are not actual deities and that sacrificing meat to idols does not somehow contaminate the meat (vv. 1–6). Nevertheless, the believer must not be satisfied with having this theological knowledge; he should aim at loving and edifying others (v. 2).

With this goal in mind, Paul calls on the Corinthians not to participate in feasts held within the precincts of an idolatrous temple (vv. 7–13). He supports his appeal with a hypothetical scenario. At an idolatrous feast a participating Christian might be observed by a fellow

---

[2] My approach to this passage parallels that of Garland, *1 Corinthians*, 347–504, who provides extensive argumentation and documentation. For somewhat similar analyses, see Fee, *First Epistle to the Corinthians*, 394–541; Thiselton, *First Epistle to the Corinthians*, 607–797.

believer with a "weak" conscience. This "weak" brother may in turn follow the first person's example and participate in the feast.

Many assume that "weak" here carries the same definition as "weak" in the semi-parallel Romans passage. As I will argue shortly, in Romans the weak brother is a Christian who isn't persuaded that he is permitted to participate in a certain activity. This doesn't seem to be what Paul has in mind in 1 Corinthians. Here the individuals in question are first identified as those who "through former association with idols, eat food as really offered to an idol" (v. 7). Paul does not attempt to correct the thinking of these people. He simply holds that if someone views eating a particular food as an idolatrous act he should not eat it.

In 1 Corinthians 8 the weakness in view is not a person's *perception* of idolatry. It is the failure of his conscience to keep him from *participating* in perceived idolatry. The individual is weak in that he caves to the pressure of someone else's example instead of following his own conscience. This results in the defiling of his conscience (v. 7).

It may also result in his destruction (1 Cor 8:11). In Paul's writings, the Greek term here (*apollumi*) consistently refers to eternal punishment.[3] Likewise, the "stumbling block" language (*proskomma*, v. 9; *skandalizō*, v. 13) is sometimes used for sin that leads to eternal punishment.[4] By eating at an idolatrous feast, the weak person will be pulled back into idolatry and, if he does not repent, will end up suffering eternal destruction.[5] The apostle is so alarmed by this possibility that he is willing to abstain from meat altogether if necessary (v. 13).

---

[3] See, for example, Rom 2:12; 1 Cor 1:18; 2 Cor 2:15; 4:3.

[4] See, for example, Matt 5:29–30, Rom 9:32–33; 11:9; 1 Pet 2:8.

[5] Fee, *First Epistle to the Corinthians*, 427–29; Garland, *1 Corinthians*, 389–90. Given Paul's teaching about the absolute security of believers (e.g., Rom 8), I conclude that a professing believer who returns permanently to a life of idolatry was never a genuine believer in the first place (cf. 1 John 2:19). This does not, however, diminish the seriousness of the warnings in 1 Corinthians 8 and elsewhere. In fact, the Spirit uses such warnings to work perseverance in the hearts of true believers. See Grudem, *Systematic Theology*, 788–809.

Paul does not side with a "strong" party in Corinth. "Strong" terminology doesn't even occur in 1 Corinthians 8:1—11:1. Paul does affirm that, in the abstract, "food will not commend us to God. We are no worse off if we do not eat, and no better off if we do" (8:8).[6] Yet our passage isn't about the abstract; it focuses on eating in a specific setting.

In this regard, categories such as "morally neutral" and "morally indifferent" (Gk. *adiaphora*) are easily misunderstood. In a nonmoral sense, food is positively good because it is created by God (1 Tim 4:1-5). And in terms of morality, food and eating do not *inherently* affect our relationship with God or our moral or spiritual condition (1 Cor 8:8). Yet Paul goes on to urge the Corinthians to glorify God through their eating and drinking (10:31), which implies that these actions may also *not* glorify God. This is because eating and drinking are done in particular *ways* and *settings* as well as with particular *motives, attitudes, associations,* and *effects*—all of which either please or displease God. Due to such factors, ultimately no human action is morally indifferent. This remains true even when we have difficulty determining which course of action honors the Lord.[7]

Paul never states that Christians have a right to eat at idolatrous feasts. In fact, his wording "this right of yours" sarcastically hints that he doesn't think believers have such a right (v. 9). Before delving into that matter, however, he expounds on how the Christian should approach the whole realm of rights.

Moving into chapter 9, Paul develops the theme of *surrendering* rights. He lists various rights that he enjoys as an apostle but that he voluntarily relinquishes for the gospel's sake (vv. 1–6). In particular, though he has a right to be remunerated financially for his ministry, he

---

[6] As argued by various commentators, this statement may have been a motto used by some Corinthian Christians to defend their actions. See, for example, Thiselton, 644–49. This is one of the points of background that is difficult to confirm.

[7] For a generally parallel view, see Frame, *Christian Life,* 168–75.

regularly declines compensation (vv. 6–18; see my discussion in chapter 7). Paul makes whatever personal adjustments he legitimately can in order to reach the lost with the message of salvation (vv. 19–23). This requires a great deal of self-denial (vv. 24–27). In highlighting his example, Paul's goal is to urge the Corinthians to deny themselves the right that some of them think they have to eat at idolatrous feasts.

But in chapter 10 the apostle goes on to argue that the Corinthians do not in fact have this right. After a strong warning based on Israel's example (vv. 1–13; again, see chapter 7 above), he states the thesis toward which he has been building: "Therefore, my beloved, flee from idolatry" (v. 14). Verses 15–22 then contend that participation in idolatrous feasts constitutes idolatry.

Here Paul focuses on the significance of the Lord's Supper. Through this ordinance believers share together in an act of fellowship with Christ (vv. 15–18). Likewise, through idolatrous feasts participants share together in an act of spiritual fellowship—not with deities but with *demons* that ultimately lie behind the idols (vv. 19–20). Fellowship with demons is utterly incompatible with fellowship with Christ, and it arouses the jealousy of God (vv. 21–22). This is why the Corinthians should avoid idolatrous feasts altogether—even though it may diminish their status in society.

First Corinthians 10:23–30 then handles some matters ancillary to the topic of idolatrous feasts. These verses keep the Corinthians from concluding that Paul is expecting them to live in total isolation from their pagan culture (cf. 5:9–10). But this section also refocuses believers on the effects of their actions on others (10:23–24).

On the one hand, the Corinthians need not be scrupulous about food outside pagan temple precincts. They may freely eat meat sold in a public market without inquiring whether it has been offered to idols (10:25–26). In a broad venue such as this, associations tend to fade away, and "Christ has not called them to be meat inspectors."[8]

---

[8] Garland, *1 Corinthians*, 490.

On the other hand, matters may become complicated when eating in an unbeliever's home (vv. 27–30). In that setting someone may announce that the meat has been sacrificed to idols, indicating that in his conscience an idolatrous association still attaches to the meat. In this case the Christian should refrain from eating in order to avoid suggesting that he is participating in or endorsing idolatry in any way.

In sum, Paul has taught the Corinthians not to eat meat that is known to have been offered to idols. This is what one would expect based on the rest of the New Testament. Earlier the "Jerusalem Council" had urged Gentile believers not to eat food offered to idols. (Acts 15:19–20, 29; 21:25). And later the ascended Christ would rebuke the churches of Pergamum and Thyatira for tolerating false teachers who influenced Christians to eat food offered to idols (Rev 2:14, 20).

Paul ends his instruction by emphasizing the Christian's motivations for a self-denying lifestyle. First, the believer aims at pleasing God—not himself, or demons (10:31). Second, like Paul, he lovingly seeks to advance the cause of the gospel in people's lives (10:32—11:1).

Application

First Corinthians 8:1—11:1 is not fundamentally about Christian liberty. This text does say that, in general, food may be enjoyed as a blessing from God (8:8; 10:25–26). But Paul puts the emphasis elsewhere. He teaches that eating is sinful when done in association with the worship of idols. Furthermore, such eating may well prompt others to sin.

This passage applies directly to contemporary cultures that still practice religious meals in connection with the worship of idols. In keeping with Paul's instructions, believers in such settings shouldn't eat food associated with idolatry. As with the Corinthians, adopting this position will likely entail painful consequences. But it also has great potential for proclaiming with clarity and conviction the truth about Jesus Christ.

"Good and necessary consequence" leads us to apply 1 Corinthians 8:1—11:1 to issues beyond idol food. Consider the following points in this regard.

We need to make sure that the issues to which we apply the passage are genuine parallels to the topic under discussion here: food, an inanimate object, something that does not intrinsically affect our moral or spiritual condition. Categorically prohibiting such things could be called legalism in our third sense. Actually, Paul classified the prohibition of divinely created foods under the heading "teachings of demons" (1 Tim 4:1)!

We must recognize that even inanimate objects may become morally problematic depending on their associations. No one lives life in the abstract. In certain contexts, otherwise good things and activities may compromise biblical truth and encourage others to sin. In such cases, the next principle is especially probing.

We need to concentrate not on upholding our rights but on loving others and protecting them spiritually. As Anthony Thiselton writes,

> The practical lessons here are profound. Paul is *not* advocating the kind of "autonomy" mistakenly regarded today as "liberty of conscience." Rather, he is arguing for the reverse. . . . *If this passage says anything at all to the ethical debates of today's world, it addresses not the overworn issue of "conscience" . . . but the impropriety of giving absolute status to "the right to choose," whatever the cost for others.*[9]

We'll see Paul reinforce this truth in our second passage.

Romans 14:1—15:13

Romans 14:1—15:13 shares some important features with 1 Corinthians 8:1—11:1 but addresses significantly different topics.[10] The differences between these texts affect how they apply to today.

Exposition

Paul warns the Roman believers against "doubtful disputations" (Rom 14:1, KJV). The underlying Greek expression refers to passing judgment

---

[9] Thiselton, *First Epistle to the Corinthians,* 644, 649 (emphasis original; Thiselton also boldfaces the expression *the right to choose*).

[10] For a listing of the differences between the passages, see Garland, *1 Corinthians,* 358–60.

(NASB) or quarrelling (ESV, NIV, NET©) over opinions (NASB, ESV, NET©) or debatable matters (NIV).[11] Paul cites two specific examples. First, one believer eats meat while another eats only vegetables (v. 2). Second, one believer regards one day above another while another regards all days alike (v. 5).[12]

In addressing these disagreements, Paul calls the more restrictive believer "weak in faith," or "weak with respect to faith." This title cannot mean that the person lacks faith in Christ for justification. The apostle would not go on to urge brotherly embrace of and deference toward a person who does not hold to a basic doctrine of the gospel (cf. Rom 16:17–18; Gal 1:8–9). Nor does "weak" in this context refer to general spiritual immaturity or unusual vulnerability to temptation. Mark Snoeberger identifies yet another mistaken definition of "weak."

> There is simply no room for using "weak" as a descriptor for Christians (fundamentalist or otherwise) who place extra-biblical fences between themselves and sin in the interest of "making no provision for the flesh in regard to its lusts" (Rom 13:14). Such practices are not manifestations of "weakness" in a Romans 14 sense, but instead expressions of wisdom. They show a wary acquaintance with the debilitating power of temptation and prudence in thwarting it. It is ludicrous at best and downright dangerous at worst to use these verses to dismiss cautious believers with a heightened sense of self-distrust as "weak," and celebrate incautious and permissive believers as "strong." This simply is not Paul's point.[13]

---

[11] For more detail on the Greek phrase, *diakriseis dialogismōn,* see Moo, *Romans,* 837, n. 45.

[12] Paul's comments in verses 17 and 21 may imply a third disagreement: drinking wine versus abstaining from wine. It can be argued, however, that the differences between modern alcoholic beverages and ancient alcoholic beverages limit the relevance of Romans 14:1—15:13 for the question of drinking alcohol today. See Jaeggli, *Christians and Alcohol.*

[13] Snoeberger, "Weakness or Wisdom?," 45–46.

What is Paul's point? What does he mean by "weak with respect to faith?" In approaching this question, note the connection between verses 1 and 2: "As for the one who is weak in faith [*pistis*], welcome him, but not to quarrel over opinions. One person believes [*pisteuō*] he may eat anything, while the weak person eats only vegetables." The Greek words for "faith" and "believes" come from the same root. Verse 2 contrasts the person who "believes" (has faith) that he may eat anything with the person who is "weak." This suggests that "faith" in verse 1 refers to the individual's conviction or persuasion as to whether a particular action is acceptable.[14]

Statements at the end of Romans 14 support this understanding. Verse 22 parallels the "faith" of the strong with his not being self-condemned about what he approves. By contrast, verse 23 equates the "doubts" of the weak with the expression *not from faith*. These statements argue that the "weak in faith" are those who are uncertain that a certain activity is permissible and therefore take a restrictive position.

We should probably also see a general connection between faith in Romans 14 and the kind of faith expounded in the epistle as a whole: faith in Jesus Christ as Savior and Lord. Cranfield explains: "The weakness in faith to which this chapter refers is not weakness in basic Christian faith but weakness in assurance that one's faith [in Christ] permits one to do certain things."[15] Presumably all believers would be classified as "weak" at some point—we all face ethical questions that we are unable to answer conclusively.[16]

Are the qualms of the weak in Romans 14 necessary? In the case of eating meat, the answer is no. Paul says regarding meat, "I know and am persuaded in the Lord Jesus that nothing is unclean in itself" (v. 14). So the weak do not fully grasp the implications of the gospel in relation

---

[14] Hodge, *Romans*, 417.

[15] Cranfield, *Romans*, 2:700. Compare Ash, *Teaching Romans, Volume 2*, 197; Moo, *Romans*, 835–36.

[16] I thank my colleague Gary Reimers for this observation.

to food.[17] But in the case of holy days, the apostle leaves the matter open-ended: "Each one should be fully convinced in his own mind" (v. 5). This implies that there is not a single correct position on the question of holy days. Presumably the weak observe holy days because they are unable to establish definitively from Scripture that Christians need not or should not observe such days. Paul's noncommittal response on the issue keeps me from portraying the weak as negatively as some commentators do.[18]

Closely related to the definition of "weak in faith" is the historical background of the debates mentioned in Romans 14. Paul never

---

[17] For a similar assessment, see Moo, *Romans, 714.*

[18] Schreiner holds that the "weak" do not sufficiently trust God in not accepting that faith in Christ implies freedom from Old Testament ritual obligations (*Romans,* 713–14). Snoeberger goes further: "What is in view in the examples supplied (eating meat, drinking, and special days) are not matters of implication, but matters to which God has spoken directly, and, as such, can be genuinely regarded as objects of *faith.* . . . [Paul is] speaking to the faith-embrace of clear biblical truth claims that are incidental to salvation" ("Weakness or Wisdom?," 35). It is difficult to see how this can be right, especially as it relates to holy days. Snoeberger says, "The issue of special days is less explicitly addressed in Scripture, but the non-necessity of observing special days may be easily deduced from certain Scriptures (e.g., Col. 2:13–17)" (32, n. 10). Several factors argue against this statement. (1) As noted above, in Romans 14:5 Paul takes a neutral position regarding holy days. (2) Unlike Romans 14, Colossians 2 is not dealing with mere observance of holy days. It rejects the insistence on holy days as part of a program for spirituality that undermined the sufficiency of Christ for sanctification. (Similarly, Galatians 4:10 opposes the observance of holy days as a condition for justification.) (3) Colossians was written several years after Romans, so the Roman believers would not have had access to the teaching of Colossians. (4) If "the non-necessity of observing special days" is "easily deduced" from Scripture, it seems odd that down to our day believers still strongly disagree over the relevance of the Sabbath for New Covenant believers. (5) If the "weak" are disbelieving clear biblical teaching, one wonders why Romans 14:1—15:13 takes such a soft approach toward them and why this passage is ultimately necessary. It seems that Paul would have simply corrected the weak and called them to faith in God's Word. Snoeberger does not provide a satisfying answer to this consideration.

states the reasoning behind the scruples of the weak. Some commentators hold that these scruples do not share a single background and/or that ascertaining the background isn't necessary for understanding and applying the passage.[19] Most commentators, however, see Romans 14 as reflecting Jew-Gentile tensions in the church at Rome.[20] These scholars argue that the weak were primarily Jewish Christians who still felt bound to ceremonial aspects of the Mosaic Law. Conversely, the strong were primarily Gentile Christians who did not have sensitivities regarding Mosaic ceremonial regulations.

This interpretation coheres with the context of Romans 14:1—15:13. Throughout the epistle Paul demonstrates a concern for the place of Jews and Gentiles in the New Covenant era (e.g., 1:16–17; 4:9–25). This concern comes to the fore in chapters 9–11, which includes a strong warning to believing Gentiles not to boast over their present position in the church (11:17–24). Furthermore, Paul's discussion of debated issues climaxes with an emphasis on the unity of Jews and Gentiles in the church (15:8–13).

The specific topics of debate in Romans 14 also fit a Jew-Gentile background naturally. The disagreement regarding holy days (v. 5) naturally suggests the Mosaic Sabbath and other sacred days. The terms *unclean* (*koinos*, 14:14) and *clean* (*katharos*, v. 20) likewise bring to mind the Mosaic laws about clean and unclean foods (Lev 11; Deut 14).

Of course, the Old Testament legitimizes the eating of meat in general (e.g., Gen 9:2–3). Yet it also records the example of Daniel and his friends, who became vegetarians in order to avoid association with the paganism of Babylon (Dan 1). Intertestamental writings indicate that other Jews adopted a similar ascetic lifestyle. So it's conceivable that

---

[19] See, for example, Haldane, *Romans*, 601–2; Lenski, *Romans*, 811–14; Morris, *Romans*, 475; Murray, *Romans*, 172–74.

[20] See, for example, Cranfield, *Romans*, 2:690–97; Hodge, *Romans*, 416–17; Moo, *Romans*, 826–33; Schreiner, *Romans*, 703–10; Snoeberger, "Weakness or Wisdom?," 30–37.

some first-century Jewish Christians abstained from meat, probably because they worried that meat sold in the marketplace had been offered to idols and/or had not been prepared in a kosher way. [21] A Jewish background explains well the sensitivities of the "weak in faith." Their applications may have been mistaken, but they would have had some biblical precedent for the restrictive positions they were taking.

Application

One's view of the background of Romans 14:1—15:13 tends to affect how he applies the passage. For instance, Douglas Moo's focus on Jew-Gentile tensions leads him to say that the only "real parallel" today is the question of Sabbath observance. [22] Yet even such scholars strive to apply the big ideas of the passage to other contemporary parallels. Paul himself encourages broader application when he concludes that it is good not to do *anything* that causes one's brother to stumble (14:21). And if we believe that Romans 14:1—15:13 is Scripture, then we will affirm that it was written for *our* instruction (15:4)—with relevance beyond its original setting (see chapter 7 above).

In this vein, Moo adds, "The value of this section is not limited to Paul's advice on these specific issues. Paul sets forth principles that are applicable to a range of issues that we may loosely classify as *adiaphora*: matters neither required of Christians nor prohibited to them." [23] I would agree with Moo's statement and his definition of *adiaphora*. But

---

[21] See Schreiner, *Romans,* 709–10.

[22] Moo, *Romans,* 881.

[23] Ibid., 881. Snoeberger's approach reflects his narrow interpretation of Romans 14:1—15:13 (see note 18 above): "Except in isolated pockets of the church where Jews are being actively evangelized, this passage has little and perhaps no *direct* applicability in today's church" ("Weakness or Wisdom?," 47). Yet even he holds to some broader use of the passage: "The application of Romans 14 extends strictly to *faith* issues (i.e., issues specifically sanctioned in Scripture) that are *non-essential* (i.e., issues that do not touch on the validity of a believer's status as a Christian)" (ibid., 37).

I would want to emphasize what has been argued throughout this book: God's requirements and prohibitions are not limited to explicit statements in Scripture. Elsewhere Moo expands his definition along these lines: "a matter [that] is not clearly prohibited in Scripture, *or prohibited by virtue of clear theological reasoning.*"[24]

On the other hand, we have to acknowledge that our deductions from Scripture and our choices in discernment are not all at the same level of certainty. Romans 14:1—15:13 does warn us against the legalism of imposing on others applications that are genuinely debatable. Regarding some applications, the solution will need to be, "Each one should be fully convinced in his own mind" (14:5). As I've noted several times, we need to evaluate applications on a case-by-case basis, assessing the biblical basis and logic behind each one. And as our study continues, I encourage you to evaluate my own applications in this way.

At the same time, we must all submit to the *full* teaching of Romans 14:1—15:13. Following is a summary of the main teachings of the passage.

The weak and the strong must not judge one another (14:1–12). The Spirit addresses both categories of believers. Each must resist the temptation to view or treat the other in a condemning way (vv. 1–3). Each is individually accountable to the Lord. And as each makes choices, the primary consideration should be not personal preferences but what would be to the Lord's advantage (vv. 4–12).

The strong will sometimes need to limit his liberty for the spiritual good of the weak (14:13–23). Several parallel terms identify the potential harm that the weak face: "a stumbling block" (*proskomma*, v. 13) or "stumble" (also *proskomma*, v. 20); "hindrance" (*skandalon*, v. 13); "grieved" (*lupeō*, v. 15); "destroy" (*apollumi*, v. 15); "destroy" (*kataluō*, v. 20); and "stumble" (*proskoptō*, v. 21). The New Testament usage of most of these terms as well as the semi-parallel discussion in 1 Corinthians 8:7–13 suggest that Paul is thinking of the worst-case scenario: a

---

[24] Moo, *Encountering,* 185 (emphasis added).

weak person may ultimately apostatize. Due to pressure from the example of the strong, he may engage in an activity even though he is unsure that the activity is acceptable. This could begin a process of spiritual decline that may lead him to abandon Christ altogether.[25]

Such an abhorrent prospect should move the strong not to exercise his liberty whenever it may put such pressure on the weak (v. 21). It also warns the weak not to participate in any activity about which they have ethical doubts (v. 23; cf. v. 14).

The strong have compelling reasons to deny themselves when necessary (15:1–13). The believer's primary question should be not whether he *can* participate in an activity but whether he *should* participate, given all the factors involved.[26] Paul encourages this selfless mentality with a series of motivations. The example of Christ (v. 3), the encouragement of Scripture (v. 4; see my discussion in chapter 7), and the enabling of God (vv. 5–6) all inspire the strong to help the weak (vv. 1–2). Finally, the work of Christ aims at bringing together diverse people in worship of God. Christians contribute to the grand goal of God's glory when they unite despite their differences on debatable matters (vv. 7–13).

Conclusion

The Apostle Paul acknowledges that biblical application can be complicated. He also instructs us about how to respond to those whose conclusions on truly doubtful applications differ from our own. This should not, however, deter us from applying Scripture. Even in teaching on matters of liberty, Paul urges a careful approach to Christian living. He calls us to focus not on our rights but on what will benefit others and what will honor God.

In fact, given the many ways we have seen the Bible itself encouraging application, one may argue for an additional, ironic definition

---

[25] See Schreiner, *Romans*, 726–44. See also my earlier discussion of 1 Corinthians 8, especially footnotes 3, 4, and 5.

[26] Moo, *Encountering*, 183.

of legalism. If legalism generally has to do with an imbalanced use of God's law, perhaps someone has become legalistic if he is satisfied with the letter or bare statement of Scripture. Maybe legalism includes the failure to appreciate the spirit of God's Word and to apply biblical ideals to every area of life.[27] Part V will help us avoid this error as we strive to develop sound procedures for application.

---

[27] I recall first hearing this line of thinking from Mark Minnick, my former pastor and now colleague.

Part V

Procedures
for Biblical Application

Chapter 11

Moving from the Bible to Life

Do you remember what it was like learning to drive? Months before reaching the minimum age for a learner's permit, you looked over the driver's manual and mastered the basics of navigating the roads. Then after breezing through the written exam, you excitedly jumped behind the wheel. Your dad didn't seem so excited. Before long his nerves were shot as you alternated randomly between wide turns and sharp turns, stopping too soon and stopping too late, under-accelerating and over-accelerating. There were so many details to remember—turn signals, yielding to traffic sometimes but not others, speed limits, and the dreaded parallel parking! You were learning the difference between theory and practice.

As we've been studying the theological basis for biblical application, much of the material has been theoretical. Along the way I've been making various points about the practice of application. The time has come to develop these, to apply our theology of application. So in chapters 11–14 I'll be recommending an approach for our ongoing study and use of biblical books. Then chapters 15–17 present a method for analyzing specific life issues in the light of Scripture.

A couple of qualifications are in order at the outset. First, I want to affirm that accurate application can happen apart from a self-conscious method. Especially because of the personal ministry of the Holy Spirit, when a believer meditates on Scripture he often arrives at applications in a kind of intuitive way. "While we interpret Scripture,

Scripture interprets us. We scrutinize the text, and the text scrutinizes us, exposing our beliefs, experiences, and secrets. We might say Scripture applies itself to us."[1] The more a Christian uses his Bible, the more this tends to be his experience, and it's a soul-stirring experience indeed.

This does not, however, argue against methodology. In order to avoid excessive subjectivity, we need to make sure that our applications are closely connected with the message of the text. A methodology helps to keep us on track here. This is especially important with the more difficult passages and the more thorny application issues. Though believers won't agree on every application, at minimum we should agree on the factors that ought to be considered in arriving at applications.

Second, I want to reiterate the reality that no method can guarantee our applications will be correct every time. We are finite and fallen after all, and any number of issues can derail us despite the best of techniques. While the Bible is inerrant, our interpretations and applications of it never will be. Our use of Scripture parallels our sanctification generally: it's progressive. We seek ongoing improvement in our application efforts, and this demands humility. Specifically, we regulate our dogmatism depending on the nature of the evidence and argumentation supporting each application. We remain open to correction. And we're willing to admit mistakes and change our views as necessary.

Methods and Models

When believers do follow a systematic application method, it's often a matter of asking a series of personally oriented questions. For example, how does a text relate to different aspects of human personality?

- *Mind:* What or how does this passage teach me to think?
- *Emotions:* What should I feel in response to the truths in this passage?
- *Will:* What decision does this passage call for?

Another common approach uses the categories found in 2 Timothy 3:16:

---

[1] Doriani, *Putting the Truth to Work*, 22.

- What *doctrine* does this passage teach me to believe?
- What sin does this passage *reprove?*
- Is there anything in my life that this passage *corrects* or sets straight?
- How does this passage *train* me to become more conformed to God's standards?

The list of questions we may ask of a passage can easily become longer. You may have heard these before:

- Is there a truth to embrace by faith and act on?
- Is there an attribute of God for which to praise him?
- Is there a sin to confess or avoid?
- Is there a command to obey?
- Is there a warning to heed?
- Is there an example to imitate or avoid?
- Is there a promise to claim?

These are helpful questions, and I've profited from them in my own reading of Scripture. But if application is limited to such questions or moves to them too quickly, we may well miss the unique richness and power of a passage. More fundamentally, we run the risk of neglecting the passage's meaning and overlooking significant differences between ourselves and the original readers.

In an effort to increase precision, scholars have developed various methods and models for biblical application. "Principlizing" is the best-known method.[2] Here we first determine the meaning of a passage in its context and the application of the passage to its original readers. Then we generalize the passage in terms of one or more universal principles that underlie its specifics. Finally, we relate the principle(s) to contemporary situations that parallel the situation of the original readers. Principlizing has also been called the "ladder of abstraction" model

---

[2] Authors who have popularized the principlizing method include Kuhatschek, *Applying the Bible,* and Veerman, *How to Apply the Bible.* On a more scholarly level, various works by Walter C. Kaiser Jr. have developed the principlizing method. For a summary and documentation, see his chapter "A Principlizing Model," in Meadors, *Four Views,* 19–50.

because it involves moving from the concreteness of the text to an abstract truth and then back down to concrete particulars in the present.[3] Or we may picture a universal principle as a bridge by which we cross over the gap between biblical times and our own times.[4]

The principlizing method has been critiqued on various grounds.[5] Establishing the principles in a passage can be a tricky business. We can state them so generally that they're not particularly helpful. Conversely, we may fasten on a minor principle while disregarding a major one. We may see a principle not because it's taught by the text but because we're importing it from another passage or, worse, from our personal or cultural predisposition. By attempting to "boil down" the Bible to principles, we can also forego the special impact of Scripture's varied genres. We dare not allow our statements of principle to supersede what God actually said. In this regard, if we focus narrowly on principles we can lose sight of the overarching redemptive story of the Bible and use Scripture legalistically in the sense of moralistically.

Many who principlize work hard to avoid the potential problems of the method.[6] Additionally, alternate approaches do not necessarily represent a total rejection of principlizing. Vanhoozer argues

---

[3] See, for example, Haddon Robinson, "The Heresy of Application," in Robinson and Larson, *Art and Craft*, 308.

[4] This is a unifying metaphor in Duvall and Hays, *Grasping God's Word*. It is also reflected in the threefold approach followed by the often helpful NIV Application Commentary series: (1) original meaning, *(2) bridging contexts,* and (3) contemporary significance.

[5] See, for example, Brown, *Scripture as Communication*, 246–48, 261–67; Clark, *To Know and Love God*, 91–98; Richard, *Preparing Expository Sermons*, 160–64; Mark L. Strauss, "A Reflection by Mark L. Strauss," in Meadors, *Four Views*, 274–77.

[6] See, for example, Duvall and Hays, 19–27; Johnson, *Expository Hermeneutics*, 213–64; Klein, Blomberg, and Hubbard, *Introduction to Biblical Interpretation*, 602–36; Osborne, *Hermeneutical Spiral*, 410–64; Köstenberger and Patterson, *Invitation to Biblical Interpretation*, 784–97; Virkler and Ayayo, *Hermeneutics*, 193–216.

for a "chastened" form of principlizing called "theodrama." Here Scripture functions like the script of an unfinished play. It records what divine wisdom looked like in particular instances in the history of redemption. We then "perform" our part in the play as we live out biblical wisdom in our situation today—not by replication but by "improvisation."[7]

We may include Vanhoozer's method in the broad category of "redemptive-historical" approaches.[8] Writers in this vein are influenced by diverse theological systems and differ on details of analysis, but they all give prominence to the Bible's redemptive storyline or metanarrative. They take special note of changes and additions God implemented as he progressively gave his revelation, and they underscore the connection between a passage and the phase of redemptive history in which it was given. More than anything, redemptive-historical writers keep Christ and his work at the heart of their interpretation and application, striving to avoid man-centeredness and legalism/moralism. I heartily concur with the concerns of the redemptive-historical approach, and I want to keep Scripture's redemptive framework and goal constantly in focus.

I also appreciate a category incorporated into various redemptive-historical models. We've seen it repeatedly in earlier chapters: the concept of *paradigms.* Somewhat distinguishable from principles, these are theological/spiritual/ethical *patterns* tied closely to the specific *purposes* that biblical authors were aiming to accomplish in the lives of the original readers in their particular stage of redemptive history. Such patterns and purposes guide us as we strive to "contextualize" God's Word faithfully in our circumstances.[9]

---

[7] See Kevin J. Vanhoozer, "A Drama-of-Redemption Model: Always Performing?," in Meadors, *Four Views,* 151–99. For fuller development, see Vanhoozer, *Drama of Doctrine,* and Vanhoozer, *Faith Speaking Understanding.*

[8] Greidanus is a major representative of the redemptive-historical school. See, for example, his work *Sola Scriptura.*

[9] Though they vary in their terminology and emphases, the works listed below emphasize redemptive history and also advocate the basic idea of

Conclusion

Further discussion of previous works on application would prove distracting here.[10] I do, however, want to acknowledge the contributions of those who have wrestled with this topic. As you can see, there is some overlap among the proposed methods. My own approach is eclectic, drawing on insights from a variety of writers. Most importantly, though, I want to synthesize, systematize, and expand on what we've learned about application from the Bible itself.

As we proceed, however, I want to avoid being formulaic. I even hesitate to speak in terms of sequential "steps" to follow. Bible study and application tend to be more fluid than this, and often several things are happening at once. While I strive to be precise, my method isn't rigid. In addition, I'm not aiming at exhaustiveness. The topics below could

---

paradigms. Daniel M. Doriani, "A Redemptive-Historical Model," in Meadors, *Four Views,* 75–120; Doriani, *Putting the Truth to Work;* Mark L. Strauss, "A Reflection by Mark L. Strauss," in Meadors, *Four Views,* 271–98; Strauss, *How to Read the Bible in Changing Times;* Al Wolters, "A Reflection by Al Wolters," in Meadors, *Four Views,* 299–319; Wolters and Goheen, *Creation Regained;* Christopher J. H. Wright, "A Reflection by Christopher J. H. Wright," in Meadors, *Four Views,* 320–46; Wright, *Old Testament Ethics.*

[10] It's beyond my scope, for example, to provide detailed evaluation of the "redemptive movement" model of William Webb. Webb holds that the New Testament may not provide the final word on a particular topic. Instead Scripture may set forth a trajectory that God's people need to continue as they develop an "ultimate ethic." This ethic may end up being substantially different from what the Bible states. For instance, Webb's approach leads him to an egalitarian position regarding male-female roles. See William J. Webb, "A Redemptive Movement Model," in Meadors, *Four Views,* 215–48. For development, see Webb, *Slaves, Women & Homosexuals,* and Webb, *Corporal Punishment.* Webb's model is based significantly on dubious conclusions regarding the Bible's teaching on slavery. It ignores the New Testament's rooting of gender roles in divine creational patterns. It also introduces an inordinate degree of subjectivity in the development of an "ultimate ethic." In Meadors, *Four Views,* various authors discuss problems with Webb's approach; see especially Al Wolters, "A Reflection by Al Wolters," 302–10. For a full-length critique, see Reaoch, *Women, Slaves, and the Gender Debate.*

be developed in much greater detail and, as suggested by the footnotes, can get rather technical. What I'm attempting to do is outline an approach to application that reflects the Scripture's own approach. Consequently, I'll be referring frequently to previous chapters in our study. I want to keep our practice rooted in our theology.

A number of times already I've emphasized that application must be firmly rooted in the biblical passage at hand. Here the material in chapters 6 and 7 is particularly instructive: cases where Scripture applies earlier Scripture illustrate how to apply a text in a way that grows out of its intended meaning. Common-sense principles of human communication also have a contribution to make. Such considerations support three commonly cited factors for interpreting and applying the Bible: *meaning* (chapter 12), *implication* (chapter 13), and *significance* (chapter 14).[11] Working carefully through each factor will move us a long way toward accurate applications.

---

[11] These categories were popularized by literary scholar E. D. Hirsch Jr. through *Validity in Interpretation* and other writings. Though Hirsch's views changed over time, conservative theologians have found his work useful because of its focus on the intended meaning of the human author. The many who rely on Hirsch include the authors listed in note 5 as well as Kaiser, *Toward an Exegetical Theology,* Kuruvilla, *Privilege the Text,* and Stein, *Basic Guide.* I've found these works helpful, but I also appreciate approaches that give a more prominent role to God as the Author of Scripture. See, for instance, Johnson, *Expository Hermeneutics,* and the writings of Poythress such as *God-Centered Biblical Interpretation.* Compare Vanhoozer, *Is There a Meaning in This Text?* Also helpful, though complicated, is Richard, "Methodological Proposals." As indicated earlier, in my categorizations and definitions I'm not following any one scholar. I trust I'm incorporating the strengths of the various views, in an accessible format.

Chapter 12

The Meaning of Meaning

In all our uses of God's Word, we must maintain a focus on the meaning of Scripture as the basis and benchmark of application. And as a starting point we need to define the term *meaning*. My general definition is as follows: *the message the author/Author intended to convey through his/his choice and arrangement of words.* This reflects the simple but profound fact that the books of the Bible constitute personal communication. All such communication centers on an idea or series of ideas that one person or group of people aims at conveying to another person or group of people.

In the case of Scripture, the unique element is that *two* authors were involved: the human author and the divine Author. Ultimately, Christians are interested in the message the Holy Spirit intends for them in a passage. He was the one who guided each human author in writing (2 Pet 1:20–21). But this very fact indicates that the message intended by the human author serves as our access to the Spirit's meaning. Thus the human author's meaning and the divine Author's meaning are inseparably linked. As we delve into these matters, our discussion will divide into two similarly linked categories: the *historical* meaning of a text and its *transhistorical* meaning.

Historical Meaning

The historical meaning is *the message intended for the original readers of a passage.* The generally accepted method for ascertaining this meaning is known as *grammatical-historical interpretation.* I don't have space for a complete defense and explanation of the grammatical-historical method, so I urge you to read further on this foundational matter.[1] But since application is so closely connected with interpretation, I'll survey the kinds of analysis that grammatical-historical interpretation carries out in order to grasp the meaning of a passage as accurately as possible. Specifically, I'll overview *historical analysis, genre analysis, contextual analysis, and linguistic analysis.* Each type of analysis aims at implementing a particular principle of grammatical-historical interpretation.

This material may seem academic and off-putting. I don't want to imply that a believer has to become a scholar in order to understand and apply the Bible. Certainly some will be able to study in more detail than others. Yet isn't a knowledge of God and his Word worth as much effort as any Christian is able to put into it? Isn't our sanctification worth an all-out pursuit of God's truth? Indeed, that is one way in which we can love him with all our minds (Matt 22:37). There I go again—making an application!

Historical Analysis

We do historical analysis because we want to *interpret each biblical passage in conformity with its historical-cultural background.*[2] This includes learning whatever we can about the background of a biblical book as a whole: its timeframe and the dominant characteristics of that timeframe, its author and his circumstances, its original recipients and their circumstances, and the purpose(s) for which the book was written. Identifying the purposes of a book and its individual passages is crucial for establishing application: whatever purposes God desires to accomplish in our

---

[1] For starters, I'd recommend Duvall and Hays, *Grasping God's Word,* and Fee and Stuart, *How to Read the Bible for All Its Worth.* For more in-depth treatment, standard resources include the works listed in note 5 of chapter 11. My summary of the grammatical-historical method is especially indebted to Fee and Stuart, *How to Read the Bible for All Its Worth;* Klein, Blomberg, and Hubbard, *Introduction to Biblical Interpretation;* Virkler and Ayayo, *Hermeneutics.*

[2] Adapted from Klein, Blomberg, and Hubbard, *Introduction to Biblical Interpretation,* 312.

lives will cohere with the purposes he aimed at in the lives of the original readers.

How do we figure out the historical-cultural background of a biblical book? Sometimes this kind of information is explicitly stated. Chapter 4 cited John 20:30–31 along these lines. Or we can piece together a fair amount from the contents of the book itself. Think of the Epistles' frequent references, direct or indirect, to problems in the churches to which they are addressed. Additionally, one book of the Bible may shed light on the historical circumstances of another book. A prophetic book will often begin by listing kings under which the prophet ministered (e.g., Mic 1:1). So we study the reigns of those kings in the Historical Books, looking for connections between those reigns and the message of the prophet. Similarly, the book of Acts provides a great deal of background for interpreting (and even dating) the Epistles.

As supplemental resources, archeology and extrabiblical history can also illuminate the background of biblical books. This is especially the case when dealing with specific historical-cultural features in individual passages. Ancient Near Eastern texts on inheritance customs help us understand the patriarchal narratives in Genesis. The study of pagan Greco-Roman religions hones our interpretation of Paul's teaching about food offered to idols (1 Cor 8–10; cf. my discussion in chapter 10). Thankfully, we have available many reference works and commentaries that compile and analyze material elucidating the historical-cultural background of biblical books.[3]

Genre Analysis

Genre analysis helps us to *interpret each biblical passage in conformity with the characteristics of its literary form.* Chapter 4 had some discussion of genres in Scripture, but the concept may still sound technical. In reality, you draw on it anytime you read anything. You don't expect a newspaper article to read like a novel, or a business letter to sound like

---

[3] For recommendations on Bible study tools, see Evans, *Guide.*

a love note. Each kind of writing has its own set of features that shape the meaning being communicated and that guide us in interpretation. This is a given of written communication, so we can expect that genre analysis plays a major role in interpreting and applying the Bible.

Following are summaries of key characteristics of the primary genres found in Scripture.

- *Historical Narrative:* As I explained in chapter 4, stories are less explicit about their meaning than other genres. They require attention to the elements of (1) setting, (2) plot, and (3) characterization (especially dialogue). Storytellers also indicate their point of view in various ways, sometimes direct (e.g., evaluative comments) but more often indirect (e.g., perspective from an "omniscient" standpoint). A *Gospel* is a unique form of narrative that differs in significant ways from a strict biography. Each Gospel arranges and shapes selections from the life of Jesus in order to highlight a particular aspect of his person and work, with a dominant focus on the events of the Passion Week.

- *Old Testament Law:* This legal material must be interpreted in light of the gracious yet conditional Mosaic Covenant of which it is part. The historical setting takes on an especially significant role here. Extrabiblical legal and treaty documents provide insight into the function of laws in the second millennium B.C. The distinction between apodictic and casuistic laws is important, as well as the fact that the laws are paradigmatic not exhaustive (see chapters 4 and 6 and the discussion below). The cultural background can help in identifying the purpose of specific laws and arriving at paradigms.

- *Old Testament Poetry:* Two features of this poetry demand special attention: various kinds of parallelism between lines and a wide array of figures of speech. Additionally, Old Testament poetry frequently uses repetition to emphasize key ideas and heighten emotional impact. The *Psalms* may be classified according to certain thematic/structural patterns that provide a framework for interpretation (e.g., praise, lament, kingship).

- *Old Testament Wisdom Literature:* The above characteristics of poetry typically apply here. Note also that the wisdom in these books isn't oriented to ironclad rules or promises. Instead it teaches how life *generally* works (*Proverbs*) as well as how to respond when there are exceptions (*Job, Ecclesiastes*).
- *Prophecy:* The Old Testament prophets were usually preachers, and their books are largely collections of sermons or oracles, typically poetical. Like the Psalms, these oracles tend to follow certain patterns (e.g., woe, salvation, lawsuit). Predictive material needs to be understood in connection with the theme of the oracle in which it occurs. *Apocalyptic* is a specialized form of prophecy that occurs to a degree in books such as Zechariah. It predicts God's final triumph over evil and makes heavy use of symbolism. The matter of symbolism relates to contextual analysis, described below, since the context is our primary guide for determining whether or not an author intends a particular statement symbolically.
- *Epistles:* These are modified letters that combine doctrinal instruction with practical direction regarding specific needs and problems among first-century churches and believers. The Epistles are more theologically loaded than other genres and call for especially detailed examination of grammar and logic.

A major reason we misinterpret and misapply Scripture is that we read one genre as if it were another. This happens especially with Old Testament narrative. Bible studies and sermons go astray when they approach Old Testament stories as though they were New Testament epistles. Readers look for specific lessons from small details in narratives when such details are not intended to be pressed for application.

For example, I once read a study of Esther 1, where King Ahasuerus deposes Queen Vashti after she refuses to showcase her beauty at his drunken feast. The commentator used this text to warn against drunkenness, to urge wives to submit to their husbands, and to exhort the church, the bride of Christ, to display her beauty to the world, i.e., evangelize. These applications fail on several points, including the matter of genre.

The first chapter of Esther belongs to the introduction to the book, the part of the plot often called the "exposition." Here the author gives background information and introduces the characters, before the key conflict of the story begins. In Esther that conflict centers on Haman's attacks against the Jews. The story about Vashti shows how God used the outrageous decisions of a pagan king to set up circumstances so that he could employ Esther to deliver the Jews. This strongly supports the theme of the book: God's providential protection of his people. In light of Esther's plot and theme, the most natural application of chapter 1 would focus on trusting the sovereign God to use even the wicked actions of governments to accomplish his redemptive purposes.

Contextual Analysis

What I said about Esther 1 overlaps with contextual analysis, which strives to *interpret each biblical passage in conformity with the layers of literary context that surround the passage.*[4] Sections of Proverbs may consist of series of unconnected verses, yet this exception suggests a rule: biblical statements don't exist in isolation. They're inseparably linked to a broader sequence of thought, and that sequence significantly shapes their meaning. Further, context is not a single piece of information but a series of layers. This has been pictured in terms of a bullseye (the passage being studied) surrounded by various concentric circles (contexts).

The circle nearest to the bullseye represents the *immediate* context, the passages most closely preceding and following the passage at hand. For studying the immediate context, chapter and verse breaks aren't always reliable. While often helpful, these editorial divisions sometimes disrupt the immediate context. We're on safer ground when we follow paragraph (prose) or strophe (poetry) divisions, typically indicated by modern versions. In any case, immediate context is most determinative of meaning because it forms the flow of thought out of which a text directly arises and to which it directly contributes.

---

[4] Adapted from Klein, Blomberg, and Hubbard, *Introduction to Biblical Interpretation,* 294.

Here's an example of a non-contextual application that hasn't gone away no matter how many times it's been challenged. In Philippians 4:13 Paul makes a reassuring declaration that has justly become famous: "I can do all things through him who strengthens me." "All things" does not, however, guarantee that a football team will win a game or that an investor will make money on a business venture. The immediate context indicates that Paul is talking about *living contentedly* in every circumstance, whether need or abundance (vv. 11–12). Applications of Philippians 4:13 ought to be natural extensions of this point. If we are going to relate the verse to sports, for instance, it's most applicable for helping a team respond correctly when it *loses* a match.[5]

The immediate context itself belongs to larger contexts. It fits into a particular *section* of a biblical book. And that section fits into the context of the *book as a whole*. We can't establish these additional contexts and their relevance for a text apart from appreciating the overall structure and theme of the book. This comes by reading a biblical book in its entirety—preferably in one sitting and preferably multiple times.

Careful Bible study regularly moves back and forth between an individual passage and its entire book. The two are self-interpreting. The more familiar we become with the whole of Genesis, the more we'll see that the main purpose of the patriarchal narratives isn't to teach lessons about family life. It's to show how God advanced his international saving plan through fallen people and how he was saving them more and more from their sin even through the consequences of their own failures.

The circles of context broaden out beyond the book under consideration. Sometimes the human *author* himself provides a broader context because he wrote other books of Scripture that relate in some way to the book one is studying. The terminology and themes of John's Gospel, for example, can shed light on his epistles and Revelation. Another circle of context comes into play if the author of a book was influenced by *earlier revelation* given through other writers. As evident

---

[5] See further, Duvall and Hays, *Grasping God's Word*, 237–41.

throughout chapters 6 and 7, this happened frequently. In the Old Testament, the Historical and Prophetic Books are largely applications of the theology of the Pentateuch. Likewise, the writers of the New Testament were immersed in and consciously adding to the teaching of the Old Testament. So arriving at an author's intent often involves interacting with other books of the Bible with which he was interacting.

Linguistic Analysis

The goal of linguistic analysis is to *interpret each biblical passage in conformity with the normal use of language.*[6] Here I've chosen the adjective *normal* over the commonly used but easily misunderstood term *literal.* Depending on genre and context, normal may be literal: "Thus the LORD saved Israel that day from the hand of the Egyptians" (Exod 14:30a). Or it may be figurative: "For the LORD God is a sun and shield" (Ps 84:11a). Again we see the interplay between the various kinds of analysis: genre and context inform language, and vice-versa.

"Normal" also tells us that the languages God used to give us his Word—Hebrew, Aramaic, and Greek—don't function in some mysterious, other-worldly way. They were ordinary human languages, and they follow standard patterns of verbal communication. The same holds true for languages into which the Scriptures are translated. So the more we understand general conventions of language, the better equipped we'll be to understand the Bible. This may sound intimidating, but it's actually encouraging. Since I teach Hebrew and Aramaic, I won't deny that studying the original languages of Scripture sharpens one's interpretation.[7] But I will affirm that you don't have to know ancient languages in order to understand God's Word. What is more necessary is also more achievable: knowledge of how language *in general* works.[8]

---

[6] Adapted from Klein, Blomberg, and Hubbard, *Introduction to Biblical Interpretation,* 325.

[7] See DeRouchie, "The Profit of Enjoying the Biblical Languages."

[8] See Silva, *God, Language, and Scripture.*

Such knowledge serves us well in dealing with individual *words* within a passage. Often word studies make more of individual terms than is defensible or helpful, especially by introducing "deep" ideas based on roots and historical origins. Were we to follow the same approach with words in our own language, the results would be amusing to preposterous.[9] The fact is that a good modern translation will make sufficiently clear the meaning of the majority of biblical words.

How do we approach words that call for detailed examination, particularly those that carry a lot of theological weight (e.g., covenant, righteousness, redemption, holiness)? We study such words in the same way that we would study words in our own language: by analyzing their *usage.* In a particular passage we look for definitional clues by considering the words that surround our word—context yet again. Then with the help of a concordance or Bible software program, we examine other passages that use the word, especially those written around the same time as our text. Narrative passages can be particularly helpful here because word meanings are fairly obvious in that genre.

More significant than the study of individual words is the study of the *syntax or arrangement* of words in sentences. Can you identify the parts of speech? Do you recall how to diagram a sentence? These are among the most valuable skills for interpreting Scripture, especially the Epistles. They enable us to analyze in detail, to trace an author's reasoning step by step. Within each sentence we strive to understand the logical connection between each main clause and its subordinate clauses and phrases. Consider the following layout of Colossians 3:1–3 (emphasis added to highlight main clauses).

---

[9] For example, the English word *pedigree* comes from a French phrase meaning "crane's foot." The connection between the two expressions is evidently a symbol commonly used to indicate succession in genealogical tables: three vertical lines that look like the claws of a crane. See *OED,* 11:424. While this etymology is an interesting bit of trivia, today it is not part of an English speaker's intention when he uses the word *pedigree* and is therefore irrelevant for interpreting a statement that includes the word.

Biblical Expression	Tag	Logical Relationship
If then you have been raised	A	Condition of C
with Christ,	B	Association of A
seek the things that are above,	C	Command #1
where Christ is,	D	Description of "above" in C
seated at the right hand of God.	E	Description of "Christ" in D
Set your mind on things that are above,	F	Command #2
not on things that are on earth.	G	Contrast to F
For you have died,	H	Cause of F/G
and your life is hidden	I	Cause of F/G
with Christ	J	Association of I
in God.	K	Sphere of I

As we work through individual sentences in this way, eventually we'll be able to map out the author's flow of thought through larger blocks of material. This is a tedious process but richly rewarding. I first did such projects as a college student. I'm not exaggerating when I say that they revolutionized my relationship with the Word of God and the God of the Word.[10]

Transhistorical Meaning

The historical meaning leads us to the transhistorical meaning: *the message intended for readers of a passage beyond the original readers.* This

---

[10] For basic instruction on analyzing grammar and logic in the New Testament, see Klein, Blomberg, and Hubbard, *Introduction to Biblical Interpretation,* 344–60. For more detail, see Huffman, *Handy Guide,* 83–106.

brings us back to the author-Author distinction. Were the human authors of Scripture intending a message for readers beyond their immediate addressees? Some clearly were. Recall some passages I've discussed in earlier chapters: Deuteronomy 29:14–15, Psalm 78:6–7, Matthew 28:20, and 2 Timothy 2:2.

What about books that don't have such indications? To the degree that a biblical author was aware he was a spokesman for God, presumably he had a sense that his writing would have something to say to all people. Yet even if we can't be sure about the relationship between the transhistorical meaning and the human author, all the data in chapters 4–7 assure us that *God's* intended communication wasn't limited to the Bible's original recipients. As the ultimate Author, *he* is communicating transhistorically. "For whatever was written in former days was written for our instruction, that through endurance and through the encouragement of the Scriptures we might have hope" (Rom 15:4).

The bigger question is whether the transhistorical meaning of a passage is identical with its historical meaning, specifically as intended by the human author. I reply that in some ways the two can differ, but in their essence they correspond.

Excluded Elements

The transhistorical meaning may exclude highly specific elements of the historical meaning. A few subcategories come into view here.

Covenantally Specific Elements

An element may be excluded from the transhistorical meaning because it is *covenantally* specific. I'm referring to the Mosaic Law in particular. The relationship between the New Testament believer and the Old Testament Law is one of the great tensions in Christian theology. On the one hand, as we've seen a number of times in our study, the Law continues to instruct us concerning the character and will of God (e.g., Matt 5:17–48; 22:35–40; Rom 13:8–10; 2 Tim 3:14–17). This includes timeless truths taught by the most narrow of Old Covenant regulations (e.g., "You shall not muzzle an ox when it is treading out the grain,"

Deut 5:24; cf. 1 Cor 9:8–11). On the other hand, the New Testament emphasizes that Christians are not under the direct, covenantal authority of the Mosaic Law (e.g., Rom 6:14; 10:4; 2 Cor 3:6–18; Gal 3:23—4:4). It also identifies several individual Mosaic laws whose stated requirements God does *not* expect of us today.

The food laws are an example (Mark 7:19; cf. Acts 10:9–16). These were unique aspects of Yahweh's arrangements for Israel as his covenant nation. So despite what Moses intended for the Israelites in Leviticus 11, in this passage the Lord is not prohibiting *us* from eating bacon or shrimp. Probably most of us are thankful that here the transhistorical meaning differs from the historical meaning!

The New Testament identifies additional covenantally specific Mosaic laws. Circumcision (e.g., Gal 6:2), the sacrificial system (e.g., Heb 8–10), and holy days (e.g., Col 2:16) come to mind. The nature of such elements suggests general categories of laws that we can expect to be specific to Israel's covenant with Yahweh: (1) requirements that functioned as *symbols* of the covenant or aspects of it, and (2) requirements that belonged to Israel's unique *worship* system.

No doubt there are other kinds of covenantally specific Mosaic laws. For instance, most theologians agree that God does not expect governments today to implement all the criminal penalties that the Law stipulated for Israelite society. Common sense goes a long way in helping us discern whether a particular regulation is restricted to Israel's covenant, though admittedly some difficulties remain. I've written on the Law elsewhere,[11] and toward the end of this chapter we'll return to its relevance for our lives.

Personally and Locally Specific Elements
Both Testaments contain other kinds of specific elements that don't belong to the transhistorical meaning. These are usually obvious, but I mention them for the sake of clarity and completeness. Consider some

---

[11] See Casillas, *The Law and the Christian.* Compare Strickland, *Five Views.*

personally specific matters in Paul's epistles. God is not telling me to welcome Phoebe (Rom 16:2) or to take Paul his cloaks, books, and parchments (2 Tim 4:13). We also find *locally* specific issues. My church can't expel the immoral man from the Corinthian church (1 Cor 5:1–13) or feel appreciated for having sent a gift to Paul (Phil 4:10–19).

Culturally Specific Elements

Finally, we can distinguish some *culturally* specific aspects of the historical meaning from the transhistorical meaning. Conservative scholars have proposed several reasonable criteria that help us sort through culturally oriented matters in Scripture.[12] I'll highlight the two criteria that seem most important.

First, *consider any reason a text states or implies for a particular duty*. A *theologically oriented* reason should especially give us pause. For instance, is a duty tightly linked to the nature of humanity or the world as God created it? First Timothy 2:12–14 bases male authority in the local church not on cultural considerations but on the order of creation. This indicates that Paul's teaching here is normative for all time, not simply a matter of first-century convention.[13]

Second, *compare the teaching at hand with the rest of the Bible*. Is it limited to a narrow setting, or is it taught throughout Scripture and addressed to multiple groups of people? The Bible argues against homosexual behavior on theological grounds, and this perspective appears in *both* Testaments (e.g., Lev 18:22; 20:13; Rom 1:26–27). So we must not view the biblical prohibition of this behavior as the product of a particular culture or timeframe (or covenant).[14]

The more I grapple with the criteria, the more I realize the danger of exaggerating cultural relativity in Scripture. Such relativity relates

---

[12] See, for example, Köstenberger and Patterson, *Invitation to Biblical Interpretation*, 790–92; Virkler and Ayayo, *Hermeneutics*, 204–9.

[13] See Grudem, *Evangelical Feminism*, 279–328.

[14] On homosexuality see DeYoung, *What Does the Bible Really Teach about Homosexuality?*; Gagnon, *Bible and Homosexual Practice*.

mostly to a handful of physical actions that symbolize deeper truths and that Christians intuitively adjust from culture to culture (e.g., the holy kiss, Rom 16:16).[15] We must exercise great caution in this area lest we dismiss a divine requirement as a human custom.

Along these lines, some comments by R. C. Sproul sound a needed warning as we close our discussion of biblical elements that we distinguish from Scripture's transhistorical message.

> *In areas of uncertainty use the principle of humility.* What if, after careful consideration of a biblical mandate, we remain uncertain as to its character as principle or custom? If we must decide to treat it one way or the other but have no conclusive means to make the decision, what can we do? Here the biblical principle of humility can be helpful. The issue is simple. Would it be better to treat a possible custom as a principle and be guilty of being overscrupulous in our design to obey God? Or would it be better to treat a possible principle as a custom and be guilty of being unscrupulous in demoting a transcendent requirement of God to the level of a mere human convention? I hope the answer is obvious.[16]

Added Richness

The transhistorical meaning may be richer than the historical meaning. We come to see this richness through the complete canon of Scripture. The human author may not have had access to every biblical book written before his time. Of course, he didn't have access to books written after his time. But since God ultimately wrote all these books, they are consistent with one another. And since he wrote all the books to form a single story, they also interpret one another.

The later books of Scripture come to the fore here. In reading a novel, don't you find that the end of the story clarifies what was going

---

[15] Grudem, *Evangelical Feminism,* 397–402.

[16] Sproul, *Knowing Scripture,* 126 (emphasis original). Sproul goes on to give some qualifications in order to prevent the principle of humility from becoming a rationale for binding others' consciences in areas of genuine liberty. He calls it "a guideline of last resort."

on in earlier chapters? The same holds true for the Bible. In particular, the New Testament gives us a more complete understanding of the Old Testament than Old Testament believers themselves enjoyed. For instance, as I explained in chapter 6, Jesus's teaching clarifies the ideals toward which the Mosaic Law was pointing (Matt 5:17–18). Similarly, the New Testament provides "end of the ages" insight into the message of Old Testament narratives (e.g., 1 Cor 10:1–13; see chapter 7 above).

Since it records so many fulfillments, the New Testament also helps us know what God was communicating through Old Testament predictive prophecies. Sometimes the prophets themselves didn't fully understand what they were revealing. God denied Daniel's request for explanation of a prophecy he recorded (Dan 12:4–13). And 1 Peter 1:10–11 says that some prophets tried to discover the details of their predictions about the Messiah, specifically "what person or time" (NASB, ESV, NET©) or "what time or what circumstances" (HCSB, cf. NIV).[17] God held them off, telling them that they were ministering to future, New Covenant believers (v. 12). In such cases, God was directing his Word more to later readers than to the original recipients!

Despite the objections of some, I'm comfortable using the term *meaning* to describe what the prophets did not grasp. More specifically, sometimes the transhistorical meaning surpasses the historical meaning intended by the human author.[18] I want to emphasize, however, that *the transhistorical meaning does not contradict or change the historical meaning.* We're talking about the *richness* or *fullness* of what the Lord was revealing through Old Testament writers.

---

[17] Grudem argues for the first rendering (*First Epistle of Peter,* 74–75). Schreiner prefers the second rendering (*1, 2 Peter, Jude,* 73–74).

[18] For a survey of the literature debating this topic and for further defense of the basic position I'm taking, see Compton, "Shared Intentions?" With Compton and others, I'm not convinced that the distinction between "sense" and "reference" sufficiently accounts for all the differences between historical and transhistorical meaning. Compare Glenny, "Divine Meaning."

Messianic Prophecies

From God's standpoint, Genesis 3:15, Psalm 22, and Isaiah 53 all point to the death of Jesus of Nazareth on a Roman cross and his suffering of the infinite wrath that our sins deserve—even though the human authors of those texts would not have known to put the matter in those terms. This is the kind of phenomenon I have in mind when I say that the divine Author could intend more than what the human authors intended. In the case of the three passages I just cited, New Testament texts establish or suggest the transhistorical meaning.

- Gen 3:15: Rom 16:20; Rev 12:9; cf. Heb 2:14.
- Ps 22: Matt 27:35/Mark 15:24/Luke 23:34/John 19:24; Matt 27:39/Mark 15:29; Matt 27:43; Matt 27:46/Mark 15:34; Luke 24:39–40/John 20:20, 25; cf. John 20:28.
- Isa 53: Matt 8:17; Luke 22:37; John 12:38/Rom 10:16; Acts 8:32–35; 1 Pet 2:22.

This is not to say, however, that we must have explicit New Testament confirmation in every case. More general themes of the complete canon may also suggest richer dimensions of earlier texts.

Am I calling for us to search for hidden meanings behind every Old Testament rock and tree? No, everything I explained about grammatical-historical interpretation is exactly what keeps us from doing that. *We can expect a demonstrable connection between the historical meaning and the transhistorical meaning.*

Let's revisit our three examples. The connection between the historical and transhistorical meanings differs in each case, but a connection exists nonetheless. In the first half of Genesis 3:15 the woman's "seed" and the serpent's "seed" are collective nouns that encompass all believers and unbelievers respectively. The wording of the second half of the verse suggests that there will be a climactic battle between an ultimate Representative of the woman's seed and the devil himself. The New Testament shows that Jesus is this Seed who finally defeats Satan.[19]

---

[19] See Vos, *Biblical Theology,* 42–44; Waltke and Fredricks, *Genesis,* 93–94, 103–4.

What about Psalm 22 and Isaiah 53? In keeping with the nature of the psalter as a whole, Psalm 22 presents itself as a pattern for God's people as they undergo intense persecution. Jesus comes in as the righteous sufferer par excellence who experiences divine deliverance through resurrection.[20] Isaiah 53 speaks more explicitly of substitutionary atonement through the Servant of the Lord. The New Testament identifies this Servant as Jesus and tells us that his death was through crucifixion.[21]

Such contextual connections are lacking in other passages where some see "deeper" meanings. We have to be especially careful in identifying symbols. For example, 1 Samuel 17 nowhere intimates that David's five smooth stones symbolize five character traits or spiritual disciplines needed for defeating the "giants" in our lives. We must also exercise great care in identifying types, symbols that anticipate future elements of God's redemptive plan. As discussed above, Esther 1 gives no hint that we should understand Vashti as a picture of the church.[22]

Just as we saw an interplay between elements of the historical meaning, we should be able to see an interplay between the historical meaning and the transhistorical meaning. As Packer writes, the transhistorical meaning "remains an extrapolation on the grammatico-historical plane, not a new projection on to the plane of allegory."[23] To change the analogy a bit, the transhistorical meaning is further down the same road as the historical meaning. It doesn't jump onto some other road. "And, though God may have more to say to us from each text than its human writer had in mind, God's meaning is never less than his."[24]

---

[20] See Patterson, "Psalm 22"; Ross, *Psalms: Volume I,* 521–51.

[21] See Motyer, *Isaiah,* 422–43; Oswalt, *Isaiah, Chapters 40–66,* 373–410.

[22] On typology, see Barrett, *Beginning at Moses,* 243–93; Payne, *Theology of the Older Testament,* 355–60. Compare Glenny, "Typology."

[23] Packer, "Hermeneutics and Biblical Authority," 4.

[24] Ibid.

Appreciating the Canonical Context

Keeping in mind this vital qualification, I'll add one more circle of context to the ones we've covered: *the entire canon of Scripture.* With this circle in view, we can appreciate how a particular passage contributes to God's larger story. We can see how the truths of the passage come to a climax toward the end of the story. And we can discern how the end of the story sheds light on God's intent through the passage.

What we need is a working knowledge of the Bible's storyline and its culmination in the person and work of Jesus Christ. At its simplest, this consists of the "macro gospel" I summarized in chapter 1: *Creation, Fall, Redemption.* But as I also said in chapter 1, redemption is God's work to restore his *kingdom* on earth. Further, this kingdom advances by means of *covenants* God makes at key points in history. As we trace these themes, we can produce a more detailed outline of the Bible.

Our grasp of Scripture's outline will grow as we read and reread the whole Bible over time. We can also learn much from others who have done the same. Many studies analyze the unifying storyline of Scripture. I've found Vaughan Roberts' approach useful. Following the lead of Graeme Goldsworthy, Roberts defines the kingdom in terms of three aspects: God' *people* in God's *place* under God's *rule and blessing.*[25] Each of these aspects unfolds in eight phases throughout Scripture. In the Appendix I give my own adaptation of Roberts's outline. Tools such as this help us understand the transhistorical meaning of a passage by summarizing the complete story to which the passage is connected.

---

[25] See *God's Big Picture;* compare Goldsworthy, *Goldsworthy Trilogy,* and Goldsworthy, *According to Plan.* Similar approaches to the Bible's metanarrative include Alexander, *From Eden to the New Jerusalem,* and Bartholomew and Goheen, *Drama of Scripture.* A major contention I have with such writers is their handling of prophecy in a way that undermines what God promised to national Israel. My adaptation of Roberts in the Appendix seeks to correct this problem. Compare Kaiser, *Promise-Plan,* and Wisdom, *Royal Destiny.* For study of the place of Israel in prophecy, see the sources listed in note 21 of chapter 7.

Only a Boy Named David

Earlier I dismissed one approach to 1 Samuel 17, and now I want to suggest a better approach—one that brings together the historical meaning and the transhistorical meaning evident from the entire canon. The books of Samuel record the beginnings of Israel's monarchy. The nation needs stability but seeks it in a human king instead of in Yahweh. God grants his people the ruler they request (1 Sam 8–10) but works in various ways to demonstrate that Yahweh himself is Israel's ultimate King. His work centers on humbling the proud and exalting the lowly, especially proud and lowly kings (1 Sam 2:1–10; 2 Sam 22:26–31).[26] By the middle of 1 Samuel, Saul's heart has become utterly proud, and the Lord has Samuel anoint a lowly shepherd to replace him (ch. 16).

The transition to this new king begins with David's victory over Goliath in 1 Samuel 17. David displays true spiritual leadership. He burns with zeal for God's glory (vv. 25–26). He stands confident in God's sovereignty (vv. 45–47). Israel's loyalty begins to shift to David in chapter 18. As the narrative unfolds, he shows remarkable faith and integrity in waiting for Yahweh to remove Saul from the throne instead of taking matters into his own hands. First Samuel ends with Saul's humiliating death, and the stage is set for David to take the throne.

But that's not all. Back in Genesis 49:10 God had promised that his final King would come from the tribe of Judah. That's the very tribe to which David belonged. As we read on in Samuel, we learn that God makes a covenant with David, promising permanent rule to his dynasty (2 Sam 7). Yet we also end up sorely disappointed with David when he abuses his power and commits adultery and murder (ch. 11). Even the model king has failed. When will there be a ruler who can be fully trusted and followed?

When we eventually open the New Testament, we find Jesus introduced as "the son of David" (Matt 1:1). God has been faithful to

---

[26] On the theme of 1 and 2 Samuel, see Arnold, *1 and 2 Samuel*, 30–40; Bell, *Theological Messages*, 131–46.

his covenant. The climactic King, the ultimate Anointed One, is here! He teaches what life in his kingdom looks like (Matt 5–7). He perfectly models that kind of life, including humility and a commitment to use his authority for the good of his people (11:28–30). And before long he yields up his life as a ransom for sinners (20:25–28).

Yet when Jesus is raised from the dead he receives authority over all nations and launches a worldwide movement to bring more and more people under his gracious rule (28:18–20). Right now the special sphere of his rule is the church (Col 1:18). But one day the entire world will bow before him as Lord (Phil 2:10–11; Rev 17:14; 19:16). In predicting the triumph of Jesus Christ over all his enemies, Revelation reflects the consummation of the truths of the story of David and Goliath.

So is 1 Samuel 17 about Yahweh's sovereignty? Does it present qualities of godly leadership? Is it designed to encourage trust in God and commitment to his glory? Or is it intended to foreshadow Christ? In view of all the layers of context involved, I believe the answer is yes![27]

Essential Correspondence

Despite differences, the transhistorical meaning corresponds to the essence of the historical meaning. I've touched on this in saying that there will be a demonstrable connection between the historical and transhistorical meanings of a text. But it's actually the main point I want to make about transhistorical meaning, and it's crucial in our quest for application.

Types of Correspondence

There are two general types of correspondence between historical and transhistorical meaning. First, the correspondence may be so close that the two are identical or virtually so. Arguing for this seems unnecessary. It's because of obvious transhistorical messages that we often apply Scripture without difficulty. I'll give some examples, though, in order to show that the Bible is not as focused on ancient times as we might think.

---

[27] For a helpful study of 1 Samuel 17, see Arnold, *1 and 2 Samuel*, 247–68. Compare Davis, *1 Samuel*, 179–91.

Though directed to specific people in ancient settings, some biblical texts are worded so broadly as to shout relevance for all readers—original or later. This happens even in the Old Testament. "I establish my covenant with you, that *never again* shall *all flesh* be cut off by the waters of the flood, and *never again* shall there be a flood to destroy *the earth*" (Gen 9:11, emphasis added). "Hear this, *all peoples!* Give ear, *all inhabitants of the world,* both low and high, rich and poor together! . . . Truly *no man* can ransom another, or give to God the price of his life" (Ps 49:1–2, 7, emphasis added). Similarly, though much of Proverbs is addressed to a specific son, its wisdom teaching presents itself as true for human beings generally. The same is true of Ecclesiastes.

Moving to the New Testament, we encounter statements such as this: "If *anyone* would come after me, let him deny himself and take up his cross and follow me. For *whoever* would save his life will lose it, but *whoever* loses his life for my sake and the gospel's will save it" (Mark 8:34–35, emphasis added). Note the breadth of 2 Peter 2:9: "The Lord knows how to rescue *the godly* from trials, and to keep *the unrighteous* under punishment until the day of judgment" (emphasis added). New Testament passages such as these are numerous indeed.[28]

Many other statements of Scripture are not as explicitly marked, yet it remains clear that their historical and transhistorical meanings are equivalent. We should include in this category any biblical teaching regarding the character of God. Since he never changes (Mal 3:6; Heb 13:8; Jas 1:17), whatever is true about him is true transhistorically. As it relates to Christian living, why would we limit "Rejoice in the Lord always: again I will say, rejoice" (Phil 4:4) to the church at Philippi? Likewise, no convincing reason exists to restrict these statements to the Jewish Christians addressed in Hebrews: "Therefore do not throw away your confidence, which has a great reward. For you have need of endurance, so that when you have done the will of God you may receive what

---

[28] See, for instance, Matt 5:3–10; 11:28–30; Luke 18:1; John 3:3, 16; Gal 1:8–9; 2 Tim 3:12; Jas 1:26–27; 1 John 2:4–6; 3:3; 2 John 9–11.

is promised" (10:35–36). I could quote at length from the Epistles. Though these letters were occasioned by first-century needs, their transhistorical message typically lies on the surface. *"Whenever we share comparable particulars (i.e., similar specific life situations) with the first-century hearers, God's word to us is the same as his word to them."*[29]

The straightforward transhistorical meaning of many passages encourages us to look for a transhistorical message in texts that are more historically conditioned and significantly different from our situation. In such cases we can expect a second type of correspondence between the historical and transhistorical meanings: correspondence on the level of *paradigms*. The rest of our chapter will concentrate on this level.

Analogies to Biblical Paradigms

We'll better appreciate the concept of paradigms when we see that something like it operates in daily life. When children are young, parents teach them basic table manners. Suppose a father sees his four-year-old son throwing carrots at his sister. The dad says, "Johnny, don't throw your carrots at Sally." Johnny reluctantly ends the game, but at dinner the next night he starts to throw peas. Frustrated, the dad responds, "Son, didn't I tell you last night not to do that?" Replies Johnny, "No, daddy, you said not to throw my carrots!"

Either Johnny is bluffing, or he hasn't caught on to paradigms. His father's statement about carrots speaks to propriety and kindness at meals, and by implication it prohibits throwing any kind of food. The context of daily family life should teach the child to take the dad's statement as paradigmatic. As the child matures, the more he will come to do so. We could get technical and ask whether on the first night the dad was consciously thinking of broad objectives and additional applications. But on the second night these would be at the forefront of his mind, and he would be sure to impress them on Johnny's mind as well!

---

[29] Fee and Stuart, *How to Read the Bible for All Its Worth*, 78 (emphasis original).

This question of intentionality surfaces in another analogy to biblical paradigms: legal codes. Abraham Kuruvilla gives an example. An 1839 London statute prohibited people from repairing a cart or carriage in a thoroughfare (except in necessary cases of accident). This was prior to the general use of motorized vehicles. Nevertheless, says Kuruvilla, "it is obvious, considering the genre of the text—legal literature—that what was being intended by 'carriage' went beyond just a 'horse-drawn buggy.' In a future-directed sense, what the law meant by 'carriage' was 'vehicle using the road' (=transhistorical intention)."[30] Consequently, the nineteenth-century law prohibits repairing cars or trucks on a road.

Kuruvilla's terms *meant* and *transhistorical intention* are debatable. It may be impossible to prove that the lawmakers were consciously thinking of the broad category "vehicle using the road." Yet few would argue with a police officer or a judge who applies the 1839 statute to cover cars and trucks. This common-sense application would presumably not require certainty regarding the authors' intent.

We encounter this same dynamic when the Bible is compared to the US Constitution.[31] Alexander Hamilton (1755–1804), famed signatory of the Constitution and one of its earliest commentators, wrote:

> We must bear in mind that we are not to confine our view to the present period, but to look forward to remote futurity. Constitutions of civil government are not to be framed upon a calculation of existing exigencies, but upon a combination of these with the probable exigencies of ages, according to the natural and tried course of human affairs.[32]

---

[30] Kuruvilla, *Privilege the Text,* 45.

[31] See, for example, ibid., 142–45; McCartney and Clayton, *Let the Reader Understand,* 161–62; Pelikan, *Interpreting the Bible and the Constitution;* Stein, *Basic Guide,* 8, 11–13, 32.

[32] Hamilton, *Federalist 34,* in *Federalist Papers,* 159; also cited in Kuruvilla, *Privilege the Text,* 31.

In other words, the Constitution, though historically situated, would speak to the widely varying situations of generations far removed from the eighteenth century.

Yet the Framers of the Constitution could not envision what all those situations would be. It is the task of later generations to ascertain how the historic document relates to their circumstances. Many today speak of the Constitution as a "living" document, holding that its meaning changes according to the views of the citizenry. More conservative interpreters follow an "originalist" approach to legal documents generally, focusing on the original meaning of the text.[33] Many within this group are specifically "textualists." Adhering closely to the wording of the Constitution, they avoid theorizing about the intent of the Framers beyond what is indicated by the text.

Textualists do allow for drawing some implications and making common-sense applications. Note the fine line maintained in these comments by Antonin Scalia and Bryan Garner:

> The omitted-case canon—the principle that what a text does not provide is unprovided—must sometimes be reconciled with the principle that a text does include not only what is express but also what is implicit. For example, when a text authorizes a certain act, it implicitly authorizes whatever is a necessary predicate of that act. Authorization to harvest wheat genuinely implies authorization to enter the land for that purpose. . . . It is part of the skill, and honest, of the good judge to distinguish between filling gaps in the text and determining what the text implies.[34]

Elsewhere Saclia writes,

> In textual interpretation, context is everything, and the context of the Constitution tells us not to expect nit-picking detail, and to give words and phrases an expansive rather than narrow interpretation—though not an interpretation that the language will not bear.

---

[33] See Calabresi, *Originalism.*

[34] Scalia and Garner, *Reading Law,* 96–97.

Take, for example, the provision of the First Amendment that forbids abridgment of "the freedom of speech, or of the press." That phrase does not list the full range of communicative expression. Handwritten letters, for example, are neither speech nor press. Yet surely there is no doubt they cannot be censored. In this constitutional context, speech and press, the two most common forms of communication, stand as a sort of synecdoche for the whole. That is not strict construction, but it is reasonable construction. . . .

Sometimes (though not very often) there will be disagreement regarding the original meaning; and sometimes there will be disagreement as to how that original meaning applies to new and unforeseen circumstances. How, for example, does the First Amendment guarantee of "the freedom of speech" apply to new technologies that did not exist when the guarantee was created—to sound trucks, or to government-licensed over-the-air television? In such new fields the Court must follow the trajectory of the First Amendment, so to speak, to determine what it requires—and assuredly that enterprise is not entirely cut-and-dried but requires the exercise of judgment.[35]

So if only in identifying issues necessary for and parallel to issues mentioned in the Constitution, textualists move beyond the text.

How does a paradigmatic approach to Scripture compare to textualism? Similar to textualism—as evident throughout this chapter—it concentrates intensely on the text and takes the original meaning as the basis for all applications. On the other hand, as we'll see below, the paradigmatic approach can be more expansive than textualism in striving to ascertain the purpose of a passage of Scripture. Why? The answer is found in some foundational points to which our study keeps returning:

- God is the ultimate Author of Scripture, and he gave his Word in order to reveal his will for humanity generally. Consequently, the Bible is replete with timeless teaching that applies to a wide variety of circumstances beyond the circumstances to which it was addressed.

---

[35] Scalia, *Matter of Interpretation*, 37–38, 45; also cited in Kuruvilla, *Privilege the Text*, 144.

- As it relates to the Old Testament specifically, Ancient Near Eastern legal codes were more intentionally paradigmatic than Western codes tend to be.[36]
- The Bible is much richer and more detailed than legal documents such as the Constitution. It contains considerable direction regarding the application of itself. In particular, Scripture's use of earlier Scripture provides an inspired model for our paradigmatic use of the Bible.

Thinking Paradigmatically

Parts II and III presented examples of biblical paradigms, and here I want to add several more. The paradigmatic approach naturally helps us with the Bible's legal material in particular. Christopher Wright proposes several questions for identifying paradigms in Old Testament laws. These are especially helpful for handling laws that don't state a universal truth but instead seem uniquely tied to Israel's covenant with Yahweh and/or Israel's ancient culture.

- What kind of situation was this law trying to promote, or prevent?
- What interests was this law aiming to protect?
- Who would have benefited from this law and why?
- Whose power was this law trying to restrict and how did it do so?
- What rights and responsibilities were embodied in this law?
- What kind of behaviour did this law encourage or discourage?
- What vision of society motivated this law?
- What moral principles, values or priorities did this law embody or instantiate?
- What motivation did this law appeal to?
- What sanction or penalty (if any) was attached to this law, and what does that show regarding its relative seriousness or moral priority?[37]

---

[36] See Stuart, *Exodus*, 442–45; cf. my discussion in chapters 4 and 6.

[37] Wright, *Old Testament Ethics*, 323.

Such questions aid us in studying the laws of Leviticus 19. These prohibitions appear in the list: "You shall not round off the hair on your temples or mar the edges of your beard. You shall not make any cuts on your body for the dead or tattoo yourselves: I am the LORD" (vv. 27–28; cf. Deut 14:1–2). What was the purpose of these rules? They banned practices of Canaanite paganism, mourning practices particularly (cf. 1 Kings 18:28). They aimed at avoiding bodily disfigurements that were associated with the worship of idols. The bodily appearance of God's people should not compromise their visible dedication to Yahweh as the only God. That's the paradigm being taught by these prohibitions.[38]

Leviticus 19 later confirms that we're right to read this chapter paradigmatically. Verse 36a says, "You shall have just balances, just weights, a just ephah, and a just hin." How do we know that this command is not limited to the specific measurements mentioned? If the words *balances* and *weights* aren't general enough, we have the broader idea stated in the immediately preceding introductory statement: "You shall do no wrong in judgment, in measures of length or weight or quantity" (v. 35).

Note also that verse 36b follows up the command with this motivation: "I am the LORD your God, who brought you out of the land of Egypt." The Israelites enjoyed a covenant relationship with a God who graciously met their needs. This fact should move them to act benevolently toward others and not take advantage of them in business transactions. As always in Scripture, the paradigm of Leviticus 19:35-36 reflects the character of God. This is a major reason we conclude that

---

[38] Harrison, *Leviticus,* 201; Rooker, *Leviticus,* 262. Others see here a general proscription of bodily disfigurement as part of upholding God's created order. See Ross, *Holiness to the Lord,* 364; Wenham, *Leviticus,* 272. This would have to be qualified, however, since the Law commanded the circumcision of Israelite and proselyte males (Exod 12:44, 48; Lev 12:3) and also designated the piercing of a servant's ear as a sign of permanent commitment to his master (Exod 21:6; Deut 15:17).

the paradigms of the Old Testament law continue to instruct us in New Testament times.[39]

The New Testament teaches by way of paradigms as well. Chapter 4 provided several illustrations, but let me mention a few more. Jesus challenged the Pharisees about the false security they felt as descendants of Abraham (John 8:31–59). Surely this teaches the more general truth that physical connection with *any* godly predecessor does not guarantee a relationship with God. Returning to 1 Corinthians 5, Paul's direction concerning the immoral man at Corinth reflects a pattern of expelling from a congregation professing believers who persist in sin. This is consistent with the teaching of Jesus in Matthew 18:17. Often the paradigms of one passage are stated explicitly in another passage, and this confirmation is reassuring. John's opposition to Diotrephes warns against the dangers of pride and divisiveness in the local church (3 John 9–11). And even if the holy kiss turns out to be merely a cultural matter, its purpose is not: demonstrating Christian affection in tangible, pure ways (Rom 16:16).

These examples show us what to do especially with passages that don't seem directly applicable to our lives. By considering the historical background, the literary context, parallel passages, and common sense we determine as best as we can the *purpose* that a text is designed to accomplish.

Conclusion

This chapter has introduced a number of technical terms and distinctions. The material has been challenging but absolutely necessary. In order to keep application as objective as possible, we must ground it in the actual meaning of Scripture. While this effort may rule out some applications, it doesn't somehow silence the Bible. Instead it helps us to arrive at applications that carry weight.

---

[39] See further, Casillas, *The Law and the Christian.*

Chapter 13

Assessing Implications

As we move from meaning to implication, our terminology admittedly becomes fuzzy. I'm using the category of implication for *any idea clearly implied by a passage that is a step or more removed from the "point(s)" of that passage.* To quote the Westminster Confession again, these are truths deduced from Scripture "by good and necessary consequence."[1]

The terms *implication* and its counterpart, *inference,* have a broader scope, however. We've already seen that we have to draw inferences in order to follow the train of thought in a passage and understand its historical meaning. In addition, inferences are necessary as we make connections between one book of Scripture and the complete canon. They're also necessary for identifying paradigms. In this chapter I'm employing "implication" and "inference" more narrowly, however. With these terms I'm speaking of implied ideas that are appreciably distinguishable from the "main point" or "basic message" of a text. We could use *conclusion, ramification,* or *extrapolation* for what I'm discussing here, though these terms may also be used in a broad sense.

Some would reject the distinctions I'm making, arguing that implication should be considered part of the *meaning* of Scripture. One reason is a fact we encountered in chapter 8: a correct deduction from a statement does not add to that statement. It merely brings out what is "there" but unexpressed.[2] Take one of our examples of implication in

---

[1] Carruthers, *Westminster Confession of Faith,* 22 (Section 1.6). See my discussion in chapter 8.

[2] Frame, *Knowledge of God,* 247.

chapter 6: Jesus's argument from Exodus 3:6 (Matt 22:23–33). Exodus 3:6 does not state the doctrine of the resurrection, yet Jesus holds that the resurrection is "in" that verse.

Another argument for subsuming implication under meaning is the divine authorship of Scripture.[3] I don't know whether Moses inferred the resurrection when he heard Yahweh say, "I am the God of your father, the God of Abraham, the God of Isaac, and the God of Jacob" (Exod 3:6a). I'm also not sure whether Moses was intending to imply the resurrection when he later recorded these words. But according to Jesus, that was at least part of *God's* intent. God intends all the implications that are accurately drawn from his Word.

On a theoretical level I find these arguments almost persuasive. In this regard, we could call implications *submeanings*.[4] On a practical level, though, caution seems in order. Two considerations incline me toward making some distinction between meaning and implication. First, the process of drawing implications from a passage can be more complex and involve more difficulties than what is involved in understanding the basic message of a text. Often a proposed implication isn't a matter of a simple syllogism. The situation becomes even more complicated when an inference is based on multiple passages. Second, I want to keep what is secondary or incidental or tangential from overpowering what is primary in a passage. That's a constant challenge in Bible study.

However we categorize implications, we'll need to assess each one on its own merits. Here you'll benefit by learning whatever you can about logic, including logical fallacies. Many writers expound this topics more capably than I could.[5] But I want to highlight two key criteria for

---

[3] Poythress, *God-Centered Biblical Interpretation,* 69–94.

[4] I'm adapting this term from Elliot Johnson, who is drawing on E. D. Hirsch. See Johnson, "Dual Authorship"; Johnson, *Expository Hermeneutics,* 13–54.

[5] Standard works include Copi, Cohen, and McMahon, *Introduction to Logic;* Toulmin, *Uses of Argument.* Explicitly Christian treatments include

evaluating implications. These came up in chapter 8 as we were considering the Westminster Confession: logical *validity* and logical *soundness*.

Logical Validity

For an argument to be valid, its conclusion(s) must follow necessarily from its premises. A trivial illustration makes this point clearly.

- Magi from the east visited the child Jesus (Matt 2:1–12).
- The magi gave Jesus three gifts (v. 11).
- Therefore, there were three (and only three) magi.

Maybe we're tempted to say that the conclusion "makes sense," but it's actually just a guess. The premises do not actually establish the conclusion. (Furthermore—to anticipate our next criterion—the second premise may be questioned: the text does not say that the magi brought *only* three gifts.)

More seriously, Job's friends reasoned wrongly in trying to help Job sort through his painful experiences.

- Job is suffering.
- God blesses the righteous with prosperity and punishes the wicked with suffering.
- Therefore, Job has been wicked.

As with our first example, this argument does not consider the possibility of alternative explanations. Though the second premise is a true statement, it doesn't account completely for the purposes of God in people's suffering. Specifically, Job's friends were not aware of the dimension of spiritual warfare behind his suffering (Job 1–2). And their invalid reasoning only exacerbated Job's anguish. Would it be too much to infer that ill-founded theological arguments can make matters worse for us as well?[6]

Here's an implication commonly drawn from the early chapters of Genesis:

Poythress, *Logic;* Tagliapietra, *Better Thinking.* See also Carson, *Exegetical Fallacies,* 87–123.

[6] See Talbert, *Beyond Suffering,* 249–68.

- After the Flood God stipulated capital punishment as the penalty for murder (Gen. 9:5–6).
- Capital punishment involves one or more human beings exercising authority over another human being. The authority in view corresponds to what we call "civil government." (Later revelation, specifically Romans 13:1–14, states that capital punishment is a function of the government.)
- Therefore, civil government began after the Flood.

Capital punishment does imply the basic idea of civil government. But this does not prove that civil government did not exist in some form prior to the Flood. We don't have definitive evidence that government existed before the Flood, but neither do we have evidence that it did *not* exist. The most we can say is that Genesis 9 gives the first recorded divine statements regarding civil government.

The conclusions described above are all possible. There *may* have been three wise men. Theoretically, Job *could* have been suffering as a result of sin. And civil government *may* have begun after the Flood. But in the technical sense these conclusions are not valid because they are not *necessary*. It isn't wrong to draw possible implications. We should, however, present them as theories not as divine certainties.

Logical Soundness

For an argument to be sound, all its premises must be true. A theological premise may be untrue for various reasons, but it's definitely untrue if it contradicts Scripture in any way. The premise must cohere both with the text under consideration and with the entirety of God's Word.

Coherence with the Text at Hand

By emphasizing coherence with the text, I'm re-emphasizing the need for grammatical-historical interpretation. Implications need to be rigorously and repeatedly checked against the actual statements of the passage at hand. Here again we see a back-and-forth movement between aspects of Bible study.

From Gideon's experience in Judges 6:36–40 some have argued as follows:

- Gideon sought an understanding of God's will by requesting a sign involving a fleece.
- God answered Gideon's request (twice).
- Therefore, "putting out a fleece"—specifying circumstantial details that will confirm divine guidance—is an appropriate way to seek an understanding of God's will.

The initial premise is not, however, consistent with the theme or the details of the Gideon story. This makes the entire argument unsound.

The book of Judges as a whole doesn't center on the judges as models of godly behavior. Instead it focuses on Yahweh's grace and faithfulness to his people, as he repeatedly delivers them despite their unfaithfulness in following the wicked ways of the Canaanites. Furthermore, this unfaithfulness shows up in various ways in the lives of the judges themselves.[7] The overall context of Judges should give us pause when we're inclined to take a particular judge as a positive example.

As we look specifically at Gideon, we sympathize with his struggles. When the angel of the Lord first appears, Gideon's questioning reflects general frustration with Israel's circumstances and perhaps even humility (vv. 11–15). God promises that he will be present with Gideon to defeat the Midianites (v. 16). Gideon asks for a confirmatory sign, and the angel acquiesces by consuming Gideon's sacrifice with fire (vv. 17–21). Gideon recognizes that he has indeed received a divine visitation and worships (v. 22–24). He then obeys the Lord and destroys his father's idolatrous shrine (vv. 25–27). He does this at night, however, "because he was too afraid of his family and the men of the town to do it by day" (v. 27). The townsmen end up not retaliating (vv. 28–32), but the note about Gideon's fear sets the tone for the next incident.

Empowered by God's Spirit, Gideon summons various Israelite tribes to fight against Midian (vv. 33–35). Even at this point, however, he is struggling to believe the Lord's earlier assurance of victory: "If you will save Israel by my hand, *as you have said*" (v. 36, emphasis added).

---

[7] On the theme of Judges, see Bell, *Theological Messages,* 119–30; Block, *Judges, Ruth,* 57–59.

That's his motive for asking for the fleece to be wet with dew and the ground to be dry. He repeats it in verse 37: "Then I shall know that you will save Israel by my hand, *as you have said*" (emphasis added).

Gideon isn't trying to discover God's will—he already knows God's will. His problem is that he doubts God's promise. His doubt is so great that he asks for the opposite sign the next day (vv. 38–40). Both times God grants Gideon's requests. This does not, however, justify the requests. It magnifies the grace of God in condescending to work with a wavering servant. We can trace throughout the rest of the Gideon narrative this emphasis on God's grace over against the weakness of Gideon. Though he finally displays courage after further divine reassurance (7:9–25), eventually he contributes to Israel's downward spiral of idolatry (8:22–27). Whatever the case, we've seen enough to challenge the implication that the fleece sign presents a model for discerning God's will.

The Lord does lead his people through his arrangement of their circumstances (e.g., 1 Cor 16:8–9; Jas 4:13–17). We may also pray that he would use circumstances to show us his will. Yet we have no right to insist that he do so in a particular way. God may choose to grant outlandish petitions from us. As with Gideon, however, this would be a statement of his exceeding patience with us, not of the legitimacy of our methods. In any case, praying for guidance differs from what Gideon was doing—doubting God's words and almost demanding that he prove himself through a miracle.[8]

Coherence with All Scripture

We can go astray with implications because we're thinking about only some passages on a topic and neglecting other relevant passages. This reminds us of the contextual circle of the entire canon. A sound implication will not contradict *any* teaching of Scripture. The doctrine of God's sovereignty provides classic case studies of implications that don't meet this criterion.

---

[8] See ibid., 272–74.

God rules over the choices of men. "I know, O LORD, that the way of man is not in himself, that it is not in man who walks to direct his steps" (Jer 10:23; cf. Prov 16:9; 20:24). "The king's heart is a stream of water in the hand of the LORD; he turns it wherever he will" (Prov 21:1). So we might reason that human beings do not make genuine choices or that our choices do not make an actual difference in our lives. Jesus would disagree. "O Jerusalem, Jerusalem . . . ! How often would I have gathered your children together as a hen gathers her brood under her wings, *and you were not willing!*" (Matt 23:37, emphasis added).

The Bible teaches that God's sovereign plan encompasses all creation (Ps 135:6), all nations (Dan 4:34–35; Acts 17:26), all individuals (Ps 139:16), and even "random" events (Prov 16:33). He "works *all things* according to the counsel of his will" (Eph 1:11, emphasis added). And he knows ahead of time what he is going to do (Isa 46:9–10). If so, then prayer must be unnecessary, right? How can it be that we actually influence the choices of God? See James 4: "You do not have, because you do not ask. You ask and do not receive, because you ask wrongly, to spend it on your passions" (vv. 2b–3).

Prior to creation God chose which individuals he would save (Eph 1:4). Furthermore, in order for these elect to believe the gospel, God must draw them—and he will do so (John 6:37, 44, 65). We might therefore conclude that evangelism is not only unnecessary but also inappropriate since it inevitably offers the gospel to many people who aren't chosen for salvation. Scripture roundly rejects such a conclusion. "Go therefore and make disciples of all nations" (Matt 28:19a). "God . . . commands all people everywhere to repent" (Acts 17:30). "For 'everyone who calls on the name of the Lord will be saved.' How then will they call on him in whom they have not believed? And how are they to believe in him of whom they have never heard? And how are they to hear without someone preaching?" (Rom 10:13–14).

God is sovereign even over human sin. He could stop evil altogether, but he doesn't. He actually uses it to accomplish his purposes: he causes the wrath of man to bring praise to himself (Ps 76:10). That's the biblical explanation for the unfair suffering of Joseph (Gen 50:20) and the Messiah (Acts 2:23; 4:27–28). But doesn't all of this imply that God is ultimately culpable for evil? James answers this one too: "Let no one say when he is tempted, 'I am being tempted by God,' for God cannot be tempted with evil, and he himself tempts no one" (1:13).

In each instance above, one set of verses could lead logically to a particular conclusion. But that conclusion is flatly contradicted by other biblical statements. In such cases we humbly give God the benefit of the doubt and accept the entirety of his Word. We accept the mysteries, trust that his logic is above ours, and devote ourselves to believing and obeying what he has graciously chosen to reveal to us (Deut 29:29).[9]

Conclusion

After the negative examples above, we need some illustrations of implications that are valid and sound. Remember four that we covered in chapter 8: the Holy Spirit's personality and the doctrine of the Trinity as well as the sinfulness of abortion and racism. Here are three more:

- The prohibition of stealing (Exod 20:15; Eph 4:28) implies the right to private property. By way of application, this right undermines the essence of communism.[10]
- Satan possesses intellect (2 Cor 11:3), emotions (Rev 12:12, 17), and a will (Rev 20:7–9). He can communicate verbally (Luke 4:1–12). He is also held accountable for his actions (Rev 20:10). Therefore, we conclude that Satan is a person not some kind of symbol for evil.[11] This reality especially motivates us to remain aware of and prepare for spiritual warfare as described in Scripture (Eph 6:10–20).[12]
- The New Testament writers regularly quote the Septuagint and other Greek translations of the Old Testament. In a number

---

[9] See further, Talbert, *Not by Chance,* 250–64.

[10] See further, Grudem, *Politics,* 261–68.

[11] See further, Dickason, *Angels,* 121–25.

[12] See further, Borgman and Ventura, *Spiritual Warfare.*

of cases the Greek wording differs significantly from the Hebrew Bible, though the basic meaning of the original passage is preserved (e.g., Heb 10:5–10/Ps 40:6–8; 1 Pet 4:18/Prov 11:31). The Greek is quoted as divinely authoritative. This implies that to the extent that a Bible translation reflects the sense of the original Scriptures, to that extent it is the Word of God.[13]

In this chapter my goal hasn't been to discourage believers from drawing implications from Scripture. Indeed, application often rests on biblical implications. We must, however, exercise great caution in this regard. We should humbly submit our conclusions to logical testing so that instead of inserting our own ideas into Scripture we are inferring the thoughts of God.

---

[13] See further, Williams and Shaylor, *God's Word in Our Hands.*

Chapter 14

Seeking Significance

Significance is a technical term for what people usually mean by the word *application*. It's *the response of a reader to the meaning and implications of a passage.* More specifically, we're concerned with how a reader *should* respond to the truths of Scripture in the particulars of his life.

Here again we run into definitional fuzziness. For one, meaning and significance can overlap considerably, especially with direct biblical commands. In addition, there's a sense in which authorial intent includes significance. The human authors intended their original readers to apply Scripture to the specific circumstances of their lives. It's true that these authors would not have known exactly what the significance would look like in every case. But the omniscient divine Author *did* know the specific significances for the original readers and all later readers, and *he* intended for people to apply his Word in all these ways.[1]

Remember also a principle we learned in chapter 6: if we're not applying the Bible to our own lives, we do not truly *understand* the Scriptures (e.g., Matt 12:1–8). Application is what proves that we "get it." Because of this, John Frame proposes eliminating altogether the distinction between meaning and significance.[2] This may, however, lead to underestimating the real differences that can exist between the original and later readers of biblical books. It may also obscure the challenges involved in applying the less direct genres of Scripture.

---

[1] Poythress, *God-Centered Biblical Interpretation*, 76–77.

[2] Frame, *Knowledge of God,* 81–85.

Doriani states the matter best: there is a boundary between meaning and significance, but it's a *permeable* boundary.[3] However we state it, we must not remain content with a description of the historical meaning of a passage or with abstract theological summaries. We move on to identify specific ways in which we need to respond to the text, and then we follow through with obedience. Only then will the sanctifying purpose of God's Word be accomplished in our lives.

We'll make progress in this direction if we identify the main ways we should respond to Scripture. Three types of response stand out.

- We worship and commune with God, engaging with him on a personal level.
- We yield internally to God's truth so that our hearts are transformed.
- We make whatever concrete changes are necessary so that our behavior reflects biblical teaching.

These categories reflect roughly the emphases of a central passage on Christian living, Romans 12:1–2.

- "I appeal to you therefore, brothers, by the mercies of God, to present your bodies as a living sacrifice, holy and acceptable to God, which is your spiritual worship" (v. 1).
- "Do not be conformed to this world, but be transformed by the renewal of your mind" (v. 2a).
- "That by testing you may discern what is the will of God, what is good and acceptable and perfect" (v. 2b).

These three types of significance also echo our earlier study of gospel sanctification. In fact, we can rephrase them so as to emphasize that they are aspects of God's ongoing work to restore us to himself and renew his image in us:

- *Relational sanctification:* Knowing God more intimately
- *Internal sanctification:* Being more like God
- *External sanctification:* Acting more like God.[4]

---

[3] Doriani, *Putting the Truth to Work,* 18–27.

[4] I thank my colleague Layton Talbert for helping me refine the wording of these categories.

When we consider significance or application, we may think primarily in terms of the third category. We want to get to "the bottom line." We want to know what action we're supposed to take. As I noted at the beginning of the book, however, application isn't limited to tangible actions. The first two types of significance are somewhat intangible, yet they are foundational. In fact, without them the third type has limited value. Unregenerate people can alter their behavior and even choose to follow many of the Bible's ethical standards. Such change may have advantages over a reckless lifestyle, but it's not gospel change—sanctification—since it doesn't proceed from a heart that is being transformed through a personal relationship with God. By the Lord's grace, the Christian enjoys this full-orbed experience of Scripture.

Relational Sanctification

Discussions of application sometimes neglect the believer's communion with God through meditation on Scripture. I believe it's a mistake to separate this devotional aspect of knowing God experientially from more cognitive interpretation of the Bible or the practical use of Scripture. After all, "the fear of the LORD is the beginning of wisdom, and the knowledge of the Holy One is insight" (Prov 9:10; cf. 1:7).

The personal nature of the Christian's relationship with God and his Word was implicit throughout my discussion of the theology of application. The gospel restores us to a personal relationship with God and aims at renewing his image in us (chapters 1–2). The Bible is a means of grace through which God sanctifies us (chapters 3 and 5). Biblical writings constitute God's speech to his people of all times (chapters 4 and 6–7). Obedience to the Bible is a loving response to God's initiating love (chapter 9).

Such considerations ought to shape the way we view Scripture. As we've seen, the Bible is not essentially a textbook of theology or a manual for living. It is God's self-disclosing speech to us. By the same token, Christianity is not fundamentally a relationship with a book. It is a relationship with God through a book. This means that application isn't merely about making ethical choices. It's about engaging with God himself—listening to him and responding to him as a person.

For confirmation of this perspective, consider the monumental Psalm 119. Here the psalmist declares that through the Word God ministers to him in various personal ways:

- Giving comfort (vv. 50, 52, 82)
- Reviving (vv. 50, 93)
- Strengthening (v. 92)
- Giving wisdom (98–100, 130)
- Giving peace (v. 165)
- Helping (v. 175).

So the psalmist meditates on Scripture with an awareness that God is present and is speaking to him. A. W. Tozer (1897–1963) passionately urged Christians along these lines:

> I think a new world will arise out of the religious mists when we approach our Bible with the idea that it is not only a book which was once spoken, but a book which is *now speaking*. . . . If you would follow on to know the Lord, come at once to the open Bible expecting it to speak to you. Do not come with the notion that it is a *thing* which you may push around at your convenience. It is more than a thing, it is a voice, a word, the very Word of the living God.[5]

I'm reminded of a similar appeal by the Puritan Thomas Watson (c. 1620–1686):

> Leave not off reading in the Bible till you find your hearts warmed. . . . . Read the word not only as a history, but strive to be affected with it. Let it not only *inform* you, but *inflame* you. . . . Go not from the word till you can say as those disciples . . . "Did not our hearts burn within us?" [Luke 24:32].[6]

As God speaks through Scripture, the writer of Psalm 119 speaks back. He moves seamlessly from meditation to prayer. Except for three introductory verses, every verse of the psalm is addressed in some

---

[5] *Pursuit of God,* 82–83.

[6] "How We May Read the Scriptures," 39.

way to Yahweh. The psalmist's responses to Scripture constitute worshipful responses to Scripture's Author:

- Love (vv. 47, 48, 97, 113, 119, 127, 140, 159, 163, 165, 167)
- Delight (vv. 16, 24, 35, 47, 70, 72, 77, 92, 103, 143, 174)
- Faith (vv. 31, 42, 43, 49, 66, 74, 81, 114, 116, 147)
- Longing (vv. 20, 40, 123, 131)
- Joy (vv. 14, 111, 162)
- Fear (vv. 120, 161)
- Praise (vv. 62, 164).

We see the same dynamic in Psalm 19. Reflection on Scripture's sanctifying ministry (vv. 7–10) shifts into a prayer for holiness (vv. 11–14). Such prayer in response to the Word is itself a vital form of application.[7] It is key to our personal interaction with God through his Word. Of what other book could it be said that reading brings one into communion with the author?

Likewise, of what other book could it be said that the author is ever present to help readers understand his book? In Psalm 119 another response to the Author of Scripture is this: "Open my eyes, that I may behold wondrous things out of your law" (v. 18). Such prayers for understanding punctuate the psalmist's meditation on Scripture (vv. 12, 26, 33, 64, 68, 108, 124-25, 135). And he affirms that God indeed performs this teaching ministry (vv. 102, 171).

We refer to this ministry as *illumination*. We noted it in chapter 3's discussion of the means of grace. We encountered it in chapter 4 as well, noting Paul's exhortation to Timothy: "Think over what I say, for the Lord will give you understanding in everything" (2 Tim 2:7). Paul also told the Corinthians that because of human depravity God's revelation cannot be truly known apart from the Holy Spirit's illuminating work (1 Cor 2:14). Additionally, the apostle prayed that the Lord would enlighten the "eyes" of the Ephesians' hearts so that they would grasp the deep gospel truths he was expounding to them (Eph 1:15–23).

---

[7] For practical help in this regard, see Whitney, *Praying the Bible*; cf. Carson, *Praying with Paul.*

Understanding God's Word and its application to our lives is a spiritual not a strictly intellectual matter. As careful as our methodology may be, we stand in desperate need of the Spirit's illumination. Our methods of Bible study must include continual prayer for this mysterious yet real work. John Owen (1616–1683) made this point forcefully:

> For a man to undertake the interpretation of any part or portion of Scripture in a solemn manner, without *invocation of God* to be taught and instructed by his Spirit, is a high provocation of him; nor shall I expect the discovery of truth from any one who so proudly and ignorantly engageth in a work so much above his ability to manage.[8]

The title of our book, *Beyond Chapter and Verse*, refers to moving beyond Scripture in the sense of relating it to contemporary life issues. But our focus on fellowship with God has underscored another, indispensable sense of the word *beyond*.

> Break Thou the Bread of Life, dear Lord, to me,
> As Thou didst break the loaves beside the sea.
> *Beyond* the sacred page I seek *Thee*, Lord;
> My spirit pants for Thee, O living Word. . . .
>
> O send Thy Spirit, Lord, now unto me,
> That he may touch my eyes, and make me see.
> Show me the truth concealed within Thy Word,
> That in Thy Book revealed I see Thee, Lord.[9]

---

[8] Owen, *Holy Spirit*, in *Works*, 4:204–5. Against some contemporary authors, I agree with Owen that illumination is not limited to the realm of significance but operates throughout the interpretive process. See McKinley, "John Owen's View of Illumination." For an overview of the doctrine of illumination, see Plummer, *40 Questions*, 143–50. For a broader study, see Brown, *The Holy Spirit & the Bible*.

[9] From "Break Thou the Bread of Life," by Mary A. Lathbury (1841–1913) and Alexander Groves (1842–1909) (emphasis added). Strauss also references this hymn in *How to Read the Bible in Changing Times*, 71. For an in-depth treatment of Bible study with a view to communion with God, see Piper, *Reading the Bible Supernaturally*.

Internal Sanctification

A thriving relationship with God cannot fail to transform us. This transformation targets the heart or inner person. We saw this in studying sanctification (chapters 2–3 and 5) and in analyzing legalism (chapter 9). "Keep your heart with all vigilance, for from it flow the springs of life" (Prov 4:23). "The good person out of his good treasure brings forth good, and the evil person out of his evil treasure brings forth evil" (Matt 12:35). Given the complexity of the human heart, internal transformation encompasses at least four major elements: *worldview, affections, virtue, and discernment.*[10] I'll briefly describe each of these.

Worldview

The heart includes the *mind* (e.g., Matt 9:4), and Romans 12:2 says that we're transformed by the renewing of our minds (cf. Eph 4:23). Growth in godliness requires that we think the way God thinks. The category of *worldview* addresses this need.

A person's worldview is his general outlook on reality. Whether or not we realize it, we all have a worldview that consists of our basic beliefs about the universe, our understanding of our own place in it, and our fundamental commitments within this framework. Together these function as a kind of lens through which we process and respond to everything. Our worldview centers on our ideas about the following:
- The origin, nature, and purpose of the world generally and humanity specifically
- What is wrong with the world and human beings
- What needs to happen for them to be set right.

These concepts in turn reflect a *story,* a narrative about how the world came into existence, how it came to be in its present state, and how it may/should/will proceed in the future.

Here we return to the "macro gospel," because the biblical storyline/worldview consists of *Creation, Fall,* and *Redemption.* The

---

[10] For more detailed studies of the heart, see Flavel, *Keeping the Heart*; Saucy, *Minding the Heart.*

more exposure we have to this storyline and the more we *believe* it as the right explanation of reality, the more we'll view the various elements of life the way God does instead of the way the unregenerate world does (Rom 12:1). We gain familiarity with the biblical storyline by regularly reading the entirety of the Bible. Our day also affords us a multitude of resources for understanding and applying the Christian worldview.[11]

Affections

Internal transformation involves more than affirming the ideals of the biblical worldview. It involves *loving* those ideals. Our *spiritual affections* come to the fore here. Jonathan Edwards (1703–1758) famously defined these as "the more vigorous and sensible exercises of the inclination and will of the soul."[12] While some overlap exists, what we call emotions or feelings are not the same as affections. Emotions tend to operate on a more surface level and can be prompted by purely physical stimuli.

Affections are our deeper proclivities—our exercise of approval and disapproval, our fundamental loves and hates, the ultimate desires that determine our life goals. The psalmist referred to the negative side: "Through your precepts I get understanding; therefore I hate every false way" (Ps 119:104). Edwards' foundational text highlights the positive side: "Though you have not seen him [Christ], you love him. Though you do not now see him, you believe in him and rejoice with joy that is inexpressible and filled with glory" (1 Pet 1:8).

Do you remember the "X-ray" questions I quoted in chapter 5? Such tools help us assess our affections biblically. They move us to plead with God to direct our hearts toward himself and his will, to nurture in us love for him and for our neighbors (Matt 22:35–40).

---

[11] The following works provide significant help for Christian worldview thinking: Colson and Pearcey, *How Now Shall We Live?*; Pearcey, *Total Truth*; Ryken, *Christian Worldview*; Smith, *Developing a Biblical Worldview*; Ward et al., *Biblical Worldview*; Wolters and Goheen, *Creation Regained*. See also Sire, *Universe Next Door*.

[12] Edwards, *Religious Affections*, 96.

Virtue

As we consider the topic of godly affections, we quickly glide into the realm of Christian *virtue*. This is a broader category of internal qualities that mirror the character of God. The most comprehensive catalog is the nine-fold fruit of the Spirit, which contrasts with the manifold works of the flesh (Gal 5:16–26). These are not fundamentally behaviors but habits of the heart. As we repeatedly encounter such qualities in Scripture—especially from the life of Christ—we are supernaturally drawn to and shaped by them (2 Cor 3:18). Relying on God's power, we cultivate them and find them growing within us (2 Pet 1:3–11; see my discussion in chapter 3).

Discernment

One other element is crucial to our internal transformation. I suppose it could be classified as a subset of virtue, but it deserves special attention: *wisdom* for making life choices, and more specifically, *discernment*. We considered this in some detail in chapter 5. There we defined discernment as the skill of making distinctions and testing matters in order to determine what course of action pleases the Lord (Heb 5:14; Eph 5:10). "To apply the Word of God to circumstances requires a kind of moral vision. Such applications require the ability to *see* the circumstances *in the light of* biblical principles. . . . Ethical discourse . . . is never merely a matter of setting forth facts and Bible passages."[13]

We've also seen how God develops discernment in us. Yes, through ongoing meditation on Scripture we increasingly internalize his thinking and desires. Yet prayer and life experience are a big part of the learning process as well (Phil 1:9-11; Heb 5:14). "There may well be some ethical questions . . . that we will not be able to answer (or even fully appreciate) until we have been in spiritual combat with the forces of darkness."[14]

---

[13] Frame, *Christian Life*, 356, 358.

[14] Ibid., 359.

External Sanctification

Finally, sanctification includes increasingly Christ-like behavior. This is that most obvious type of significance: concrete actions taken in response to God's Word. Such actions are associated especially with divine commands. As explained in chapter 4, these may be *generic* imperatives that need to be implemented in specific ways (e.g., "Honor your father and your mother," Exod 20:12). Or they may be *specific* imperatives that establish paradigms for any number of parallel particulars (e.g., "Do not get drunk with wine," Eph 5:18). Yet our behavior isn't oriented to commands only. Every genre of Scripture reveals actions of the God whom we were created and re-created to imitate. Every genre of Scripture teaches paradigms that foster Christ-like conduct.

Discernment comes back into view under the heading of external sanctification. On details that God does not explicitly address in his Word, how will we determine which specific actions to take or not take? We make an assessment on the basis of the biblical truth we do have. We ascertain what issues in our lives are appropriate *parallels* to topics under discussion in Scripture.

Think back on some of the passages I've discussed so far in Part V. Here are the kinds of discernment questions that need to be asked in order to determine the significance of these passages.

- Pagan body markings (Lev 19:27–28): In my culture, what physical appearances should I avoid so that my testimony for Christ isn't compromised?
- Righteous measurements (Lev 19:35–36): What temptations to cheat others do I need to resist in my financial dealings?
- Gideon's fleece (Judg 6:36–40): How is unbelief keeping me from doing what God has called me to do?
- David and Goliath (1 Sam 17): How is God's name being defamed in my environment? What faith-filled actions should I take to promote his glory in the world?
- The holy kiss (Rom 16:16): What are some tangible, pure ways through which I can demonstrate affection for my fellow church members?

Some particulars of significance will be the same for all Christians. But with various details of external sanctification that are not specified in Scripture, significance may legitimately differ from Christian to Christian. Such applications may also change over time since circumstances change. It's impossible to state comprehensively which matters are absolute and which are variable. In sorting through issues of discernment, however, two matters become especially important: the ongoing exercise of *logic* and the role of *conscience*.

Logic Revisited

What we saw about logic in dealing with implications *applies* to the category of significance as well. We'll need to give particular attention to logic when identifying parallels between issues in Scripture and issues in our own lives. The process here can be boiled down as follows:
- God told the original recipients of Scripture to do (or not do) X.
- Y in our day parallels X in biblical times.
- Therefore, God is telling us to do (or not do) Y.

Such an argument rises or falls on whether the middle premise is true. If it isn't, the conclusion/significance/application fails.

Consider the Jehovah's Witnesses' prohibition of blood transfusions.[15] In part, their case goes like this:
- The Bible prohibits eating blood (Gen 9:4; Lev 17:10–12; Deut 12:15; Acts 15:20, 28–29).
- Blood transfusions are analogous to eating blood.
- Therefore, the Bible prohibits blood transfusions.[16]

This argument is *valid* because its premises, if true, lead to the conclusion. It isn't *sound,* however: even if the first premise holds throughout the New Covenant age, the middle premise is not true. Jehovah's Witnesses argue for the analogy between blood transfusions and blood-eating through a further parallel: the similarity between transfusions and intravenous feeding. This connection does not work.

---

[15] I am adapting this example from Sire, *Scripture Twisting,* 84–88.

[16] See *Truth That Leads to Eternal Life,* 163–69.

Intravenous feeding inserts nutrients into the body for consumption. Transfused blood performs a different function, continuing to circulate throughout the body.

Cults aren't the only groups that use weak arguments. Christians can fall into the same trap. Especially given the decadence of our age, we must humbly embrace and thoroughly apply the Bible's teaching on clothing and modesty (e.g., 1 Tim 2:9–10).[17] On the other hand, unsound argumentation damages one's credibility on this issue. This has sometimes happened with the clothing law in Deuteronomy 22:5a:

- "A woman shall not wear a man's garment."
- Pants are a man's garment.
- Therefore, a woman must not wear pants.

I don't see any reason that Deuteronomy 22:5a would not apply directly under the New Covenant. Here again, though, the middle premise of the application argument is problematic.

This becomes clear as we move to the second half of the verse: "Nor shall a man put on a woman's cloak." The word for "cloak" (*simlāh*) is a general one that can also be used for a male's outer garment (e.g., Gen 37:4; Isa 3:6).[18] This indicates that Deuteronomy 22:5 is not addressing particular types of clothing but *styles* of clothing that were gender-specific in the culture of the day. Whether in the ancient or modern worlds, style is primarily what distinguishes the clothing of men and women. In Moses's day robes were worn by men as well as women. Down to our day, men in various cultures wear dress-like attire. The style of such attire is what indicates the gender for which it is designed. Likewise, the pants most women wear are styled specifically for women.

---

[17] See, for example, Peace and Keller, *Modesty*.

[18] The term translated "garment" in Deuteronomy 22:5a (*kelî*) is similarly general. It can refer to a wide variety of implements, including weapons and military gear (e.g., Gen 27:3; Judg 18:11). Consequently, Deuteronomy 22:5a may be focusing on implements of warfare. But the parallel with "cloak" (*simlāh*) in 5b suggests clothing of various kinds. The KJV's translation is helpfully broad: "The woman shall not wear that which pertaineth unto a man."

What Deuteronomy 22:5 prohibits is cross-dressing or trans-vestitism. Some archeological evidence suggests that in the ancient Near East transvestitism was practiced as part of pagan religious rituals. As is often the case today, this was probably associated with homosexuality.[19] When a woman wears pants, however, she is not typically practicing transvestitism. At one time in the twentieth century, the trend of women wearing pants may have been associated with the feminist movement, but this connection no longer prevails. Even if it did, however, Deuteronomy 22:5 wouldn't be the most convincing verse to use. Feminism's effort to remove distinctions between the sexes isn't equivalent to trans-vestitism. On the other hand, Deuteronomy 22:5 does have relevance for contemporary "trans-gender" trends. The passage emphasizes the need to uphold the divinely assigned distinction between male and female, even in the area of dress.[20] We distract from such vital issues, however, when we engage in dubious applications.

Our closing chapters will pose some contemporary parallels to biblical situations that I trust you'll find more compelling. But I recognize that we encounter genuine challenges in identifying such parallels. Specifically, the middle premise in an application argument may not be clearly untrue, but it may to some degree be uncertain and therefore debatable. In this regard, one author encourages preachers to evaluate each potential application and ask whether it is "necessary, probable, possible, improbable, or impossible."[21] Another one writes, "It's a mark of maturity when Christians can recognize that their applications have different levels of authority."[22]

---

[19] See Craigie, *Deuteronomy*, 287–88; McConville, *Deuteronomy*, 337; Thompson, *Deuteronomy*, 234.

[20] See DeRouchie, "Confronting the Transgender Storm; compare DeRouchie, *How to Understand and Apply the Old Testament*, 444–49.

[21] Haddon Robinson, "The Heresy of Application," in Robinson and Larson, *Art and Craft*, 309.

[22] Naselli, *How to Understand and Apply the New Testament*, 323.

The Role of Conscience

The process of discerning the significance of Scripture for our lives inevitably involves our consciences. The less certain an application is, however, the more one's individual conscience becomes the determining factor. So we need to understand what the conscience is and what it does. Occasionally the Bible refers to the conscience with broad terms: "heart" (1 Sam 24:5; 2 Sam 24:10; 1 John 3:21) and "mind" (Rom 1:28). But the key word for conscience is the Greek *syneidēsis,* and it occurs thirty times in the New Testament. Most helpful for definition is Romans 2:15, which presents the conscience as bearing witness within Gentiles. Here the conscience functions in connection with the awareness that God gives Gentiles regarding his moral law. It is also linked with "their thoughts alternately accusing or else defending them" (NASB). This and other passages lead us to define the conscience as *man's moral consciousness, his God-given capacity for distinguishing between good and evil.*[23]

The Christian aims to have a conscience that is *good* (Acts 23:1; 1 Tim 1:5, 19; Heb 13:18; 1 Pet 3:16), *blameless* (Acts 24:16), or *clear* (1 Tim 3:9; 2 Tim 1:3). In other words, we strive to live in such a way that our conscience does not condemn us for wrongdoing. Sin causes the conscience to be *defiled* (1 Cor 8:7; Titus 1:15), *wounded* (1 Cor 8:12), or *evil* in the sense of *guilty* (Heb 10:22). When we fail, thankfully, the blood of Jesus remains available for the cleansing of the conscience (Heb 9:9, 14; 10:2, 22; cf. 1 Pet 1:21).

An accurately functioning conscience is a key aspect of progressive sanctification, a powerful tool of the Holy Spirit (e.g., Acts 23:1; 24:16; Rom 9:1; 13:5; 1 Tim 1:5, 19). Yet any number of factors may influence our consciences in one direction or another. These include our culture, our family and upbringing, our religious background, our past failures, and even our personalities. In this regard, the New Testament presents various ways in which the conscience may not operate properly.

---

[23] See BDAG, 967.

- The conscience may *vacillate,* unable to come to a conclusion, or be *overly sensitive,* registering permissible things as sinful. As we saw in chapter 10, Romans 14 uses the expression *weak in faith* to describe these problems (vv. 1–2, 22–23).
- As we also saw in chapter 10, 1 Corinthians 10 uses the description *weak* for another conscience problem: *the propensity to yield to external pressure rather than yielding to one's own conscience* (vv. 7, 10).
- Sinning against conscience can lead to a *seared* conscience, one that is insensitive to wrongdoing, incapable of making accurate judgments (1 Tim 4:2; cf. "a debased mind," Rom 1:28).

Such sobering possibilities urge all Christians to take the following steps with regard to conscience. These points overlap with our study of Romans 14, but they deserve emphasis the more we look at specific applications.

- Unless your conscience is moving you to disobey a clear command of God, don't violate it. "Whatever does not proceed from faith is sin" (v. 23).
- Focus on responding to your own conscience not on correcting that of others. God is well able to direct each of his people (v. 4). "Each one should be fully convinced in his own mind" regarding matters that are not clearly commanded or prohibited by biblical statement or implication (v. 5).
- Fill your mind with Scripture humbly and repeatedly. Over time the Spirit will use the Word to adjust any hypersensitivity or insensitivity of your conscience (Rom 12:2).[24]

The Importance of External Sanctification

At times we'll differ on issues of conscience, but we dare not throw up our hands in indifference. The difficulties involved in matters of external sanctification do not make such matters unimportant. On the contrary, the pursuit of godly conduct serves as the acid test of a genuine response to God's Word. Earlier I mentioned that some measure of external

---

[24] See further, Ash, *Discovering the Joy of a Clear Conscience*; Naselli and Crowley, *Conscience;* MacArthur, *Vanishing Conscience.*

change may happen apart from internal transformation. My point here is that internal transformation *necessarily* issues in actions that please the Lord. "If you love me, you will keep my commandments" (John 14:15). "So also faith by itself, if it does not have works, is dead" (Jas 2:17).

An authentic experience of God's grace leads us to "renounce ungodliness and worldly passions, and to live self-controlled, upright, and godly lives in the present age." To quote Tozer again,

> Truth divorced from life is not truth in its Biblical sense, but some- thing else and something less. . . . The Bible . . . is more than a volume of hitherto unknown facts about God, man and the universe. It is a book of exhortation based upon those facts. . . . No man is better for knowing that God in the beginning created the heaven and the earth. The devil knows that, and so did Ahab and Judas Iscariot. No man is better for knowing that God so loved the world of men that he gave his only begotten Son to die for their redemption. In hell there are millions who know that. Theological truth is useless unless it is obeyed. The purpose behind all doctrine is to secure moral action.[25]

Applications in Interaction

The three types of significance are inseparable and interact in a variety of ways. Generally speaking, application flows from communion with God to internal transformation to behavioral change. This is what George Müller (1805–1898) learned and then taught others. Daily he would meditate on Scripture primarily to get his soul "happy in the Lord." Out of this experience grew his faith-filled prayer life and his selfless ministry as a preacher and humanitarian.[26]

Yet application can move in other directions too. Our spiritual affections naturally (or I should say, supernaturally) enrich our experi- ence of communion with God. So do our Spirit-enabled acts of obedience. As chapter 9 explained, the Lord uses our obedience to

---

[25] *Of God and Men*, 26–27; also cited in Robinson, *Biblical Preaching*, 72.

[26] See *Life of Trust*, 204–8.

deepen our intimacy with him (John 14:21, 23) and our assurance that we are his children (2 Pet 5:1–11). Additionally, he employs external acts of obedience to transform our inner man further. Our worldview, affections, virtue, and discernment are like muscles that become stronger with use (recall Heb 5:14).

In highlighting these interactions among applications, the point is not that we need to figure out which direction we're moving every time we read our Bibles. Gospel sanctification does require, however, that we pursue all three types of significance on a regular basis. Stated negatively, we must not limit ourselves to the kinds of applications that we find the easiest or most appealing.

Conclusion

The chart on the next page provides a snapshot of the concepts we've covered in chapters 12–14. Notice that the lines that divide meaning, implication, and significance are dotted. They represent the fact that the distinctions among these factors are not hard and fast.

I don't want to complicate the chart, but several more arrows could be added. As we have seen, the different aspects of Bible study and application interact with one another in various ways. In fact, the more we apply a passage the better we understand it. So you could picture a large arrow circling from significance back to meaning. The cycle continues throughout our lives as we pursue an increasingly greater grasp of and obedience to God's Word. This is akin to what scholars call "the hermeneutical spiral."[27]

---

[27] See Osborne, *Hermeneutical Spiral,* 22–23.

Meaning

Historical meaning

Analyze:
1. Background
2. Genre
3. Context
4. Language

Transhistorical meaning

Identify:
1. Any excluded elements of the historical meaning
2. Richer dimensions in light of the entire canon and its complete revelation of the gospel of Jesus Christ
3. Essential correspondence with the historical meaning, including paradigms

Implication

Identify any ideas clearly implied by the passage

The argument for an implication must be:
1. Logically *valid:* its conclusion must follow necessarily from its premises
2. Logically *sound:* all its premises must be true (more specifically, cohering with the text at hand and with all Scripture)

Significance

1. *Relational sanctification:* Knowing God more intimately
   Includes responding to him on a personal level and praying for illumination
2. *Internal sanctification:* Being more like God
   Includes nurturing worldview, affections, virtue, discernment
3. *External sanctification:* Acting more like God
   Involves exercising discernment, determining present parallels to biblical issues; requires special attention to logic and conscience

Chapter 15

Moving from Life to the Bible

Some time ago my van's speedometer broke. It started defaulting to various places above the zero line. For a while it got stuck at eighty miles per hour: when I was doing sixty, it looked like I was doing 140. That is a bit unnerving if you're not used to it. But repairing the speedometer would be pricey.

I'm not too worried, though. In a matter of seconds I found a free speedometer app for my smartphone. Now I just set the phone on the dashboard, and it tells me how fast I'm going. When I told my mechanic what I was doing, he replied that he was doing the same thing about his own broken speedometer!

The ability to run apps is what makes a smartphone smart. Because of apps you can use your phone to take a selfie, edit out your imperfections, and then post the photo online. You can also check your email, play thousands of games, buy pizza, order furniture, find coupons for your pizza and your furniture, get directions, listen to podcasts, find and share recipes, watch movies, open your garage door, control your room temperature, video-conference with someone across the globe, scan documents, and translate documents (sort of).

On your phone you can track your time, your spending, your eating, your exercise, your sleep, your to-do list, your children and the apps they're using, your friends and the fun they're supposedly having, your sports teams, the weather, the news, the stock market, and the deer you're trying to hunt. I read books on my phone, but I haven't found

255

an app that can write books. So there's an app for *almost* everything. In fact, if it weren't for apps, we might as well go back to cheap flip phones.

Likewise, how profitable would the ancient books of Scripture be if it weren't for applications? What has been driving this book is the conviction that application enables us to experience the life-transforming ministry of God's Word. Continuing that emphasis, this chapter briefly outlines a method to follow when we're examining a specific matter of conduct and go to the Bible looking for direction.

Unlike the previous chapter, here I will be suggesting steps to follow. In any analysis of life issues, however, more is happening than completing steps. "Ethical judgment involves the application of a *norm* to a *situation* by a *person.*"[1] The last component is convicting. Our thinking and our choices are inevitably influenced by who we *are* as individual *people.* So we can't isolate any one decision from our overall sanctification. That's one reason this chapter comes toward the end of the book.

God-glorifying choices about conduct grow out of the soil of a godly heart. Several internally oriented elements ought to permeate the whole process of moving from life to the Bible and then back again. I'll list three that are especially crucial. After all we've covered, these won't come as a surprise.

- *Prayer,* relying on the Holy Spirit for illumination as well as enabling to obey (Ps 25:4–5; Eph 1:15–18; 5:18).
- *Humility,* remaining teachable before the Lord—surrendered to doing whatever he directs—and ruthlessly honest about ourselves, our relationships, our circumstances, and our culture (Ps 25:8–9; Rom 12:1–2).
- *Diligence,* earnestly pursuing an accurate understanding of God's Word and will (Eph 5:10; 2 Tim 2:15).

The appeal in Proverbs 2:1–8 captures all of these ideas and begins our discussion on the right note:

My son, if you receive my words and treasure up my commandments with you, making your ear attentive to wisdom and inclining your

---

[1] Frame, *Christian Life,* 33.

heart to understanding; yes, if you call out for insight and raise your voice for understanding, if you seek it like silver and search for it as for hidden treasures, then you will understand the fear of the LORD and find the knowledge of God. For the LORD gives wisdom; from his mouth come knowledge and understanding; he stores up sound wisdom for the upright; he is a shield to those who walk in integrity, guarding the paths of justice and watching over the way of his saints.

Assuming this posture, how do we go about evaluating a particular aspect of conduct? I suggest four broad steps: *define terms, search Scripture, seek counsel,* and *formulate response.*

Define Terms

First, *define the issue precisely.* An inaccurate definition can create confusion from the outset. Many words and expressions related to the Christian life are variously understood. This is especially the case with buzzwords such as "social justice." A related difficulty is that some terms represent whole categories of issues. "Stewardship" comes to mind. Such terms need to be divided into subtopics. If not, distinct issues may get collapsed, or you may simply end up overwhelmed. Conversely, many specific terms are tied to broader biblical themes. "Gossip," for instance, comes under the theme of speech or the tongue and is addressed through various terms, descriptions, and comments. Such connections can open up more biblical material than you might have originally considered. In this regard, the definition step may involve noting categories and passages that are preliminary or foundational to your topic.

Search Scripture

Second, *search the Scriptures, studying passages relevant to your topic.* Begin by surveying God's Word as a whole, looking for pertinent data. Here a topical Bible or a Bible dictionary or encyclopedia can help greatly.[2] You

---

[2] See, for example, Kohlenberger, *Zondervan NIV Nave's Topical Bible;* Tenney and Silva, *Zondervan Encyclopedia of the Bible.* Our day affords the unparalleled opportunity of software that can perform quick searches of these kinds of resources. See especially www.logos.com.

might discover a sequence of passages all the way through the Scriptures or just a few verses here and there. Especially if specific texts are sparse, can you draw implications for your subject from texts on parallel subjects or on more general themes?

Following the recommendations in chapters 12–14, study your selected passages in as much detail as necessary to grasp their relevance for the issue you're analyzing. Then distill the results of your study and organize the main ideas in a coherent way. This may take various forms. You could put together a simple list of key arguments or principles. Tracing a topic along the biblical storyline/worldview may not work well in every case but is probably the ideal approach.

- *Creation:* What was God's original ideal for this?
- *Fall:* How has sin corrupted this?
- *Redemption:* How is Christ now restoring this to its original ideal along the way to its ultimate form in his final kingdom?

A complementary strategy distinguishes between structure and direction.

- The *structure* of a thing is its essence, its nature as God created it to be. In considering structure, observe creation as well as the Scriptures. Despite the fall, does the created order continue to reflect any patterns that suggest what God intends for the issue you're studying?
- *Direction* refers to the way a thing is turned or used. How does sin turn it away from God, pervert it? How is God graciously working to return it to its intended character and purpose, to renew it so that it glorifies him?[3]

Seek Counsel

Third, *seek counsel from several mature believers.* "Where there is no guidance, a people falls, but in an abundance of counselors there is safety" (Prov 11:14).[4] Take the initiative to ask for input about your subject from your spiritual leaders and other Christians who have a track record

---

[3] Wolters and Goheen, *Creation Regained,* 10–11, 59–63, 87–89.

[4] See also Prov 15:22; 19:20; 20:18; 24:6; Heb 13:7, 17.

of making wise choices. Share with them the results of your study and ask for their evaluation. Seeking godly counsel may also include reading biblically trustworthy writers, whether historic or contemporary. This is what I'll concentrate on as I discuss some sample issues in the remainder of the book.

The Bible greatly values the wisdom gained by those who are older, and so should we (Prov 16:31; 1 Pet 5:5). Yes, you'll need to exercise discernment even concerning the counsel you receive. Yet humility includes a healthy measure of self-distrust and a willingness to be instructed, challenged, and corrected by others. Proverbs goes so far as to say, "Whoever trusts in his own mind is a fool" (28:26a; cf. 12:15).

Formulate Response

Fourth, *in response to what you've discovered in the previous steps, formulate clearly a position on the topic at hand.* After reviewing the material you've collected, articulate your conclusions. Be as concrete as possible regarding what you will and will not think and do regarding the issue. This may require further reflection on the texts you studied or on other biblical passages and patterns. As you develop your position, keep it connected to the gospel, sanctification, and the heart.

Once you've formulated the application, what remains is to implement it in your life. In essence this refers to obedience. On the other hand, you'll need to assess the degree to which your application is determined by personal factors such as your conscience regarding debatable matters. This will affect how you interact with other Christians about the issue (Rom 14:1—15:13; see chapters 10 and 14 above).

Conclusion

The steps I've laid out are simple enough. Depending on the issue you're analyzing, however, you may face any number of interpretive challenges and difficult practical questions. You may be tempted to give up the effort and settle for a vague or non-committal approach. Why be so intentional? Why do all this work?

People are typically willing to work hard to pursue a goal that has sufficiently captured their imagination. So I want to remind you of the goal that I've emphasized throughout our study. God has graciously distinguished and redeemed us in order to make us like Jesus Christ for his ultimate glory (Rom.8:28–30). This breathtaking objective is worth all the effort required to apply God's Word to our lives. Keep it in the forefront of your thoughts as our book concludes with a few case studies.

Chapter 16

Work and Church

In our final two chapters I'll follow the steps suggested in chapter 15 as I discuss three matters of "external sanctification." These issues differ from one another in their nature and in the way Scripture addresses them. Consequently, I'll be organizing the material in different ways. I'm intentionally striving for variety because variety characterizes life. Of course, I won't be analyzing the issues exhaustively. Due to the broad scope of this book, my discussion will have to be highly selective and condensed. This chapter takes up the topics of work and local-church membership, and the next chapter discusses the subject of music.[1]

Work

One reason I've chosen work as our first topic is that it illustrates the biblical-storyline approach so clearly. Yet work is a vital subject in its own right. If for no other reason, we ought to think carefully about our work because it takes up such a large proportion of our time. Scripturally, however, there's much more going on with work than punching a clock from eight to five.

Define Terms

Though the term *work* can refer to any kind of activity, I'm using it in the narrower sense of one's job, occupation, or employment. I am not,

---

[1] For additional discussions that serve as helpful case studies in application, consider the following: Dyer, *From the Garden to the City;* MacArthur et al., *Right Thinking;* Tripp, *War of Words;* and the series Biblical Discernment for Difficult Issues published by Bob Jones University Press.

however, describing this as "gainful" employment because I don't want to exclude the nonpaid occupations of many such as students, homemakers, and those who do volunteer work of various kinds.

The concept of work belongs to the doctrine of vocation or calling. This is the truth that God calls individuals to various privileges and responsibilities. These include specific life situations such as one's occupation (1 Cor 7:17–24). The Lord tends to indicate his call as the believer evaluates his abilities (Exod 4:11), desires (1 Cor 7:36–39; 1 Tim 3:1), and circumstances (Prov 16:9); seeks wise counsel (Prov 11:14; 20:18); and prays (Jas 4:13–17).

Search Scripture

While the Bible won't tell you what occupation to pursue, it contains much teaching on the place of work in God's plan and how to work. Each movement in the biblical storyline addresses the theme of work.

Creation

The Creation account presents God himself as a worker (Gen 2:2). Work is therefore part of his original, good plan for the beings he made in his image. The Lord equips and commissions the human race to exercise dominion over the earth for his glory (Gen 1:26–28; Ps 8). This requires work, illustrated in Adam's responsibility to "cultivate" and "keep" the Garden of Eden (2:15, NASB) and his naming of the animals (vv. 19–20). Adam's work mirror's God's work of organizing creation and naming its elements (Gen 1).

Fall

The curse didn't create work, but it did complicate work considerably. One consequence of man's sin is that work became toilsome as nature resists man's efforts to subdue it (Gen 3:17–19). Other realities such as the unpredictable outcome of one's occupation make work frustrating (Eccl 2:18–23). Additionally, various aspects of human depravity have an impact on the realm of work. Especially prominent is the propensity to laziness (e.g., Prov 6:6–11; 24:30–34).

Redemption

Despite the challenges of work in a fallen world, God instructs and enables his people to engage in it faithfully. Restored to their Creator, their ultimate motivation for work becomes what it was at Creation: the glory of God. This was the motivation of Jesus in his earthly work (e.g., John 4:34; 9:4). And it makes work doable in the most challenging of work environments. Paul repeatedly urges both slaves and masters to view their work as service to Christ (Eph 6:5–9; Col. 3:22—4:1). The implication is unavoidable: if even slaves may honor the Lord in their occupations, how much more should other workers do the same?

The original goal of exercising dominion over the world continues in force (Gen 1:26–28; 9:1–7). Other functions of work also redound to God's glory: providing for one's needs and the needs of one's family (2 Thess 3:10–12; 1 Tim 5:8); giving to the needy (Eph 4:28; 1 Tim 6:17–19); and presenting a credible gospel testimony to unbelievers (1 Thess 4:11–12). God also intends that we enjoy the material benefits that result from our work (Eccl 3:9–13; 5:18–20).

The most emphasized characteristic of the work of the redeemed is diligence. Proverbs has a great deal to say about this (e.g., 10:4–5; 12:11, 24, 27). Other biblical books likewise underscore the importance of zeal and industry in one's occupation (e.g., Eccl 9:10; Col 3:23; 2 Thess 3:10–12). With respect to one's employer, a lack of diligence amounts to theft (an application of passages such as Exod 20:15 and Eph 4:25).

On the other hand, the Bible warns against an excessive devotion to work and its benefits. Even if the Old Testament Sabbath law doesn't apply directly to Christians, it at least teaches a pattern of incorporating regular rest into our work cycle (Exod 20:8–11; Deut 5:12–15; cf. Gen 2:2–3).[2] More generally, the biblical work ethic includes a restful trust in God for the grace to work and for the results of one's work. Psalm 127 warns against the anxiety that drives much "workaholism,"

---

[2] Regarding the Sabbath, see Carson, *From Sabbath to Lord's Day.*

saying that the Lord can provide for his people "even when they sleep" (v. 2, NET©). No doubt greed is also a major factor here, and the Bible calls this idolatry (Col 3:5). When redemption is consummated and the curse is removed, the New Creation will feature a perfect blend of work (Rev 7:15; 22:1–5) and rest (Heb 4:11–11).

Seek Counsel

Christian theology has produced a wealth of wise reflection on the theme of work. This flows particularly from the Protestant Reformation. One of many Roman Catholic views that the Reformers countered was the rigid distinction between the clergy and the laity, including the tendency to devalue the "secular" work done by the laity. Applying various biblical truths, the Reformers sought to encourage believers with a sense of the dignity of their particular callings.[3]

The Lutheran tradition especially develops the idea that work is a means through which God works in the world. Spurred on by love for their neighbors, workers serve others (an application of Matt 22:39). Thus when we work we are instruments of God to meet the needs of fellow human beings. If God providentially works through pagan civil government, we can expect him to work through other vocations as well (an implication drawn from Romans 13:1–6). Human work is a kind of mask behind which God hides as he accomplishes his purposes in the world. This perspective instills in workers a strong sense of purpose even in mundane tasks.[4]

Other strands of the Reformation emphasize that work, its products, and the abilities it requires inherently glorify God. These all reflect his multi-faceted character. They also contribute to his original mandate that humanity maximize the beauty and usefulness of creation (Gen 1:26–28). Similarly, work is a matter of stewardship, faithfully

---

[3] For a helpful contemporary statement of a Reformation work ethic, see Ryken, *Redeeming the Time.* Compare Keller, *Every Good Endeavor.*

[4] See, for example, Veith, *God at Work.*

employing the skills and resources the Lord has graciously supplied (an application of passages such as Matt 25:14-30 and 1 Cor 4:2). When a worker thinks in these terms, he finds powerful motivation to work hard and pursue excellence.[5]

Formulate Response

Our study of the theme of work leads to several imperatives. First, *view work as dignified.* Work is more than a burden and more than a means of making a living. It's integral to our glorious purpose as those who are being remade in God's image. Nurturing this mindset is foundational to the remaining applications.

Second, *rely on God for the grace to work.* He is the one who calls us to our work, and he is the source of the strength and wisdom we need to carry it out. Praying for divine enabling throughout the workday is the natural, biblical way to express dependence on God.

Third, *work diligently.* We work so that God will be glorified and so that he can use us to bless others. Therefore we do the best work we possibly can. In pursuit of this goal, we avoid activities that unnecessarily distract from work. Here one should obviously observe any parameters set by his employer. Each believer will also need to identify and avoid those distractions that tempt him particularly. Excessive personal conversations with coworkers and personal Internet activity are examples of common distractions.

Fourth, *don't idolize work.* Resist any tendency to let work dominate life unduly. Adequate periods of rest should be incorporated into one's weekly schedule. Family members should feel free to share with us any concerns they may have about workaholic patterns in our lives. We should also avoid financial ambitions and commitments that drive us to work excessively.

Fifth, *approach work as an opportunity for the gospel.* We want others to see the Savior as they observe our work. We develop positive

---

[5] See, for example, Helm, *The Callings.*

relationships with coworkers and other work contacts, seeking to share the message of Christ with them (while observing our employers' wishes regarding the use of work time).

Local-Church Membership

In dealing with work, we've been looking at the Christian in society. We move now to the smaller circle of the local church.

Define Terms

When a person is converted to Christ, he immediately becomes a member of the body of Christ, the group of all true believers in the present age (Matt 16:18; Eph 1:22-23; 5:25). Practically, this universal church functions through local churches, assemblies in distinct geographical locations (e.g., "the church in Jerusalem," Acts 8:1; "the church at Antioch," Acts 13:1). In general, I define the local church as a group of baptized believers who have voluntarily agreed to pursue together God's mission for the local church: to make and mature disciples of Jesus Christ (Matt 28:18–20; Eph. 4:11–16). More specifically, as taught in the Reformation tradition, a local church is marked particularly by the faithful preaching of God's Word (1 Tim 4:13; 2 Tim 4:1–2), the biblical administration of the ordinances (Matt 28:19; 1 Cor 11:17–34), and the exercise of discipline (Heb 10:24–25; Matt 18:15–20).[6]

In speaking of membership in such a church, I'm not limiting myself to any particular mechanism for becoming a member. Rather, I'm dealing with the core idea of *a definite, voluntary commitment to a local church* as one expression of personal faith in Christ, the Head of the church.

Search Scripture

Since local churches didn't exist until Pentecost (Acts 2), we won't find any specific data on our topic in the Old Testament. In terms of the biblical storyline, however, the local church is central to what God is

---

[6] See article 29 of the Belgic Confession in Schaff, *Creeds,* 419–21.

doing to accomplish his plan of redemption in the present age (see especially the entire Epistle to the Ephesians and 1 Tim 3:14–16). It's true that no verse says in so many words, "Thou shalt join a church." Nevertheless, as we read the New Testament story, we encounter various lines of evidence arguing for local-church membership.

The Teaching of Jesus

In Matthew our Lord speaks of the church only briefly, but his comments are far reaching and lay the groundwork for the teaching of the rest of the New Testament. In Matthew 16:18 Jesus predicts that he will build his church. Then he gives to Peter, as the representative of the apostles through whom he would found the church, "the keys of the kingdom of heaven" (v. 19). This is the authority to recognize people as members of Christ's kingdom based on their confession of faith in him (cf. John 20:23).

In Matthew 18 Jesus implies that this authority passes on to his disciples generally and includes the authority of church discipline. As with "the keys of the kingdom," when a local church agrees to excommunicate a professing believer who won't repent of sin, it is expressing the will of God in heaven (compare 16:19 with 18:17–20). Furthermore, when Christ receives universal authority as the Messianic King, church discipline is part of the "all that I have commanded you" to be taught to disciples in all nations (Matt 28:18–20).[7]

For our purposes the upshot is this: Jesus depicts discipleship to himself as including a committed relationship with a group of other disciples who exercise oversight toward one another. This involves excluding from the group those whose lives clearly do not match their profession. Here we have to ask: how can one be excluded from a group of which he is not somehow a member?

---

[7] For more on Jesus's teaching about the church, see Blomberg, *Matthew*, 250–56, 278–81, 431–34; Carson, "Matthew," 413–27, 455–58, 664–70; Turner, *Matthew*, 402–8, 443–47, 689–92. Compare Leeman, *Surprising Offense*, 169–227.

The Pattern in Acts

The accounts of early churches in Acts develop more specifically the lo-cal-church concept sketched out by Jesus. In particular, conversion, baptism, and incorporation into the local church are closely linked. For those living in Jerusalem, what was involved in the positive response to the message that Peter preached on Pentecost? It included several com-ponents: repentance/faith in Christ, baptism, and assimilation into the assembly at Jerusalem (Acts 2:37–41). This was a "package deal." And it resulted in ongoing participation in the practices of the church (v. 42): "the apostles' teaching and the fellowship . . . the breaking of bread and the prayers." Of course, the actual means of salvation was repent-ance/faith, yet the other aspects appear as inseparable corollaries. Note verse 47a especially: "And the Lord added to their number day by day those who were being saved." Here the number of the saved and the number in the assembly are equivalent.

Acts doesn't provide details regarding the founding of every first-century church, but what general paradigm does it reflect? The ministry of Paul is especially instructive. As he traveled from city to city, he didn't merely lead individuals to Christ. His consistent practice was to gather them into identifiable assemblies so that they would worship their Lord and live out their faith together. See, for example, Acts 14:21–23; 15:41; 16:5; and 20:17–38.

The Instruction of the Epistles

Naturally, the Epistles contain the most explicit material on the be-liever's relationship to the local church. They depict the life of the Christian as interwoven with and interdependent on other Christians. As we saw in chapter 3, a strong connection exists between the local church and the believer's sanctification. Note the corporate language in Ephesians 4:11–16 (emphasis added):

> And he gave the apostles, the prophets, the evangelists, the shepherds
> and teachers, to equip *the saints* for the work of ministry, for building
> up the body of Christ, until *we all* attain to the unity of the faith and

of the knowledge of the Son of God, to mature manhood, to the measure of the stature of the fullness of Christ, so that *we* may no longer be children, tossed to and fro by the waves and carried about by every wind of doctrine, by human cunning, by craftiness in deceitful schemes. Rather, speaking the truth in love, *we* are to grow up in every way into him who is the head, into Christ, from whom *the whole body*, joined and held together by *every joint* with which it is equipped, when *each part* is working properly, makes *the body* grow so that it builds itself up in love.

Growth into Christ-likeness is presented as a joint effort that involves the entire church, a kind of "team sport." It takes the contribution of "every joint" and "each part" for each of us individually and for the church as a whole to become all that God wants us to be. This body concept implies an established and intimate relationship among the parties involved.

A major component here is the ministry of the leaders of the local church. Indeed, in Ephesians 4 the reference to "the shepherds and teachers" (v. 11) indicates that the outworking of this text is primarily on the level of the local church. The Epistles assume that the Christian has a pastor or pastors to whom he looks for spiritual feeding and guidance (e.g., 1 Thess 5:12–13; Heb 13:17). Sheep need shepherds, that is, under-shepherds (1 Pet 5:1–4).

At the same time, the Epistles call for the regular exercise of diverse spiritual gifts by a variety of Christians. The passages on this topic take for granted that an assembly exists and that the people in the assembly know who else belongs to it so that they can perform their ministries toward one another (Rom 12:3–8; 1 Cor 12–14; 1 Pet 4:10–11). In connection with spiritual gifts, Romans 12:5 says, "So we, though many, are one body in Christ, and individually members one of another." The local church is the main sphere in which this spiritual reality is experienced practically.

Another emphasis in the Epistles is the oversight and discipline that Jesus introduced in Matthew 18. Excommunication remains necessary in extreme cases (e.g., 1 Cor 5), again assuming a defined group.

But discipline isn't limited to excommunication. It encompasses various levels of accountability, including regular exhortation among Christians (e.g., Heb. 3:12–13; 10:23–25). Such exhortation happens most effectively within committed relationships.

The Pastoral Epistles contribute significantly to our topic. Paul commissions Timothy and Titus to firm up various organizational matters in churches at Ephesus and Crete respectively (1 Tim 3:14–15; Titus 1:5). The apostle covers such topics as the following:

- Role distinctions depending on gender and age (1 Tim 2:11–15; Titus 2:2–8)
- Leadership qualifications, duties, remuneration (1 Tim 3:1–13; 5:17–18; 2 Tim 2:24–26; 4:1–5; Titus 1:5–9)
- A roll of widows (1 Tim 5:13–16)
- Steps for handling problems (1 Tim 5:19–25; Titus 3:10–11).

Such policies and procedures imply that first-century local churches were well-defined bodies with a recognizable constituency.

Toward the end of the first century, the Apostle John makes a striking comment in relation to the local church. Speaking of false teachers, he writes: "They went out from us, but they were not of us; for if they had been of us, they would have continued with us. But they went out, that it might become plain that they all are not of us" (1 John 2:19). This does not imply that if someone leaves a particular local church at any time he is not regenerate. It does imply, however, that, attachment to an orthodox assembly is an expected result of regeneration.[8]

Seek Counsel

I'll reference just a few of the many writers who provide helpful discussions of church membership. From some of the same passages I cited above, the London Baptist Confession (1689) infers that Christ "*commandeth* [believers] to walk together in particular societies or churches,

---

[8] Commenting on the statement, "For if they had been of us, they would have continued with us," Burdick writes: "This contrary-to-fact statement is built upon the principle that genuine believers persevere in the faith and in their association with other believers" (*Letters of John,* 195).

for their mutual edification and the due performance of that public worship, which he requireth of them in the world."[9] Samuel Waldron explains:

> Christ's command to his people to walk together in particular churches is more than simply another one of his precepts. This precept creates the structure or context in which the Great Commission ... is carried out. Jesus desires that his disciples be taught to observe all that he commanded. How shall this be accomplished? By the creation of local churches, with local teacher-elders. Jesus commands such churches in Matthew 18:15–20. If Jesus commands that offences be brought to the church and commands the church to rebuke such offences and ultimately to exclude the impenitent, then necessarily he commands the existence of such local churches.[10]

There's a commendable example of a "good and necessary consequence" drawn from Scripture.

Jonathan Leeman has written one of the most extensive treatments of our topic. He targets contemporary cultural "baggage" that often stands in the way of church membership and discipline: individualism, consumerism, commitment phobia, and skepticism.[11] Leeman argues that such problems betray a deficient view of love. God's love operates in connection with his holiness, and his people are called to reflect the same kind of love. This means that the Christian's relationship to the church must include commitment and accountability.[12] Leeman's probing analyses include the following:

> One of the chief tragedies of evangelicalism today is that it has lost sight of the wonderful, life-giving force of authority. We've been carried away by culture. More than we realize, we view ourselves as

---

[9] Section 26.5, cited in Waldron, *Modern Exposition,* 307 (emphasis added).

[10] Ibid., 317.

[11] *Surprising Offense,* 39–74.

[12] Ibid., 77–126.

independent agents charged with determining how best to grow, serve, and love in the faith. Yes, we may listen to others, defer to others, and accept guidance from others, but in the final analysis we view ourselves as our own coaches, portfolio managers, guides, judges, and the captains of our own ships in a manner that is more cultural than biblical. In short, an underdeveloped theology conspires with our anti-authority and individualistic instincts to deceive us into claiming that we love all Christians everywhere equally while excusing ourselves from loving any of those Christians specifically, especially submissively. Unsurprisingly, churches are shallow, Christians are weak, and God's people look like the world.[13]

In connection with love, the analogy of marriage makes important points regarding church membership. Christians who attend a church indefinitely without joining have been compared to a man and a woman who live together without getting married. They want the benefits of marriage without the commitment. In reality, they're forfeiting some of the benefits. Worse, they're hurting each other in ways they may not even realize. They're also confusing onlookers.[14]

Formulate Response

Our application will come as no surprise: *join a church!* Given the emphasis of the passages on our topic, however, Jonathan Leeman's way of stating the matter seems more accurate: "Christians don't join churches; they submit to them."[15] To be sure, church authority can be abused, as when a pastor attempts to micromanage the lives of his church members. But such abuse doesn't argue against the legitimate authority of the local church.

In fact, the issue of authority helps address the question of exactly how one becomes a member of a church. In one church a candidate

---

[13] Ibid., 216.

[14] Mack and Swavely, *Life in the Father's House,* 51–52; citing Lane, *Members One of Another,* 66.

[15] *Church Membership,* 30.

may be asked to give a public testimony. In another he may sign a covenant or take membership vows. Some congregations vote on new members, while others don't. Such details are not stipulated in Scripture but are practical measures taken in order to implement the Bible's more general instruction about the church. It would seem that a church and/or its leadership are operating within their authority when they determine whatever membership process they will follow. After all, they make other decisions about church-wide affairs such as the location and times of their services and the congregation's financial commitments. As long as no biblical teaching is being violated, complying with the established method for becoming a member provides a Christian with his first opportunity to display proper submission to a local church.

While our discussion has centered on becoming a church member, this is, of course, only a first step. Sadly, church rolls may overflow with names of people who aren't participating actively in the life of the church. Membership is only as valuable as the commitment it represents. How do we apply fully the passages we've considered? Relying on God's grace, we strive to fulfill faithfully the *duties* of church membership that our discussion has noted. We attend services regularly and remain teachable under the preaching of God's Word. We submit to the rightful authority of our church leaders. We use our spiritual gifts to build up the body. We minister to the needs of our brothers and sisters through our time, funds, energy, and prayers. We work with them to reach the lost with the gospel.[16]

Conclusion

Since work and church play such a large part in God's plan for our lives, they deserve our careful thought and faithful participation. Thankfully, the Bible provides considerable instruction to direct the believer. Our survey of these subjects has illustrated a number of the emphases of this

---

[16] For detail on the duties of church membership, see Anyabwile, *What Is a Healthy Church Member?*; Mack and Swavely, *Life in the Father's House;* Whitney, *Spiritual Disciplines within the Church.*

book: the motivational power of the gospel, the need for accurate interpretation, the importance of the biblical storyline, the role of implications and paradigms, and the necessity of practical implementation. May your work life and your church life be more God-honoring and fruitful as a result.

Chapter 17

Ending in Song

Our final case study, music, is more complex than the topics of work and church membership. Naturally, it's also more controversial. While the discussion below is only a starting point, I trust that it will provide a reliable foundation for making wise choices in this area.

Define Terms

Defining music may seem unnecessary, but precision can only help. Music is a way of organizing *sound* in time. Its main properties are pitch (highness or lowness), dynamics (loudness or softness), tone color (e.g., "bright" vs. "dark"), and duration. These are arranged in patterns to produce rhythm, melody, harmony, and texture ("layers" of sound).[1] Musical sound may suggest ideas, generate emotions, and give pleasure. When music includes *lyrics,* it communicates ideas more explicitly.

Music belongs to some broader categories. First, it is an aspect of *culture.* Here is a standard definition of culture in a general sense: "An historically transmitted pattern of meanings embodied in symbols, a system of inherited conceptions expressed in symbolic forms by means of which men communicate, perpetuate, and develop their knowledge about and attitudes toward life."[2] Note the close connection between culture and "attitudes toward life." To one degree or another, a people's culture reflects their *worldview.* This holds true for music as well as for more propositional elements of culture such as literature.

---

[1] See Kamien and Kamien, *Music,* 1–55.

[2] Geertz, *Interpretation of Cultures,* 89.

Second, music is a form of *art*. This term refers to "the expression or application of human creative skill and imagination . . . producing works to be appreciated primarily for their beauty or emotional power."[3] Products of creativity or imagination, music and other art forms are expressions of *human nature*. Further, they are aimed particularly at displaying *beauty* and/or moving people *emotionally*.

Search Scripture

The subordination of music to culture and art widens our scope as we search for biblical material. Here the distinction between *structure* and *direction* serves us well (see chapter 15).

Structure

The development of culture and art reflect two fundamentally good realities of human existence taught in Genesis 1:26–28. First, God made man in his own image. What kind of God are we designed to mirror? Among other traits, he is a God who creates and enjoys beauty. Genesis' Creation account makes this point in dazzling terms. We also have this early statement about aesthetics: "And out of the ground the LORD God made to spring up every tree that is *pleasant to the sight* and good for food" (Gen 2:9a, emphasis added). Likewise, music is a manifestation of God's love for beauty (e.g., Ps 96:6). Second, God commissioned man to exercise dominion over the earth, to maximize its resources and capabilities, to make it increasingly useful and productive. Music is one arena in which to pursue this dominion mandate. It contributes to human flourishing by harnessing and shaping elements of sound.

Direction

Human beings may "bend" music in a positive or a negative direction.[4] The positive direction encompasses various forms of music. In addition

---

[3] Jewell and Abate, *Oxford American Dictionary,* 88.

[4] For much of the biblical argumentation that remains in this chapter, I am indebted to my colleague Peter Davis, who holds a doctorate in piano pedagogy as well as degrees in Bible.

to entertaining generally (e.g., Job 21:12), music appears as a normal and evidently appropriate way to celebrate diverse life experiences:

- Farewells (Gen 31:27)
- Military victories (1 Sam 18:6)
- Romantic love (Song 1:1)
- Grief (Jer 9:10, where NET© translates the Hebrew word *qinah* as "mournful song")
- Homecomings (Luke 15:24–25).

Some music is oriented to God directly and honors him in a unique way, e.g., "the songs of the LORD" (1 Chron 25:7, KJV) and "spiritual songs" (Eph 5:19; Col 3:16). Such songs can also have an edifying effect on oneself and on other believers (Job 35:10; Eph 5:19; Col 3:16).[5]

The Bible indicates that musical sound can have positive effects on listeners. Many passages refer generally to the *delight* produced by beautiful music. Descriptions such as "sweet" (Ps 81:2) and "glorious" (Ps 66:2) make this point. Similarly, music can convey *joy* (Job 21:12; 1 Chron 15:16). Harp music helped Saul experience *peace* (1 Sam 16:23).

On the other hand, Scripture teaches that sin has tainted every part of human nature and culture (e.g., Gen 6:5; Eph 4:17–19). Here we need to consider especially the New Testament's teaching concerning "the world" (Gk. *kosmos*). I'm not referring to the physical earth or to humanity in general but to "the bad part of culture,"[6] driven by the desires of the flesh, the desires of the eyes, and the pride of life (1 John 2:16). Based on detailed study of the relevant biblical material, my colleague Randy Leedy provides a more specific definition:

> *The world is a spiritual kingdom ruled by Satan, in unremitting conflict with the kingdom of God, consisting visibly of the mass of living people who do not know God, and who, in response to satanic allurement that plays upon and preys upon fallen human nature, corrupt the various aspects of God's earthly creation into avenues for the gratification of self*

---

[5] On the translation and interpretation of Col 3:16, see Moo, *Letters to the Colossians and to Philemon*, 285–90.

[6] Frame, *Christian Life*, 866.

instead of the glory of God, thereby incurring eternal judgment and destruction.[7]

God commands us not to love the world (1 John 2:15–17). In the words of Romans 12:2, we must not be conformed to this age (Gk. *aiōn*). Using different terms, Ephesians 5 speaks to the same issue. Paul urges us to "try to discern what is pleasing to the Lord" (v. 10; see my discussion in chapter 5). Then he says, "Take no part in the unfruitful works of darkness, but instead expose them. For it is shameful even to speak of the things that they do in secret" (vv. 11–12).

In fact, the Bible doesn't shrink from specifying sinful proclivities of particular cultures. Titus 1 contains one of the more "politically incorrect" biblical texts along these lines. Here the Apostle Paul deftly but bluntly critiques the culture of the island of Crete: "One of the Cretans, a prophet of their own [probably Epimenides], said, 'Cretans are always liars, evil beasts, lazy gluttons.' This testimony is true. Therefore rebuke them sharply" (vv. 12–13b).

Given the depravity of man and the ingenuity of Satan in directing the world, we have ample reason to expect that music may be shaped and used in such a way as to promote sinful agendas and influence people away from God. The Bible's first reference to human music seems to hint at this. The invention of musical instruments appears as a natural expression of the dominion mandate, alongside the beginnings of animal breeding and metallurgy (Gen. 4:20–22). Yet the fact that the inventor of musical instruments was Jubal, son of wicked Lamech in the line of wicked Cain, raises the possibility that music can be used for evil ends (v. 21). Waltke and Fredricks go so far as to say, "The arts and sciences, appropriate extensions of the divine cultural mandate, are here expressed in a depraved culture as means of self-assertion and violence, which climaxes with Lamech's song of tyranny."[8]

---

[7] Leedy, *Love Not,* 69 (emphasis original). For application of the biblical teaching on worldliness to a variety of life issues, see Hughes, *Set Apart.*

[8] Waltke and Fredricks, *Genesis,* 100.

As we continue reading Scripture, we encounter music with clearly negative connotations. There are songs of drunkards (Ps 69:12), fools (Eccl 7:5), and prostitutes (Isa 23:15–16). One wonders what exactly it is that makes such songs problematic: the lyrics, the sound, or both? But if musical sound itself can encourage good dispositions such as peace and joy (1 Sam 16:23; 1 Chron 15:16; cf. Gal 5:22), could it not also promote works of the flesh such as sensuality, anger, and carousing (Gal 5:19–21)? This seems to be a sound inference.

Seek Counsel

Christian theologians and musicians have provided plenty of instruction for evaluating music, especially worship music, from a biblical perspective. I'd certainly recommend that you read works on this topic.[9] Here, though, I want to share some more general perspectives on culture as a whole. I'm placing this material under "Seek Counsel" because it is not found in the Bible. Instead it is gleaned from life observation. As I've pointed out before, we will often need to use information outside the Bible in order to apply the Bible.

A common method for classifying culture centers on three categories: high (or classical, or fine) culture, folk (or traditional) culture, and pop culture.[10] These aren't airtight compartments, and we won't be able to place every cultural product neatly into one of these categories. But as generalizations they provide valuable insights for evaluating music. By way of loose analogy, we're talking about the differences among a five-star steakhouse (high), an authentic Mexican restaurant (folk), and a fast-food hamburger joint (pop).

What are some general characteristics of these types of culture? *High* culture is marked by traits such as transcendence and timelessness,

---

[9] I would especially recommend Makujina, *Measuring the Music.* Other works that I've profited from include Aniol, *Sound Worship;* Aniol, *Worship in Song;* Gordon, *Why Johnny Can't Sing Hymns.*

[10] My discussion here is based largely on Myers, *All God's Children and Blue Suede Shoes.* Compare Aniol, *Worship in Song,* 59–78.

substance, discipline of form, and delayed gratification. High-culture ideals correspond closely with certain emphases of Christian theology. *Folk* culture shares some qualities with high culture but is more oriented to the average person and is therefore simpler and more accessible. Folk culture is the medium typically used to perpetuate the values of specific ethnic groups and other communities. When it blends substance with accessibility, it has considerable potential for propagating Christianity, especially within particular groups.

We may characterize *pop* culture in terms opposite to high culture: an excessive concern with novelty and the current generation, superficiality, an emphasis on individual expression, freedom of form, and immediate gratification. The name *pop* doesn't imply that other kinds of culture aren't popular. But it does make the point that pop culture is *extremely* popular on a *wide* scale. The modern development of mass media allowed for the quick and broad dissemination of new ideas, leading to a further characteristic of pop culture: commercialism. In pop culture those who can harness the media go after the masses— they regularly redefine culture in order to make money, often by appealing to a lowest common denominator in society.

We shouldn't conclude that every product of pop culture is inherently wrong. After all, I began chapter 15 by talking about my smartphone, and I just used it to check my social media accounts. I've also eaten my share of fast food. Yet these illustrations actually support the point I want to make: pop culture raises significant concerns. Its focus on immediate gratification tends to overemphasize experience and emotion while de-emphasizing the mind. Here we need to recognize that "the medium is the message."[11] Sentimental culture cultivates sentimental people. Worse still, the inclination toward a lowest common denominator means that pop culture has great potential for appealing to the flesh (cf. Rom 13:14).

---

[11] See McLuhan, *Understanding Media;* Postman, *Amusing Ourselves.*

I'll highlight just one more tendency of pop culture: its emphasis on youth. Even secular analysts have been critical of this tendency. Musicologist Julian Johnson writes,

> Contemporary commercial music is, above all, the music of youth. Young people spend more time and money on music than any other sector of society, and since our cultural diet is primarily market-led, it follows that our dominant musical culture is that of youth. . . . This music is used, like other areas of fashion, as part of teenage rites of passage that include formulating individual identities in relation to collective groups, articulating independence from a parental generation, and coping with excessive libidinal energy in the absence of other obvious outlets for it. . . .

> What remains hard to understand is why adult culture should also be shaped to such a degree by what is, after all, youth culture. But the distinction I am making is of course not clearly defined in contemporary culture. Our collective fascination with the imagery of youth and youthfulness effectively dissolves any boundaries between the cultural diets of children, adolescents, and adults. Seven-year-old children and thirty-seven-year-old adults are equally fascinated, it seems, by a musical culture defined almost exclusively by the images of singers between the ages of seventeen and twenty-seven.[12]

Even if this is a little overstated, doesn't it resonate with what you've observed overall? Let me ask one other question: how does it square with biblical teaching?

In critiquing pop culture, I'm not implying that other types of culture are trouble free. In addition, cultural elitism is a danger to avoid. It does not, however, strike me as the greatest danger in our day. If we're committed to gospel-driven holiness, we dare not minimize the obvious moral degeneration that pop culture has promoted in recent history.

---

[12] Johnson, *Who Needs Classical Music?*, 44–45. I thank Amy Schoneweis, a fellow church member, for directing my attention to Johnson's work. For evidence of how pop culture's youth emphasis has shaped contemporary church life, see Bergler, *Juvenilization*.

Formulate Response

Scripture doesn't specify how to assess the moral direction of a piece of music. This is an act of discernment. To fine-tune our discernment, we do well to evaluate three specific aspects of music: *lyrics, sound,* and *associations.* As I discuss each aspect below, I'm making an effort to apply biblical criteria such as we find in a verse I highlighted in chapter 5, Philippians 4:8: "Finally, brothers, whatever is true, whatever is honorable, whatever is just, whatever is pure, whatever is lovely, whatever is commendable, if there is any excellence, if there is anything worthy of praise, think about these things."

Lyrics

I'm dealing with lyrics first because they're the most objective. Since we are accountable even for the careless words that come out of our mouths, we must be alert to the words that we speak and hear (Matt 12:36). Words certainly have moral import. They reflect the condition of one's heart (Matt 12:34) and can be used for blessing or cursing (Prov 18:21; Jas 3:9–10). According to Ephesians 4:25–32, our words must not be false, carnal, vulgar, or expressive of bitterness or sinful anger. Instead they should be truthful, edifying, and kind. These requirements apply to words that are sung as well as to those spoken in conversation.

For instance, the lyrics of many pop songs are explicitly ungodly. If such words are inappropriate for God's people to speak, why would we choose to listen to them as a form of entertainment? Along these lines, Johnson raises a thought-provoking question about the ironies of our age: "Why are we so concerned about food additives, the presence of genetically modified crops, or the lives of battery hens and yet so utterly unconcerned about the content of the cultural products with which we feed our minds?"[13]

We should evaluate with even greater care the words of our worship songs. Such songs are presented to God as an offering, which

---

[13] Johnson, *Who Needs Classical Music?,* 121.

requires special reverence and caution (Eccl 5:1–2). Worship songs are also supposed to build others up spiritually (Eph 5:19; Col 3:16; Heb 13:15). Here the Psalms and other biblical songs serve as our greatest resource. They not only provide specific words to sing but also illustrate the *kinds* of lyrics that delight the heart of God.[14] Our Lord is pleased with words that represent him accurately. He is honored by texts that uphold his exalted position even while praising him for his condescending grace. Can you think of recent or older worship songs that don't meet up to this criterion?

Sound

Composers combine elements of sound in various ways in order to produce the effects they desire—emotional effects particularly. This seems self-evident, a truth we learn by observing the created order. God created music with the potential for having such effects. The music that accompanies a movie scene is designed to support and enhance the thematic content of that scene. In watching a movie, we can intuitively tell the difference between music that is happy, sad, suspenseful, reflective, romantic, or triumphant. We may also pick up on problematic moods suggested by music: rage or licentiousness, for example.

At this point I'm not going to get into details about chords and beats. I am not a musician, and those kinds of arguments are often unpersuasive. As a nonverbal means of communication, musical sound is not as precise as verbal communication. In particular, identifying isolated musical elements as intrinsically good or evil seems strained.

A work of art, however, is greater and more communicative than the sum of its parts. So we should do the best we can to evaluate the overall aural "drift" of a piece of music, asking especially whether it has negative effects. Does it suggest or prompt sinful desires (Gal 5:19–21; 1 John 2:16)? Here we shouldn't limit our evaluation to a song's tune or instrumentation. Other factors can affect the impact of music.

---

[14] See O'Donnell, *God's Lyrics.*

At a concert, for instance, the overall atmosphere, the *style* of singing, and even the physical appearance of the singer can intensify the effect of the experience—for good or ill.

Evaluating musical sound becomes especially important with worship music. Biblical teaching on worship repeatedly emphasizes the holiness of God (e.g., 1 Chr 16:29; 2 Chr 20:21 Ps 29:1–2; 93:5; 96:9). How can we offer to a holy God music that encourages people toward sin? Indeed, Yahweh specifically warned Israel not to worship him according to the wicked ways of the Canaanites (Deut 12:29–32).

Sin isn't the only issue to consider, however. Worship music expresses and fosters right emotions toward God (e.g., Ps 98:4–6). Yet this can easily slip into *emotionalism*. Especially when a pop style of music is used for worship music, it can become difficult to determine whether one is actually engaged with the Lord emotionally or simply experiencing an artificial "buzz" from the music. So we must honestly assess our worship music by this principle: "I will sing praise with my spirit, but I will sing with my mind also" (1 Cor 14:15).[15]

Associations

Music often carries associations that are somewhat distinguishable from its other aspects. An idea and/or a feeling is generated not only by the musical sound and any lyrics but also by a symbolic connection between the music and its culture. We need to consider such associational "baggage" in our evaluation of music.

Every culture has symbols that communicate nonverbally by way of association. To give an extreme illustration, most people react when they see a swastika. There's nothing inherently wrong with the shape and intersection of lines that form this symbol, and historically it has been used for various purposes. Yet decades after the end of the Third Reich, the swastika retains a strong and disturbing identification

---

[15] For general discussions of worship, see Chapell, *Christ-Centered Worship;* Peterson, *Engaging with God;* Reimers, *Glory Due his Name;* Ross, *Recalling the Hope of Glory.*

with the Nazi holocaust. Consequently, the symbol is rightly avoided. Other examples come to mind: various bodily gestures, flags, articles and styles of clothing—and songs. The associations of such things may change over time. At one point beards were heavily associated with the rebellion of the hippie movement, but that symbolism doesn't continue today. Thus associations have to be evaluated on an ongoing basis.

As many have said, we need to "exegete" the culture as well as the Scriptures. To figure out the associations of a cultural element, probably the most helpful step we can take is simply to consult the culture—or the world—itself. What are the associations of rock music, for example? It's a matter of historical record that to a significant degree this genre arose as a vehicle for the expression of immorality, hedonism, and rebellion.[16] Has this connection faded away?

Pop star Janet Jackson doesn't think so. In 2008 Larry King interviewed Jackson on his television program, introducing her as "sexier . . . smarter . . . and slimmer than ever." As the two talk about the lyrics of some of her songs, the adjectives *racy* and *sensual* are used openly. After a conversation about some of Jackson's personal struggles, attention turns to the issue of recreational drugs. Here Jackson says, "I am so against drugs and that whole thing. *But at the same time, that's kind of what this field is about. It's like drugs, sex and rock and roll.*" She goes on to affirm that despite the prevalence of drugs in her industry, she hadn't used drugs. The discussion ends on a sad note, however.

Jackson: I've seen it, but I've never—thank God.
King: Thank God.
Jackson: Knock on wood.[17]

---

[16] See, for example, Cottrell, *Sex, Drugs, and Rock 'N' Roll*; Friedlander, *Rock & Roll*. On the origins of Contemporary Christian Music, see Stowe, *No Sympathy for the Devil*.

[17] CNN "Larry King Live" Transcript, 28 February 2008 (emphasis added). I thank Steve Hankins, my associate dean, for making me aware of this interview.

In citing this example, I'm not arguing that every song in the rock genre and related genres actively promotes carnal behavior. Rather, I'm raising the question of associations: at least in general, what does this kind of music represent in society?

Christians ought to consider this question because the Scriptures call on us to exercise care regarding our personal purity and our testimony before others. We strive to live in a way that unquestionably portrays the holy character of the God we worship (Matt 5:14–16; 1 Pet 2:11–12). We want to maintain a visible distinction from the sinful agendas of the world (Rom 12:2; 1 John 2:15–17; Jas 4:4). With this in mind, what should be our response to cultural practices that represent worldly values?

Remember chapter 10's study of 1 Corinthians 8:1—11:1. That passage doesn't fit music exactly because Paul is discussing meat, an object that itself has no moral or spiritual effect on people (8:8). As we've seen, the same cannot be said about music. But must we not infer that if even the associations of meat matter, the associations of music matter as well? If so, the Lord would have us consider earnestly the following questions as they relate to music:

- *How can I most contribute to the advance of the gospel* (9:1–27; 10:32–33)?
- *Will my participation likely influence someone to sin* (10:23–30)?
- *What decision will glorify God* (1 Cor 10:31)?

Finally, if it seems that a musical issue falls in the category of genuinely debatable matters (Rom. 14:1—15:13), the questions are similarly probing:

- *What is to the Lord's advantage* (14:6–9)?
- *Will I be able to justify my decision before God's judgment seat* (14:10–12)?
- *Will my participation likely prompt someone to violate his conscience* (Rom. 14:13–21)?
- *Is my own conscience in doubt* (14:22–23)?

Conclusion

It's appropriate that our final chapter should close with such questions. Although this book's study of application has included much detail, undoubtedly it hasn't answered every question you have about the subjects I've raised. I'm not sorry for that, though. My goal hasn't been to apply the Bible for you but to help you apply it yourself. Indeed, given the vastness of Scripture and the complexities of life, we will all spend the rest of our time on earth growing in the skill of moving beyond chapter and verse.

Epilogue

Though this book has sometimes required technicality, my interest in the topic of biblical application is not academic. It is deeply personal. Perhaps some background will help you understand my heart as I've written.

As a consequence of the Spanish-American War, in 1898 the island of Puerto Rico became a territory of the United States of America. One of the blessings resulting from this development was the dissemination of the gospel on the island, following centuries of Roman Catholic domination under Spain. During those early days of religious liberty, my great-grandfather accepted Christ as Savior through the witness of a missionary sent out by a major American denomination. My grandfather also came to Christ and went on to serve as a pastor with that denomination.

This was the family into which my father was born and through which he was converted. In his youth Dad came to believe that God had called him to vocational ministry, and he was assured of a scholarship to his denomination's seminary. He wondered if he should study elsewhere, however.

In the early 1950s Dad found himself stationed in Germany, serving as a medic in the US Army. As the Korean War was winding down, his thoughts turned to the future and to his need for ministerial training. One day he was looking at a Christian magazine and was intrigued by an ad for a school named Bob Jones University (BJU) in Greenville, SC.

Around that time evangelist Billy Graham traveled to Germany to preach to the soldiers. Dad attended a rally and afterward took the opportunity to ask Graham for some advice. As the story goes, when

Dad inquired whether Graham knew anything about BJU, the evangelist replied, "It's a great school. If you want to learn to preach, that's the place to go."

This brief recommendation would have far-reaching and ironic consequences. Dad returned home and announced that he would be turning down his denominational scholarship and would be attending BJU. He endured the expected resistance and pursued his goal, thanks to the GI Bill.

Dad's years at BJU proved formative in many ways, not the least of which was that he met a godly young lady who would become my mother. I'll focus on another part of the experience, however. Those years witnessed the turning point in the controversy between "fundamentalism" and "new evangelicalism."[1] That point came when fundamentalists, led by Bob Jones Sr. and others, separated from Billy Graham over the ecumenism formalized in his 1957 New York crusade.

My father became convinced of the fundamentalist position, and this determined the direction of his ministry. When he returned to Puerto Rico, it was as an independent missionary. The more he learned of the theological liberalism within the denomination of his upbringing, the more he concluded that he could not participate. For nearly fifty years Dad served faithfully as an evangelist, church planter, and educator.

All of this is to say that I grew up as a second-generation fundamentalist. I came to faith in Jesus Christ through the influence of fundamentalist parents. They and a host of preachers and teachers also taught me the separatist principles of fundamentalist Christianity. I've seen the principles implemented in many situations. And I've witnessed firsthand the sacrifices—relational, financial, and otherwise—that are often required in order to maintain those principles.

---

[1] See Beale, *In Pursuit of Purity;* Murray, *Evangelicalism Divided;* Marsden, *Reforming Fundamentalism;* Pickering and Houghton, *Biblical Separation;* Sidwell, *Set Apart.* Compare Naselli and Hansen, *Four Views.*

I've also observed plenty of controversy regarding fundamentalism, and that brings me to the subject of this book. To one degree or another, fundamentalism has been marked by adherence to core doctrinal truths of Christianity—the fundamentals—and ecclesiastical separation from those who deny or compromise those truths. A related characteristic has been an emphasis on holiness of lifestyle or "personal separation." This has included much teaching on self-discipline as well as warnings and taboos against activities considered worldly or spiritually unhealthy.

Fundamentalism's approach to holiness has been subjected to all manner of criticism. The movement has been dismissed as obscurantist, man-centered, isolationist, hypocritical, legalistic, and abusive. Fundamentalism's diversity makes it impossible to assess the movement in a generalized way, especially as the lines of ecclesiastical demarcation have grown fuzzy. In fact, twenty-first-century fundamentalism does not seem cohesive enough to qualify as a single movement. Additionally, for various reasons some who have historically borne the name *fundamentalist* question whether that label is worth using anymore. We also need to distinguish between the ideals of fundamentalism and the personal fallibility of its adherents and leaders. My own experience in one stream of fundamentalism has been positive in many respects. Nonetheless, the accusations against the movement(s) are serious and call for sober self-evaluation.

As I look back on my years in fundamentalism, I'm especially grateful for the devotion and steadfastness of my parents. Both of them passed from this life into the presence of Christ during the preparation of this book. That has made the completion of the project especially poignant. It also inspires me as I look forward. I'm burdened about the legacy I am leaving my own children as well as my church members and students. I pray that this study will provide reliable assistance to them and to any believer, fundamentalist or otherwise, who is striving to base the pursuit of holiness firmly on Scripture.

One of my major concerns has been to root holiness and application in the gospel. This was drilled into me by a former professor at BJU. He wrote,

> One of the foremost objectives in my ministry has been to bring students to see and understand something of the Savior: who he is, and what he has done, and what their place in him is. I have often grieved, having expounded some essential gospel truth such as justification by faith or union with Christ, that so many students confessed they had never heard such truths before. The general consensus seems to be that whereas the gospel message is essential for evangelism, edification requires something beyond those simple facts. Such a reaction to the gospel betrays a sad unfamiliarity with its power and scope. Although I have rejoiced to see many come into the true liberty of the gospel, I have lamented that what I teach from the Scripture seems so novel to many. . . .
>
> I have told my students, perhaps thousands of times over the years, that *right thinking about the gospel produces right living in the gospel.* It is truth, not activity, which makes Christianity distinct. We cannot ignore the link between gospel doctrine and gospel duty if we hope to approach genuine Christian life and successful Christian living.[2]

I'm moved as I recall the impact such teaching had on my life. My heart cries out, "Yes! That's the kind of fundamentalism I want!"

By the time I started teaching at BJU, however, I began to encounter problems in an opposite direction. Due in part to excesses within the "gospel-centered" movement in broader evangelicalism,[3] concern for practical holiness seemed to be on the wane. One day I was teaching on the doctrine of sanctification. Afterward a student approached me and asked, "What do you mean by 'personal holiness?' I thought I was righteous in Christ." I don't think the problem was a lack of clarity on my part. As I spoke with the student, it became evident that

---

[2] Barrett, *Complete in Him,* 2–3 (emphasis original).

[3] On the gospel-centered movement, see the sources listed in note 29 of chapter 1.

he had been influenced by a particular theology, one that gives the impression that because of justification by faith the pursuit of experiential holiness doesn't matter all that much.

I hope I was able to point this young man in a more biblical direction. The theology he was expressing is *not* what I want for myself or my children. As I emphasized in chapters 1 and 2, the gospel cannot be separated from sanctification. Christ saves us for the very purpose of restoring us into the image of God.

I also don't want a version of Christianity that is satisfied with the letter of Scripture, that fails to internalize its spirit and seek its implications for contemporary life. I fear legalism in all forms, including minimalism. Nor do I want to be naïve about the godlessness of the world, complacent about carnality in the name of Christian liberty or cultural engagement.

On the other hand, I recognize that we face genuine difficulties as we try to work out the details of sanctification. This is definitely an area where fundamentalism needs growth. It's one thing to teach positions and practices. It's another to teach the reasons for them. And when we do give attention to our reasons, sometimes we discover that they aren't too convincing. We need a solid biblical rationale for application generally and a sensible method for arriving at specific applications.

Fundamentalist educational institutions have often been criticized for insisting that students abide by extrabiblical codes of conduct. Leaders must place such codes in proper theological context, keeping clear the Bible's teaching on the gospel and sanctification. They need to have solid reasons for their rules and explain those reasons carefully. They should also regularly evaluate the need for particular rules as well as the amount of emphasis they place on rules generally. In principle, however, I don't find a rule objectionable just because it is extrabiblical. After all, citizens, employees, and soldiers submit to the extrabiblical rules of their superiors every day. So I'm not necessarily bothered when my children are called on to submit to a Christian school's extrabiblical rules, nor do I think that such rules are inherently legalistic.

Here is what I *am* concerned about: my children are quickly completing their years in a Christian school. Presumably, they will soon be moving out from under my roof. They will be living as adults in a godless world. How will they be able to thrive for the Lord?

By God's own gracious working within them, more and more the biblical worldview will need to shape their affections, their thinking, and their choices. They will need to sort through life issues and exercise discernment based on that worldview. They will also need to interact biblically with other believers concerning questions of Christian living.

My focus isn't on my children's "standards" of conduct. I'm burdened about their sanctification overall, their love for and likeness to Jesus Christ. Fundamentally, holiness is motivated by loyalty not to men or movements or even doctrines but to Christ himself. And that loyalty is nurtured through an intimate relationship with the Lord through his Word.

I also long for my children to represent Christ well to a lost world. Reaching unbelievers with the gospel is going to require a firm grounding in Scripture, the ability to handle God's Word in a way that is clear and compelling.

Every aspect of the Christian life is tied in some way to the believer's understanding of and response to Scripture. Consequently, as a father I need to teach my children how to use their Bibles. I also need to model biblical application for them. Primarily, this book has been my effort to think through these matters "from the ground up" so that I can disciple my children more effectively. If they are better equipped to apply God's Word to their lives, I will rejoice over his grace. If you are helped as well, I'll have even more reason to praise our Lord.

Appendix

The Storyline of Scripture[1]

Kingdom Phase	People	Place	Rule and Blessing
Pattern Kingdom	Adam and Eve	Eden, original dwelling of God on earth	Perfect communion with God Perfect human relationships Perfect dominion over earth
Perished Kingdom	Seed of woman	Outside of Eden	Opposition to rebellion and curse Common and special grace
Promised Kingdom	Seed of Abraham	Canaan	Abrahamic Covenant: Seed, Land, Universal Blessing
Partial Kingdom	Israel	Canaan and tabernacle Jerusalem and temple	Exodus Sinaitic Covenant Conquest of Canaan Monarchy Davidic Covenant
Prophesied Kingdom	Israel	Exile and return New temple New Creation	National and universal judgments Davidic Messiah New Covenant

---

[1] Adapted from Roberts, *God's Big Picture.*

Kingdom Phase	People	Place	Rule and Blessing
Present Kingdom	Jesus Christ: Second Adam and Ideal Israelite	Jesus Christ: New temple	Jesus Christ: Davidic King and Mediator of New Covenant
Proclaimed Kingdom	Church: Jews and Gentiles in one body	All nations Church and believer as temple	New Covenant preached to world Heightened ministry of Holy Spirit
Perfected Kingdom	All humanity, centered on restored Israel	Jerusalem and temple	Unprecedented spiritual and material blessings during Millennium
	All believers	New Creation/ New Jerusalem God himself as temple	Perfect communion with God Perfect human relationships Perfect dominion over earth

Bibliography

Adams, Jay E. *A Call for Discernment: Distinguishing Truth from Error in Today's Church.* 1987. Reprint, Woodruff, SC: Timeless, 1998.

———. *Temptation: Applying Radical Amputation to Life's Sinful Patterns.* Resources for Biblical Living. Phillipsburg, NJ: Presbyterian & Reformed, 2012.

———. *What to Do on Thursday: A Layman's Guide to the Practical Use of the Scriptures.* Phillipsburg, NJ: Presbyterian and Reformed, 1982.

Akin, Daniel L., ed. *A Theology for the Church.* Nashville: B&H, 2007.

Aland, Barbara, et al., eds. *The Greek New Testament.* 4th rev. ed. Stuttgart, Germany: Deutsche Bibelgesellschaft, 2001.

Alexander, T. Desmond. *From Eden to the New Jerusalem: An Introduction to Biblical Theology.* Grand Rapids: Kregel, 2009.

Anderson, Lorin W., et al, eds. *A Taxonomy for Learning, Teaching, and Assessing: A Revision of Bloom's Taxonomy of Educational Objectives.* Complete ed. New York: Longman, 2001.

Aniol, Scott. *Sound Worship: A Guide to Making Musical Choices in a Noisy World.* N.p.: Religious Affections, 2010.

———. *Worship in Song: A Biblical Approach to Music and Worship.* Winona Lake, IN: BMH, 2009.

Anyabwile, Thabiti M. *What Is a Healthy Church Member?* 9Marks. Wheaton: Crossway, 2008.

Archer, Gleason L., and Gregory Chirichigno. *Old Testament Quotations in the New Testament: A Complete Survey.* Chicago: Moody, 1983.

Arnold, Bill T. *The NIV Application Commentary: 1 and 2 Samuel.* Grand Rapids: Zondervan, 2003.

Ash, Christopher. *Discovering Joy the of a Clear Conscience.* Phillipsburg, NJ: Presbyterian & Reformed, 2014.

———. *Teaching Romans, Volume 1: Unlocking Romans 1–8 for the Bible Teacher.* Proclamation Trust Teaching the Bible Series. Fearn, Scotland: Christian Focus, 2009.

———. *Teaching Romans, Volume 2: Unlocking Romans 9–15 for the Bible Teacher.* Proclamation Trust Teaching the Bible Series. Fearn, Scotland: Christian Focus, 2009.

Augustine. "On Christian Doctrine." Translated by J. F. Shaw. In *A Select Library of the Nicene and Post-Nicene Fathers of the Christian Church,* edited by Philip Schaff, 2:513–97. 1886. Reprint, Grand Rapids: Eerdmans, 1956.

Baer, D. A., and R. P. Gordon, "חסד." In *NIDOTTE,* 2:211–18.

Barrett, Matthew. *God's Word Alone—The Authority of Scripture: What the Reformers Taught . . . and Why It Still Matters.* The Five Solas Series. Grand Rapids: Zondervan, 2016.

Barrett, Michael P. V. *Beginning at Moses: A Guide to Finding Christ in the Old Testament.* Greenville, SC: Ambassador-Emerald International, 1999.

———. *Complete in Him: A Guide to Understanding and Enjoying the Gospel.* Greenville, SC: Ambassador-Emerald International, 2000.

———. *Love Divine and Unfailing: The Gospel according to Hosea.* The Gospel According to the Old Testament. Phillipsburg, NJ: Presbyterian & Reformed, 2008.

Bartholomew, Craig G., and Michael W. Goheen. *The Drama of Scripture: Finding Our Place in God's Story.* 2nd ed. Grand Rapids: Baker, 2014.

Bauer, David R., and Robert A. Traina. *Inductive Bible Study: A Comprehensive Guide to the Practice of Hermeneutics.* Grand Rapids: Baker, 2011.

Bauer Walter, Frederick W. Danker, W. F. Arndt, and F. W. Gingrich. *Greek-English Lexicon of the New Testament and Other Early Christian Literature.* 3rd ed. Chicago: University of Chicago Press, 2000.

Beale, David O. *In Pursuit of Purity: American Fundamentalism since 1850.* Greenville, SC: Unusual, 1986.

Beale, G. K. *Handbook on the New Testament Use of the Old Testament.* Grand Rapids: Baker, 2012.

—————, ed. *The Right Doctrine from the Wrong Texts? Essays on the Use of the Old Testament in the New.* Grand Rapids: Baker, 1994.

Beale, G. K., and D. A. Carson, ed. *Commentary on the New Testament Use of the Old Testament.* Grand Rapids: Baker, 2007.

Bell, Robert D. *The Theological Messages of the Old Testament Books.* Greenville, SC: Bob Jones University Press, 2010.

Berding, Kenneth, and Jonathan Lunde, eds. *Three Views on the New Testament Use of the Old Testament.* Counterpoints: Bible & Theology. Grand Rapids: Zondervan, 2007.

Berg, Jim. *Changed into His Image: God's Plan for Transforming Your Life.* 2nd ed. Greenville, SC: Bob Jones University Press, 2018.

—————. *Essential Virtues: Marks of the Christ-Centered Life.* Greenville, SC: Bob Jones University Press, 2008.

Bergler, Thomas. *The Juvenilization of American Christianity.* Grand Rapids: Eerdmans, 2012.

Berkhof, Louis. *Systematic Theology.* 4th ed. Grand Rapids: Eerdmans, 1939.

Bernard, Thomas Dehany. *The Progress of Doctrine in the New Testament.* 1864 Bampton Lectures. 2nd ed. Boston: Gould and Lincoln, 1869.

Best, Megan. *Fearfully and Wonderfully Made: Ethics and the Beginning of Human Life.* Kingsford, NSW, Australia: Matthias, 2012.

Block, Daniel. *Judges, Ruth.* NAC. Nashville: B&H, 2002.

Blomberg, Craig L. *Matthew.* NAC. Nashville: B&H, 1992.

—————. *The NIV Application Commentary: 1 Corinthians.* Grand Rapids: Zondervan, 1994.

Bloom, Benjamin S., ed. *Taxonomy of Educational Objectives: Handbook I: Cognitive Domain.* New York: David McKay, 1956.

Bock, Darrell L. *Luke, Volume 2: 9:51—24:53.* BECNT. Grand Rapids: Baker, 1996.

Bock, Darrell L., and Mitch Glaser, eds. *The People, the Land, and the Future of Israel: Israel and the Jewish People in the Plan of God.* Grand Rapids: Kregel, 2014.

Bock, Darrell L., with Benjamin I. Simpson. *Jesus according to Scripture: Restoring the Portrait from the Gospels.* 2nd ed. Grand Rapids: Baker, 2017.

Bolton, Samuel. *The True Bounds of Christian Freedom.* 1645. Reprint, Edinburgh: Banner of Truth, 1964.

Bonar, Andrew. *The Everlasting Righteousness or, How Shall Man Be Just with God?* 1874. Reprint, Edinburgh: Banner of Truth, 1993.

———. *Memoir and Remains of Robert Murray M'Cheyne.* Enlarged ed. 1892. Reprint, Edinburgh: Banner of Truth, 1966.

Borgman, Brian, and Rob Ventura. *Spiritual Warfare: A Biblical and Balanced Perspective.* Grand Rapids: Reformation Heritage, 2014.

Bridges, Jerry. *The Discipline of Grace: God's Role and Our Role in the Pursuit of Holiness.* Colorado Springs: NavPress, 1994.

———. *The Practice of Godliness.* Colorado Springs: NavPress, 1996.

Bridges, Jerry, and Bob Bevington. *The Great Exchange: My Sin for His Righteousness.* Wheaton: Crossway, 2007.

Briggs, Richard S. *Reading the Bible Wisely: An Introduction to Taking Scripture Seriously.* Rev. ed. Eugene, OR: Cascade, 2011.

Brown, Paul E. *The Holy Spirit & the Bible: The Spirit's Role in Relation to Biblical Hermeneutics.* Ross-shire, Great Britain: Christian Focus, 2002.

Brown, Jeannine K. *Scripture as Communication: Introducing Biblical Hermeneutics.* Grand Rapids: Baker, 2007.

Bruce, F. F. *The Epistle to the Hebrews.* NICNT. Grand Rapids: Eerdmans, 1990.

———. *The Gospel of John: Introduction, Exposition and Notes.* Grand Rapids: Eerdmans, 1983.

———. *Romans: An Introduction and Commentary.* 2nd ed. TNTC. Downers Grove: InterVarsity, 1985.

Buice, Josh, ed. *The New Calvinism: New Reformation or Theological Fad?* Ross-shire, Great Britain: Christian Focus, 2018.

Burdick, Donald W. *The Letters of John the Apostle: An In-Depth Commentary.* Chicago: Moody, 1985.

Caird, G. B. *The Language and Imagery of the Bible.* 1980. Reprint, Grand Rapids: Eerdmans, 1997.

Calabresi, Steven G., ed. *Originalism: A Quarter Century of Debate.* Washington, DC: Regnery, 2007.

Calvin, John. *Commentaries on the Epistle of Paul the Apostle to the Romans.* Translated by John Owen. Calvin's Commentaries, 500th Anniversary ed., 19/2:1–592. 1849. Reprint, Grand Rapids: Baker, 2009.

———. *Institutes of the Christian Religion*. 2 vols. Translated by Ford Lewis Battles. Edited by John T. McNeill. The Library of Christian Classics. Louisville: Westminster John Knox. 1960.

Capill, Murray. *The Heart Is the Target: Preaching Practical Application from Every Text*. Phillipsburg, NJ: Presbyterian & Reformed, 2014.

Campbell, Donald K., and Jeffrey L. Townsend. *A Case for Premillennialism: A New Consensus*. Chicago: Moody, 1992.

Carson, D. A. *The Difficult Doctrine of the Love of God*. Wheaton: Crossway, 2000.

———. *Exegetical Fallacies*. 2nd ed. Grand Rapids: Baker, 1996.

———. *The Farewell Discourse and Final Prayer of Jesus: An Exposition of John 14–17*. Grand Rapids: Baker, 1980.

———. *From Sabbath to Lord's Day: A Biblical, Historical, and Theological Investigation*. 1982. Reprint, Eugene, OR: Wipf & Stock, 1999.

———. *The Gospel according to John*. PNTC. Grand Rapids: Eerdmans, 1993.

———. "Matthew." In *The Expositor's Bible Commentary,* rev. ed. edited by Tremper Longman III and David E. Garland, 9:23–670. Grand Rapids: Zondervan, 2010.

———. *Praying with Paul: A Call to Spiritual Reformation*. 2nd ed. Grand Rapids: Baker, 2014.

Carson, D. A., and Douglas J. Moo. *An Introduction to the New Testament*. 2nd ed. Grand Rapids: Zondervan, 2005.

Carruthers, S. W., ed. *Westminster Confession of Faith*. Glasgow: Free Presbyterian Publications, 1995.

Casillas, Ken. *The Law and the Christian: God's Light within God's Limits*. Biblical Discernment for Difficult Issues. Greenville, SC: Bob Jones University Press, 2007.

Challies, Tim. *The Discipline of Spiritual Discernment*. Wheaton: Crossway, 2007.

Chalmers, Thomas. "The Expulsive Power of a New Affection." In *The Works of Thomas Chalmers: Complete in One Volume,* 81–88. Philadelphia: Towar & Hagan, 1830.

Chapell, Bryan. *Christ-Centered Preaching: Redeeming the Expository Sermon*. 2nd ed. Grand Rapids: Baker, 2005.

————. *Christ-Centered Worship: Letting the Gospel Shape Our Practice.* Grand Rapids: Baker, 2009.

————. *Holiness by Grace: Delighting in the Joy That Is Our Strength.* Wheaton: Crossway, 2001.

Ciampa, Roy E., and Brian S. Rosner. *The First Letter to the Corinthians.* PNTC. Grand Rapids: Eerdmans, 2010.

Clark, David K. *To Know and Love God: Method for Theology.* Foundations of Evangelical Theology. Wheaton: Crossway, 2003.

Clowney, Edmund. *The Message of 1 Peter.* BST. Leicester, England: InterVarsity, 1988.

CNN "Larry King Live" Transcript. 28 February 2008. http://transcripts.cnn.com/TRANSCRIPTS/0802/28/lkl.01.html.

Coleman, William L. *The Pharisees' Guide to Total Holiness.* Minneapolis: Bethany, 1982.

Collins, Brian C. "Scripture, Hermeneutics, and Theology: Evaluating Theological Interpretation of Scripture." PhD diss., Bob Jones University, 2011.

Colson, Charles, and Nancy Pearcey. *How Now Shall We Live?* Wheaton: Tyndale, 1999.

Compton, Jared M. "Shared Intentions? Reflections on Inspiration and Interpretation in Light of Scripture's Dual Authorship." *Themelios* 33 (2008) 23–33.

Conn, Harvie M., ed. *Inerrancy and Hermeneutic: A Tradition, a Challenge, a Debate.* Grand Rapids: Baker, 1988.

Corley, Bruce, Steve W. Lemke, and Grant I. Lovejoy, eds. *Biblical Hermeneutics: A Comprehensive Introduction to Interpreting Scripture.* 2nd ed. Nashville: B&H, 2002.

Copi, Irving M., Carl Cohen, and Kenneth McMahon. *Introduction to Logic.* 14th ed. New York: Pearson, 2010.

Cosgrove, Charles H. *Appealing to Scripture in Moral Debate: Five Hermeneutical Rules.* Grand Rapids: Eerdmans, 2002.

Cotterell, Peter, and Max Turner. *Linguistics and Biblical Interpretation.* Downers Grove, IL: InterVarsity, 1989.

Cottrell, Robert C. *Sex, Drugs, and Rock 'N' Roll: The Rise of America's 1960s Counterculture.* Lanham, MD: Rowman & Littlefield, 2015.

Craigie, Peter C. *The Book of Deuteronomy.* NICOT. Grand Rapids: Eerdmans, 1976.

Cranfield, C. E. B. *A Critical and Exegetical Commentary on the Epistle to the Romans.* 2 vols. ICC. Edinburgh: T. & T. Clark, 1975.

Culver, Robert Duncan. *Systematic Theology: Biblical and Historical.* Ross-shire, Great Britain: Christian Focus, 2005.

Danby, Herbert. *The Mishnah: Translated from the Hebrew with Introduction and Brief Explanatory Notes.* London: Oxford University Press, 1933.

Davis, Andrew M. *An Infinite Journey: Growing toward Christlikeness.* Greenville, SC: Ambassador International, 2014.

Davis, Dale Ralph. *1 Samuel: Looking on the Heart.* Focus on the Bible. Ross-shire, Great Britain: Christian Focus, 2000.

Davis, John Jefferson. *Evangelical Ethics: Issues Facing the Church Today.* 4th ed. Phillipsburg, NJ: Presbyterian and Reformed, 2015.

Decker, Rodney J. "The Church's Relationship to the New Covenant." *Bibliotheca Sacra* 152 (1995) 290–305, 431–56.

Demarest, Bruce. *The Cross and Salvation.* Foundations of Evangelical Theology. Wheaton: Crossway, 1997.

DeRouchie, Jason S. "Confronting the Transgender Storm: New Covenant Reflections on Deuteronomy 22:5." *JBMW* 21 (2016) 58–69.

———. *How to Understand and Apply the Old Testament: Twelve Steps from Exegesis to Theology.* Phillipsburg, NJ: Presbyterian & Reformed, 2017.

———. "The Profit of Employing the Biblical Languages: Scriptural and Historical Reflections." *Themelios* 37 (2012) 32–50.

DeYoung, Kevin. *The Hole in Our Holiness: Filling the Gap between Gospel Passion and the Pursuit of Godliness.* Wheaton: Crossway, 2012.

———. *What Does the Bible Really Teach about Homosexuality?* Wheaton: Crossway, 2015.

DeYoung, Kevin, and Greg Gilbert. *What Is the Mission of the Church? Making Sense of Social Justice, Shalom, and the Great Commission.* Wheaton: Crossway, 2011.

Dieter, Melvin E., et al. *Five Views on Sanctification.* Counterpoints Series. Grand Rapids: Zondervan, 1987.

Dickason, C. Fred. *Angels: Elect & Evil.* Rev. ed. Chicago: Moody, 1995.

Doriani, Daniel M. *Getting the Message: A Plan for Interpreting and Applying the Bible*. Phillipsburg, NJ: Presbyterian & Reformed, 1996.

———. *Putting the Truth to Work: The Theory and Practice of Biblical Application*. Phillipsburg, NJ: Presbyterian & Reformed, 2001.

Dunn, James D. G. *Romans 1–8*. WBC. Dallas: Word, 1988.

Dutcher, Greg. *Killing Calvinism: How to Destroy a Perfectly Good Theology from the Inside*. N.p.: Cruciform, 2012.

Duvall, J. Scott, and J. Daniel Hays. *Grasping God's Word: A Hands-On Approach to Reading, Interpreting, and Applying the Bible*. 2nd ed. Grand Rapids: Zondervan, 2005.

Dyer, John. *From the Garden to the City: The Redeeming and Corrupting Power of Technology*. Grand Rapids: Kregel, 2011.

Edwards, James R. *The Gospel according to Mark*. PNTC. Grand Rapids: Eerdmans, 2002.

Edwards, Jonathan. *A Treatise concerning Religious Affections*. Edited by John E. Smith. The Works of Jonathan Edwards. New Haven: Yale University Press, 1959.

Ellingworth, Paul. *The Epistle to the Hebrews: A Commentary on the Greek Text*. NIGTC. Grand Rapids: Eerdmans, 1993.

Emlet, Michael R. *CrossTalk: Where Life & Scripture Meet*. Greensboro, NC: New Growth, 2009.

Erickson, Millard J. *Evangelical Interpretation: Perspectives on Hermeneutical Issues*. Grand Rapids: Baker, 1993.

Estes, Daniel J. "Audience Analysis and Validity in Application." *Bibliotheca Sacra* 150 (1993) 219–29.

Evans, John. *A Guide to Biblical Commentaries and Reference Works*. 10th ed. Grand Rapids: Zondervan, 2016.

Fabarez, Michael. *Preaching That Changes Lives*. Nashville: Nelson, 2002.

Fee, Gordon D. *The First Epistle to the Corinthians*. Rev. ed. NICNT. Grand Rapids: Eerdmans.

Fee, Gordon D., and Douglas Stuart. *How to Read the Bible for All Its Worth*. 4th ed. Grand Rapids: Zondervan, 2014.

Feinberg, John S., and Paul D. Feinberg. *Ethics for a Brave New World*. Wheaton: Crossway, 1993.

Ferguson, Everett. *Backgrounds of Early Christianity*. 2nd ed. Grand Rapids: Eerdmans, 1993.

Ferguson, Sinclair B. *The Christian Life: A Doctrinal Introduction.* Edinburgh: Banner of Truth, 1981.

———. *Devoted to God: Blueprints for Sanctification.* Edinburgh: Banner of Truth, 2016.

———. *From the Mouth of God: Trusting, Reading, and Applying the Bible.* Rev. ed. Edinburgh: Banner of Truth, 2014.

———. *The Holy Spirit.* Contours of Christian Theology. Downers Grove, IL: InterVarsity, 1996.

———. *The Whole Christ: Legalism, Antinomianism, and Gospel Assurance—Why the Marrow Controversy Still Matters.* Wheaton: Crossway, 2016.

Flavel, John. *Keeping the Heart.* 1667. Reprint, Morgan, PA: Soli Deo Gloria, 1998.

Flusser, David. *Judaism and the Origins of Christianity.* Edited by Brad Young. Jerusalem: Magnes, 1988.

Frame, John M. *The Doctrine of the Christian Life.* A Theology of Lordship. Phillipsburg, NJ: Presbyterian & Reformed, 2008.

———. *The Doctrine of the Knowledge of God.* A Theology of Lordship. Phillipsburg, NJ: Presbyterian & Reformed, 1987.

———. *The Doctrine of the Word of God.* A Theology of Lordship. Phillipsburg, NJ: Presbyterian & Reformed, 2010.

France, R. T. *The Gospel according to Matthew: An Introduction and Commentary.* TNTC. Leicester, England: InterVarsity, 1985.

Friedlander, Paul. *Rock & Roll: A Social History.* 2nd ed. Cambridge, MA: Westview, 2006.

Fung, Ronald Y. K. *The Epistles to the Galatians.* NICNT. Grand Rapids: Eerdmans, 1988.

Gagnon, Robert A. J. *The Bible and Homosexual Practice: Texts and Hermeneutics.* Nashville: Abingdon, 2001.

Garland, David E. *1 Corinthians.* BECNT. Grand Rapids: Baker, 2003.

———. *2 Corinthians.* NAC. Nashville: B&H, 1999.

———. *The NIV Application Commentary: Mark.* Grand Rapids: Zondervan, 1996.

Garrett, Duane A. *Hosea, Joel.* NAC. Nashville: B&H, 1997.

Geisler, Norman L. *Christian Ethics: Contemporary Issues and Options.* 2nd ed. Grand Rapids: Baker, 2010.

Geertz, Clifford. *The Interpretation of Cultures.* New York: Basic, 1973

Gillespie, George. *A Treatise of Miscellany Questions.* Edinburgh: University of Edinburgh, 1649.

Glenny, W. Edward. "The Divine Meaning of Scripture: Explanations and Limitations." *The Journal of the Evangelical Theological Society* 38 (1995) 481–500.

———. "Typology: A Summary of the Present Evangelical Discussion." *JETS* 40 (1997) 627–38.

Goldman, Lawrence, ed. *The Federalist Papers.* Oxford World's Classics. Oxford: Oxford University Press, 2008.

Goldsworthy, Graeme. *According to Plan: The Unfolding Revelation of God in the Bible.* Downers Grove, IL: InterVarsity, 1991.

———. *The Goldsworthy Trilogy.* Milton Keynes, England: Paternoster, 2000.

———. *Gospel-Centered Hermeneutics: Foundations and Principles of Evangelical Biblical Interpretation.* Downers Grove, IL: InterVarsity 2006.

Gordon, T. David. *Why Johnny Can't Sing Hymns: How Pop Culture Rewrote the Hymnal.* Phillipsburg, NJ: Presbyterian & Reformed, 2010.

Greidanus, Sidney. *The Modern Preacher and the Ancient Text: Interpreting and Preaching Biblical Literature.* Grand Rapids: Eerdmans, 1988.

Green, Bradley G. *Covenant and Commandment: Works, Obedience and Faithfulness in the Christian Life.* NSBT. Downers Grove, IL: InterVarsity, 2014.

Green, Gene L. *The Letters to the Thessalonians.* PNTC. Grand Rapids: Eerdmans, 2002.

Grudem, Wayne. *1 Peter: An Introduction and Commentary.* TNTC. Leicester, England: InterVarsity, 1988.

———. *Evangelical Feminism and Biblical Truth: An Analysis of More Than 100 Disputed Questions.* Colorado Springs: Multnomah, 2004.

———. *Politics—according to the Bible: A Comprehensive Resource for Understanding Modern Political Issues in Light of Scripture.* Grand Rapids: Zondervan, 2010.

———. *Systematic Theology: An Introduction to Biblical Doctrine.* Grand Rapids: Zondervan, 1994.

Guthrie, Donald. *The Pastoral Epistles: An Introduction and Commentary.* TNTC. Leicester, England: InterVarsity, 1957.

Guthrie, George H. *Read the Bible for Life: Your Guide to Understanding & Living God's Word.* Nashville: B&H, 2011.

Hafeman, Scott J. *The NIV Application Commentary: 2 Corinthians.* Grand Rapids: Zondervan, 2000.

Hagner, Donald A. *Matthew 1–13.* WBC. Dallas: Word, 1993.

Haldane, Robert. *Commentary on Romans.* 1853. Reprint, Grand Rapids: Kregel, 1988.

Hand, Brian. *Upright Downtime: Making Wise Choices about Entertainment.* Biblical Discernment for Difficult Issues. Greenville, SC: Bob Jones University Press, 2008.

Hansen, Collin. *Young, Restless, Reformed: A Journalist's Journey with the New Calvinists.* Wheaton: Crossway, 2008.

Harrison, R. K. *Leviticus: An Introduction and Commentary.* TOTC. Leicester, England: InterVarsity, 1980.

Hays, J. Daniel. *From Every People and Nation: A Biblical Theology of Race.* NSBT. Downers Grove, IL: InterVarsity, 2003.

Hays, Richard B. *The Moral Vision of the New Testament: A Contemporary Introduction to New Testament Ethics.* London: T & T Clark, 1997.

Hays, Richard B., Stefan Alkier, and Leroy A. Huizenga, eds. *Reading the Bible Intertextually.* Waco, TX: Baylor University Press, 2009.

Helm, Paul. *The Callings: The Gospel in the World.* Edinburgh: Banner of Truth, 1987.

Hendricks, Howard G., and William D. Hendricks. *Living by the Book: The Art and Science of Reading the Bible.* Rev. ed. Chicago: Moody, 2007.

Henrichsen, Walter, and Gayle Jackson. *Studying, Interpreting, and Applying the Bible.* Grand Rapids: Zondervan, 1990.

Hill, Michael. *The How and Why of Love: An Introduction to Evangelical Ethics.* Kingsford, NSW, Australia: Matthias, 2002.

Hirsch, E. D. Jr. *The Aims of Interpretation.* Chicago: University of Chicago, 1976.

———. *Validity in Interpretation.* New Haven: Yale University Press, 1967.

Hodge, Charles. *A Commentary on Ephesians.* GSC. 1856. Reprint, Edinburgh: Banner of Truth, 1964.

———. *A Commentary on Romans.* Rev. ed. GSC. 1864. Reprint, Edinburgh: Banner of Truth, 1972.

Hoehner, Harold W. *Ephesians: An Exegetical Commentary.* Grand Rapids: Baker, 2002.

Hoekema, Anthony A. *Created in God's Image.* Grand Rapids: Eerdmans, 1986.

———. *Saved By Grace.* Grand Rapids: Eerdmans, 1989.

Holmes, Arthur F. *Ethics: Approaching Moral Decisions.* 2nd ed. Contours of Christian Philosophy. Downers Grove, IL: InterVarsity, 2007.

Horn, Samuel E. "A Biblical Theology of Christian Liberty: An Analysis of the Major Pauline Passages in Galatians, Colossians, I Corinthians, and Romans." PhD diss., Bob Jones University, 1995.

Huffman, Douglas S. *The Handy Guide to New Testament Greek: Grammar, Syntax, and Diagramming.* Grand Rapids: Kregel, 2012.

Hughes, Philip E. *The Second Epistle to the Corinthians.* NICNT. Grand Rapids: Eerdmans, 1962.

Hughes, R. Kent. *Set Apart: Calling a Worldly Church to a Godly Life.* Wheaton: Crossway, 2003.

Jaeggli, Randy. *Christians and Alcohol: A Scriptural Case for Abstinence.* Biblical Discernment for Difficult Issues. Greenville, SC: Bob Jones University Press, 2014.

———. *Love, Liberty, and Christian Conscience.* Biblical Discernment for Difficult Issues. Greenville, SC: Bob Jones University Press, 2007.

———. *More Like the Master: Reflecting the Image of God.* Greenville, SC: Ambassador-Emerald, 2004.

Jewell, Elizabeth J., and Frank Abate, eds. *The Oxford American Dictionary.* New York: Oxford University Press, 2001.

Johnson, Elliott E. "Dual Authorship and the Single Intended Meaning of Scripture." *BSac* 143 (1986): 218–27.

———. *Expository Hermeneutics: An Introduction.* Grand Rapids: Zondervan, 1990.

Johnson, Julian. *Who Needs Classical Music? Cultural Choice and Musical Value.* New York: Oxford University Press, 2002.

Johnson, Marcus Peter. *One with Christ: An Evangelical Theology of Salvation*. Wheaton: Crossway, 2013.

Jones, Mark. *Antinomianism: Reformed Theology's Unwelcome Guest?* Phillipsburg, NJ: Presbyterian & Reformed, 2013.

Kaiser, Walter C. Jr. *The Promise-Plan of God: A Biblical Theology of the Old and New Testaments*. Grand Rapids: Zondervan, 2008.

————. *Toward an Exegetical Theology: Biblical Exegesis for Preaching and Teaching*. Grand Rapids: Baker, 1981.

————. *What Does the Lord Require? A Guide for Preaching and Teaching Biblical Ethics*. Grand Rapids: Baker, 2009.

Kaiser, Walter C. Jr., and Moisés Silva. *Introduction to Biblical Hermeneutics: The Search for Meaning*. Rev. ed. Grand Rapids: Zondervan, 2007.

Kamien, Roger, with Anita Kamie. *Music: An Appreciation*. 7th brief ed. New York: McGraw-Hill, 2011.

Keener, Craig S. *The Gospel according to Matthew: A Socio-Rhetorical Commentary*. Grand Rapids: Eerdmans, 2009.

Keller, Timothy. *Every Good Endeavor: Connecting Your Work to God's Work*. New York: Dutton, 2012.

Kevan, Ernest. *The Grace of Law: A Study in Puritan Theology*. 1963. Reprint, Morgan, PA: Soli Deo Gloria, 1993.

Kistler, Don, ed. *Law and Liberty: A Biblical Look at Legalism*. Orlando: Northampton, 2013.

Klein, William W., Craig L. Blomberg, and Robert L. Hubbard Jr. *Introduction to Biblical Interpretation*. 3rd ed. Grand Rapids: Zondervan, 2017.

Knight, George W. III. *The Pastoral Epistles: A Commentary on the Greek Text*. NIGTC. Grand Rapids: Eerdmans, 1992.

Koehler, Ludwig, and Walter Baumgartner. *The Hebrew and Aramaic Lexicon of the Old Testament*. Study ed. Revised by Walter Baumgartner and Johann Jakob Stamm. Translated by M. E. J. Richardson. Leiden: Brill, 2001.

Kohlenberger, John R. III. *Zondervan NIV Nave's Topical Bible*. Premier Reference Series. Grand Rapids: Zondervan, 1999.

Kohler, Ludwig, and Walter Baumgartner. *The Hebrew and Aramaic Lexicon of the Old Testament*. Study ed. Revised by Walter Baumgartner and Johann Jakob Stamm. Translated by M. E. J. Richardson. Leiden: Brill, 2001.

Köstenberger, Andreas J., and Richard D. Patterson. *Invitation to Biblical Interpretation: Exploring the Hermeneutical Triad of History, Literature, and Theology*. Invitation to Theological Studies Series. Grand Rapids: Kregel, 2011.

Kruger, Michael J. *Canon Revisited: Establishing the Origins and Authority of the New Testament Books*. Wheaton: Crossway, 2012.

Kruse, Colin G. *John: An Introduction and Commentary*. TNTC. Grand Rapids: Eerdmans, 2004.

———. *The Letters of John*. PNTC. Grand Rapids: Eerdmans, 2000.

———. *Paul's Letter to the Romans*. PNTC. Grand Rapids: Eerdmans, 2012.

Kuhatschek, Jack. *Applying the Bible*. Grand Rapids: Zondervan, 1990.

Kuruvilla, Abraham. *Privilege the Text! A Theological Hermeneutic for Preaching*. Chicago: Moody, 2013.

———. *Text to Praxis: Hermeneutics and Homiletics in Dialogue*. Library of New Testament Studies. London: T&T Clark International, 2009.

Lane, Eric. *Members of One of Another*. London: Evangelical, 1968.

———. *Psalms 1–89: The Lord Saves*. Focus on the Bible Series. Rossshire, Great Britain: Christian Focus, 2006.

Lane, Timothy S., and Paul David Tripp. *How People Change*. 2nd ed. Greensboro, NC: New Growth, 2008.

Lane, William L. *The Gospel according to Mark: The English Text with Introduction, Exposition and Notes*. NICNT. Grand Rapids: Eerdmans, 1974.

———. *Hebrews 1–8*. WBC. Nashville: Word, 1991.

Larson, Craig Brian. *Interpretation and Application*. The Preacher's Toolbox. Peabody, MA: Hendrickson, 2012.

Leedy, Randy. *Love Not the World: Winning the War against Worldliness*. Biblical Discernment for Difficult Issues. Greenville, SC: Bob Jones University Press, 2012.

Leeman, Jonathan. *The Church and the Surprising Offense of God's Love: Reintroducing the Doctrines of Church Membership and Discipline*. 9Marks. Wheaton: Crossway, 2010.

———. *Church Membership: How the World Knows Who Represents Jesus*. 9Marks Building Healthy Churches Series. Wheaton: Crossway, 2012.

Leggett, Donald A. *The Levirate and Gō'ēl Institutions in the Old Testament with Special Attention to the Book of Ruth.* Cherry Hill, NJ: Mack, 1974.

Lenski, R. C. H. *The Interpretation of St. Paul's Epistle to the Romans.* Commentary on the New Testament. 1936. Reprint, Peabody, MA: Hendrickson, 1998.

Letham, Robert. *Union with Christ in Scripture, History, and Theology.* Phillipsburg, NJ: Presbyterian & Reformed, 2011.

Lloyd-Jones, D. Martyn. *Romans, An Exposition of Chapter 6: The New Man.* Edinburgh: Banner, of Truth, 1972.

Longman, Tremper III. *Reading the Bible with Heart and Mind.* Colorado Springs: NavPress, 1997.

Lundgaard, Kris. *The Enemy Within: Straight Talk about the Power and Defeat of Sin.* Phillipsburg, NJ: Presbyterian & Reformed, 1998.

Luther, Martin. "Luther at the Diet of Worms, 1521." Translated by Roger A. Hornsby. In *Luther's Works, American Edition, Volume 32: Career of the Reformer II,* edited by George W. Forrell and Helmut T. Lehmann, 101–31. Philadelphia: Muhlenberg, 1958.

MacArthur, John, et al. *Right Thinking in a World Gone Wrong.* Eugene, OR: Harvest House, 2009.

MacArthur, John F. Jr. *The Vanishing Conscience.* Dallas: Word, 1994.

Mack, Wayne A., and Dave Swavely. *Life in the Father's House: A Member's Guide to the Local Church.* Rev. ed. Phillipsburg, NJ: Presbyterian & Reformed, 2006.

Makujina, John. *Measuring the Music: Another Look at the Contemporary Christian Music Debate.* 3rd ed. N.p.: Religious Affections, 2016.

Marsden, George M. *Reforming Fundamentalism: Fuller Seminary and the New Evangelicalism.* Grand Rapids: Eerdmans, 1987.

Marshall, I. Howard, with Kevin J. Vanhoozer and Stanley E. Porter. *Beyond the Bible: Moving from Scripture to Theology.* Grand Rapids: Baker, 2004.

Marshall, Walter. *The Gospel Mystery of Sanctification.* 1692. Reprint, Grand Rapids: Reformation Heritage, 1999.

Mathis, David. *Habits of Grace: Enjoying Jesus through the Spiritual Disciplines.* Wheaton: Crossway, 2016.

McCartney, Dan, and Charles Clayton. *Let the Reader Understand: A Guide to Interpreting and Applying the Bible.* 2nd ed. Phillipsburg, NJ: Presbyterian and Reformed, 2002.

McConville, J. G. *Deuteronomy.* AOTC. Leicester, Apollos, 2002.

McCracken, Brett. *Gray Areas: Navigating the Space between Legalism & Liberty.* Grand Rapids: Baker, 2013.

McCune, Rolland. *A Systematic Theology of Biblical Christianity, Volume 1: Prolegomena and the Doctrines of Scripture, God, and Angels.* Detroit: Detroit Baptist Theological Seminary, 2008.

————. *A Systematic Theology of Biblical Christianity, Volume 3: The Doctrines of Salvation, the Church, and Last Things.* Detroit: Detroit Baptist Theological Seminary, 2010.

McDermott, Gerald R. *The New Christian Zionism: Fresh Perspectives on Israel and the Land.* Downers Grove, IL: InterVarsity, 2016.

McGraw, Ryan M. *By Good and Necessary Consequence.* Explorations in Reformed Confessional Theology. Grand Rapids: Reformation Heritage, 2012.

McKinley, David J. "John Owen's View of Illumination: An Alternative to the Fuller-Erickson Dialogue." *BSac* 154 (1997) 93–104.

McLuhan, Marshall. *Understanding Media: The Extensions of Man.* Critical ed. Berkeley, CA: Gingko, 2013.

McQuilkin, Robertson. *Understanding and Applying the Bible.* Rev. ed. Chicago: Moody, 2009.

McQuilkin, Robertson, and Paul Copan. *An Introduction to Biblical Ethics: Walking in the Way of Wisdom.* 3rd ed. Downers Grove, IL: InterVarsity, 2014.

Meadors, Gary T., ed. *Four Views on Moving beyond the Bible to Theology.* Counterpoints: Bible & Theology. Grand Rapids: Zondervan, 2009.

Melick, Richard R. *Philippians, Colossians, Philemon.* NAC. Nashville: B&H, 1991.

Mickelsen, A. Berkeley. *Interpreting the Bible.* Grand Rapids: Eerdmans, 1963.

Mitchell, C. Ben. *Ethics and Moral Reasoning: A Student's Guide.* Reclaiming the Christian Intellectual Tradition. Wheaton: Crossway, 2013.

BIBLIOGRAPHY

Montgomery, John Warwick, ed. *God's Inerrant Word: An International Symposium on the Trustworthiness of Scripture.* Minneapolis: Bethany, 1974.

Moo, Douglas J. *Encountering the Book of Romans: A Theological Survey.* 2nd ed. Encountering Biblical Studies. Grand Rapids: Baker, 2014.

———. *The Epistle to the Galatians.* BECNT. Grand Rapids: Baker, 2013.

———. *The Epistle to the Romans.* NICNT. Grand Rapids: Eerdmans, 1996.

———. *The Letters to the Colossians and to Philemon.* PNTC. Grand Rapids: Eerdmans, 2008.

Morris, Leon. *1 Corinthians: An Introduction and Commentary.* Rev. ed. TNTC. Leicester, England: InterVarsity, 1985.

———. *The Epistle to the Romans.* PNTC. Grand Rapids: Eerdmans, 1988.

Motyer, J. Alec. *The Prophecy of Isaiah: An Introduction and Commentary.* Downers Grove, IL: InterVarsity, 1993.

Mounce, William D. *Pastoral Epistles.* WBC. Nashville: Thomas Nelson, 2000.

Müller, George. *The Life of Trust: Being a Narrative of the Lord's Dealings with George Müller Written by Himself.* Final ed. Boston: Crowell, 1898.

Muller, Richard A. *Dictionary of Latin and Greek Theological Terms.* Grand Rapids: Baker, 1985.

Muller, Richard A., and Rowland S. Ward. *Scripture and Worship: Biblical Interpretation and the Directory for Public Worship.* The Westminster Assembly and the Reformed Faith: A Series. Phillipsburg, NJ: Presbyterian & Reformed, 2007.

Munson, Paul, and Joshua Farris Drake. *Art and Music: A Student's Guide.* Reclaiming the Christian Intellectual Tradition. Wheaton: Crossway, 2014.

Murray, Iain. H. *Evangelicalism Divided: A Record of Crucial Change in the Years 1950 to 2000.* Edinburgh: Banner of Truth, 2000.

Murray, John. *Collected Writings of John Murray, Volume 2, Select Lectures in Systematic Theology.* Edinburgh: Banner of Truth, 1977.

———. *Divorce.* Philadelphia: Presbyterian & Reformed, 1976.

313

———. *The Epistle to the Romans: The English Text with Introduction, Exposition and Notes.* Grand Rapids: Eerdmans, 1959.

———. *Principles of Conduct: Aspects of Biblical Ethics.* Grand Rapids: Eerdmans, 1957.

———. *Redemption—Accomplished and Applied.* Grand Rapids: Eerdmans, 1955.

Myers, Ken. *All God's Children and Blue Suede Shoes: Christians and Popular Culture.* Wheaton: Crossway, 1989, 2012.

Naselli, Andrew David. *No Quick Fix: Where Higher Life Theology Came from, What It Is, and Why It's Harmful.* Bellingham, WA: Lexham, 2017.

———. *How to Understand and Apply the New Testament: Twelve Steps from Exegesis to Theology.* Phillipsburg, NJ: Presbyterian & Reformed, 2017.

Naselli, Andrew David, and Collin Hansen, eds. *Four Views on the Spectrum of Evangelicalism.* Counterpoints: Bible & Theology. Grand Rapids: Zondervan, 2011.

Naselli, Andrew David, and J. D. Crowley. *Conscience: What It Is, How to Train it, and Loving Those Who Differ.* Wheaton: Crossway, 2016.

Naudé, Jackie A. "קדֹשׁ." In *NIDOTTE,* 3:877–87.

Newheiser, Jim. *Marriage, Divorce, and Remarriage: Critical Questions and Answers.* Phillipsburg, NJ: Presbyterian & Reformed, 2017.

Newman, Louis E. *Past Imperatives: Studies in the History and Theory of Jewish Ethics.* Suny Series in Jewish Philosophy. Albany: State University of New York Press, 1998.

Nicole, Roger. "The New Testament Use of the Old Testament." In *Revelation and the Bible: Contemporary Evangelical Thought,* edited by Carl F. H. Henry, 135–51. Grand Rapids: Baker, 1958.

Nicole, Roger R., and J. Ramsey Michaels, eds. *Inerrancy and Common Sense.* Grand Rapids: Baker, 1980.

Niehaus, Jeffrey. "Amos." In *The Minor Prophets: An Exegetical and Expository Commentary,* edited by Thomas Edward McKomiskey, 1:315–494. Grand Rapids: Baker, 1992.

Nolland, John. *The Gospel of Matthew: A Commentary on the Greek Text.* NIGTC. Grand Rapids: Eerdmans, 2005.

O'Donnell, Douglas Sean. *God's Lyrics: Rediscovering Worship through Old Testament Songs*. Phillipsburg, NJ: Presbyterian & Reformed, 2010.

Osborne, Grant R. *The Hermeneutical Spiral: A Comprehensive Introduction to Biblical Interpretation*. Rev. ed. Downers Grove, IL: InterVarsity, 2006.

Oswalt, John N. *The Book of Isaiah, Chapters 40–66*. NICOT. Grand Rapids: Eerdmans, 1998.

Owen, John. *Overcoming Sin and Temptation*. Edited by Kelly M. Kapic and Justin Taylor. Wheaton: Crossway, 2006.

———. ΠΝΕΥΜΑΤΟΛΟΓΙΑ *or, A Discourse Concerning the Holy Spirit* (1674-1692). Vols. 3 and 4 of *The Works of John Owen*, edited by William H. Goold. 1850-53. Reprint, London: Banner of Truth, 1966-1967.

Packer, J. I. *Concise Theology: A Guide to Historic Christian Beliefs*. Carol Stream, IL: Tyndale, 1993.

———. "Hermeneutics and Biblical Authority." *Themelios* 1 (1975) 3-12.

———. *Keep in Step with the Spirit: Finding Fullness in Our Walk with God*. Rev. ed. Grand Rapids: Baker, 2005.

———. *A Quest for Godliness: The Puritan Vision of the Christian Life*. Wheaton: Crossway, 1990.

———. *Rediscovering Holiness*. Ann Arbor: Servant, 1992.

———. *Truth and Power: The Place of Scripture in the Christian Life*. Wheaton: Harold Shaw, 1996.

Patterson, Richard D. "Psalm 22: From Trial to Triumph." *JETS* 47 (2004) 213–33.

Paulsen, Michael Stokes, and Luke Paulsen. *The Constitution: An Introduction*. New York: Basic, 2015.

Payne, J. Barton. *The Theology of the Older Testament*. Grand Rapids: Zondervan, 1962.

Peace, Martha, and Kent Keller. *Modesty: More Than a Change of Clothes*. Phillipsburg, NJ: Presbyterian & Reformed, 2015.

Pearcey, Nancy. *Total Truth: Liberating Christianity from Its Cultural Captivity*. Study guide ed. Wheaton: Crossway, 2005.

Pelikan, Jaroslav. *Interpreting the Bible and the Constitution*. A John W. Kluge Center Book. New Have: Yale University Press, 2004.

Peterson, David. *Engaging with God: A Biblical Theology of Worship.* Downers Grove, IL: InterVarsity, 1992.

———. *Possessed by God: A New Testament Theology of Sanctification and Holiness.* NSBT. Downers Grove, IL: InterVarsity, 1995.

Pickering, Ernest, with Myron Houghton. *Biblical Separation: The Struggle for a Pure Church.* 2nd ed. Schaumburg, IL: Regular Baptist, 2008.

Pipa, Joseph, and J. Andrew Wortman, eds. *Written for Our Instruction: The Sufficiency of Scripture for All of Life.* Taylors, SC: Southern Presbyterian, 2001.

Piper, John. *Reading the Bible Supernaturally: Seeing and Savoring the Glory of God in Scripture.* Wheaton: Crossway, 2017.

Piper, John, and David Mathis, eds. *Act the Miracle: God's Work and Ours in the Mystery of Sanctification.* Wheaton: Crossway, 2013.

Plummer, Robert L. *40 Questions about Interpreting the Bible.* 40 Questions Series. Grand Rapids: Kregel, 2010.

Porter, Stanley E., and Beth M. Stovell, eds. *Biblical Hermeneutics: Five Views.* Downers Grove, IL: InterVarsity, 2012.

Postman, Neil. *Amusing Ourselves to Death: Public Discourage in the Age of Show Business.* 20th anniversary ed. New York: Penguin, 2005.

Powlison, David. *How Does Sanctification Work?* Wheaton: Crossway, 2017.

———. *Seeing with New Eyes: Counseling and the Human Condition through the Lens of Scripture.* Phillipsburg, NJ: Presbyterian & Reformed, 2003.

Poythress, Vern S. *God-Centered Biblical Interpretation.* Phillipsburg, NJ: Presbyterian and Reformed, 1999.

———. *Logic: A God-Centered Approach to the Foundation of Western Thought.* Wheaton: Crossway, 2013.

———. *The Shadow of Christ in the Law of Moses.* Phillipsburg, NJ: Presbyterian & Reformed, 1991.

Pratt, Richard L. Jr. *He Gave Us Stories: The Bible Student's Guide to Interpreting Old Testament Narratives.* Phillipsburg, NJ: Presbyterian & Reformed, 1990.

Radmacher, Earl D., and Robert D. Preus, eds. *Hermeneutics, Inerrancy, and the Bible.* Grand Rapids: Zondervan, 1984.

Rae, Scott B. *Moral Choices: An Introduction to Ethics.* 3rd ed. Grand Rapids: Zondervan, 2009.

Ralston, Timothy J. "Showing the Relevance: Application, Ethics, and Preaching." In *Interpreting the New Testament Text: Introduction to the Art and Science of Exegesis,* edited by Darrell L. Bock and Buist M. Fanning, 293–310. Wheaton: Crossway, 2006.

Reaoch, Benjamin. *Women, Slaves, and the Gender Debate: A Complementarian Response to the Redemptive-Movement Hermeneutic.* Phillipsburg, NJ: Presbyterian & Reformed, 2012.

Reimers, Gary. *The Glory Due His Name: What God Says about Worship.* Biblical Discernment for Difficult Issues. Greenville, SC: Bob Jones University Press, 2009.

Reymond, Robert L. *A New Systematic Theology of the Christian Faith.* Nashville: Thomas Nelson, 1998.

Richard, Ramesh. "Methodological Proposals for Scripture Relevance." *BSac* 143 (1986) 14–25, 123–33, 205–17, 302–13.

———. *Preparing Expository Sermons: A Seven-Step Method for Biblical Preaching.* Grand Rapids: Baker, 2001.

Roberts, Vaughan. *God's Big Picture: Tracing the Storyline of the Bible.* Downers Grove, IL: InterVarsity, 2002.

Robinson, Haddon W. *Biblical Preaching: The Development and Delivery of Expository Messages.* 3rd ed. Grand Rapids: Baker, 2014.

Robinson, Haddon W., and Craig Brian Larson, eds. *The Art and Craft of Biblical Preaching.* Grand Rapids: Zondervan, 2005.

Rooker, Mark F. *Leviticus.* NAC. Nashville: B&H, 2000.

Ross, Allen P. *A Commentary on the Psalms: Volume 1 (1–41).* Kregel Exegetical Library. Grand Rapids: Kregel, 2011.

———. *Holiness to the LORD: A Guide to the Exposition of the Book of Leviticus.* Grand Rapids: Baker, 2002.

———. *Recalling the Hope of Glory: Biblical Worship from the Garden to the New Creation.* Grand Rapids: Kregel, 2006.

Ryken, Leland. *Redeeming the Time: A Christian Approach to Work and Leisure.* Grand Rapids: Baker, 1995.

Ryken, Philip Graham. *Christian Worldview: A Student's Guide.* Reclaiming the Christian Intellectual Tradition. Wheaton: Crossway, 2013.

Ryle, J. C. *Holiness: Its Nature, Hindrances, Difficulties, and Roots.* Enlarged ed. 1879. Reprint, Darlington, England: Evangelical Press, 1979.

Sanders, Fred. *The Deep Things of God: How the Trinity Changes Everything.* 2nd ed. Wheaton: Crossway, 2017.

Satterthwaite, Philip E., and David F. Wright, eds. *A Pathway into the Holy Scripture.* Grand Rapids: Eerdmans, 1994.

Saucy, Robert L. *Minding the Heart: The Way of Spiritual Transformation.* Grand Rapids: Kregel, 2013.

Scalia, Antonin. *A Matter of Interpretation: Federal Courts and the Law.* Edited by Amy Gutmann. Princeton, NJ: Princeton University Press, 1997.

Scalia, Antonin, and Bryan A. Garner. *Reading Law: The Interpretation of Legal Texts.* St. Paul: Thomson/West, 2012.

Schaff, Philip. *The Creeds of Christendom, with a History and Critical Notes.* Revised by David S. Schaff. Vol. 3. 1931. Reprint, Grand Rapids: Baker, 2007.

Scharf, Greg R. *Let the Earth Hear His Voice: Strategies for Overcoming Bottlenecks in Preaching God's Word.* Phillipsburg, NJ: Presbyterian & Reformed, 2015.

Schnittjer, Gary Edward. *The Torah Story: An Apprenticeship on the Pentateuch.* Grand Rapids: Zondervan, 2006.

Schreiner, Thomas R. *1, 2 Peter, Jude.* NAC. Nashville: B&H, 2003.

———. *Faith Alone—The Doctrine of Justification: What the Reformers Taught . . . and Why It Still Matters.* The Five Solas Series. Grand Rapids: Zondervan, 2015.

———. *Galatians.* ZECNT. Grand Rapids: Zondervan, 2010.

———. *Paul, Apostle of God's Glory in Christ: A Pauline Theology.* Downers Grove, IL: InterVarsity, 2001.

———. *Romans.* BECNT. Grand Rapids: Baker, 1998.

Schultz, Richard L. *Out of Context: How to Avoid Misinterpreting the Bible.* Grand Rapids: Baker, 2012.

Selvaggio, Anthony T., ed. *The Faith Once Delivered: Essays in Honor of Wayne R. Spear.* The Westminster Assembly and the Reformed Faith: A Series. Phillipsburg, NJ: Presbyterian & Reformed, 2007.

Sidwell, Mark. *Set Apart: The Nature and Importance of Biblical Separation.* Greenville, SC: Bob Jones University Press, 2016.

Sigal, Phillip. *The Halakhah of Jesus of Nazareth according to the Gospel of Matthew.* Studies in Biblical Literature. 1986. Reprint, Atlanta: Society of Biblical Literature, 2007.

Silva, Moisés. *God, Language, and Scripture.* Foundations of Contemporary Interpretation, vol. 4. Grand Rapids: Zondervan, 1990.

———. *Philippians.* 2nd ed. BECNT. Grand Rapids: Baker, 2005.

Simpson, J. A., and E. S. C. Weiner, eds. *The Oxford English Dictionary.* 20 vols. Oxford: Oxford University Press, 1989.

Sire, James W. *Scripture Twisting: 20 Ways the Cults Misread the Bible.* Downers Grove, IL: InterVarsity, 1980.

———. *The Universe Next Door: A Basic Worldview Catalog.* 5th ed. Downers Grove, InterVarsity, 2009.

Smith, Billy K., and Frank S. Page. *Amos, Obadiah, Jonah.* NAC. Nashville: B&H, 1995.

Smith, C. Fred. *Developing a Biblical Worldview: Seeing Things God's Way.* Nashville: B&H, 2015.

Smith, Scotty. *Everyday Prayers: 365 Days to a Gospel-Centered Faith.* Grand Rapids: Baker, 2011.

Snoeberger, Mark A. "Weakness or Wisdom? Fundamentalists and Romans 14.1—15.13." *Detroit Baptist Seminary Journal* 12 (2007) 29–49.

Spinney, Robert G. *Are You Legalistic? Grace, Obedience, and Antinomianism.* Hartsville, TN: Tulip, 2007.

Sproul, R. C. *Knowing Scripture.* Rev. ed. Downers Grove, IL: InterVarsity, 2009.

Stein, Robert H. *A Basic Guide to Interpreting the Bible: Playing by the Rules.* 2nd ed. Grand Rapids: Baker, 2011.

Sterrett, T. Norton, and Richard L. Schultz. *How to Understand Your Bible.* 3rd ed. Downers Grove, IL: InterVarsity, 2010.

Stonehouse, N. B., and Paul Woolley, eds. *The Infallible Word: A Symposium by the Members of the Faculty of Westminster Theological Seminary.* 2nd ed. 1967. Reprint, Phillipsburg, NJ: Presbyterian and Reformed, 2002.

Storms, Sam. *Tough Topics: Biblical Answers to 25 Challenging Questions.* Wheaton: Crossway, 2013.

Storms, Sam, and Justin Taylor, eds. *For the Fame of God's Name: Essays in Honor of John Piper.* Wheaton: Crossway, 2010.

Stott, John R. W. *The Message of Romans: God's Good News for the World.* BST. Downers Grove, IL: InterVarsity, 1994.

―――. *The Message of the Sermon on the Mount.* BST. Downers Grove, IL: InterVarsity, 1978.

Stowe, David W. *No Sympathy for the Devil: Christian Pop Music and the Transformation of Evangelicalism.* Chapel Hill, NC: University of North Carolina Press, 2011.

Strauss, Mark L. *How to Read the Bible in Changing Times: Understanding and Applying God's Word Today.* Grand Rapids: Baker, 2011.

―――. "Sadducees." In *Dictionary of Jesus and the Gospels,* 2nd ed. edited by Joel B. Green, 823–25. Downers Grove, IL: InterVarsity, 2013.

―――, ed. *Remarriage after Divorce in Today's Church: 3 Views.* Counterpoints: Church Life. Grand Rapids: Zondervan, 2006.

Strickland, Wayne, ed. *Five Views on Law and Gospel.* Counterpoints: Bible & Theology. Grand Rapids: Zondervan, 1999.

Stuart, Douglas K. *Exodus.* NAC. Nashville: B&H, 2006.

Swavely, Dave. *Who Are You to Judge? The Dangers of Judging and Legalism.* Phillipsburg, NJ: Presbyterian & Reformed, 2005.

Swindoll, Charles R. *The Grace Awakening.* Dallas: Word, 1990.

Tagliapietra, Ron. *Better Thinking and Reasoning.* Greenville, SC: Bob Jones University Press, 1995.

Talbert, Layton. *Beyond Suffering: Discovering the Message of Job.* Greenville, SC: Bob Jones University Press, 2007.

―――. *Not by Chance: Learning to Trust a Sovereign God.* Greenville, SC: Bob Jones University Press, 2001.

Tenney, Merrill C., and Moisés Silva, eds. *The Zondervan Encyclopedia of the Bible.* Rev. ed. 5 vols. Grand Rapids: Zondervan, 2009.

Thielman, Frank. *Ephesians.* BECNT. Grand Rapids: Baker, 2010.

―――. *The NIV Application Commentary: Philippians.* Grand Rapids: Zondervan, 1995.

Thiselton, Anthony. *The First Epistle to the Corinthians.* NIGTC. Grand Rapids: Eerdmans, 2000.

Tiessen, Terrance. "Toward a Hermeneutic for Discerning Universal Moral Absolutes." *JETS* 36 (1993) 189–207.

Thomas, Robert L. *Evangelical Hermeneutics: The New Versus the Old.* Grand Rapids: Kregel, 2002.

Thomas, W. H. Griffith. *St. Paul's Epistle to the Romans: A Devotional Commentary.* Grand Rapids: Eerdmans, 1946.

Thompson, J. A. *Deuteronomy: An Introduction and Commentary.* TOTC. Downers Grove, IL: InterVarsity, 1974.

Toulmin, Stephen E. *The Uses of Argument.* Updated ed. New York: Cambridge UP, 2003.

Tozer, A. W. *Of God and Men.* Harrisburg, PA: Christian, 1960.

———. *The Pursuit of God.* Harrisburg: Christian Publications, 1948.

Tripp, Paul David. *War of Words: Getting to the Heart of Your Communication Struggles.* Resources for Changing Lives. Phillipsburg, NJ: Presbyterian & Reformed, 2000.

The Truth that Leads to Eternal Life. New York: Watchtower, 1968.

Turner, David L. *Matthew.* BECNT. Grand Rapids: Baker, 2008.

Turretin, Francis. *Institutes of Elenctic Theology.* 3 vols. Translated by George Musgrave Giger. Edited by James T. Dennison Jr. Phillipsburg, NJ: Presbyterian & Reformed, 1992.

Ulrich, Dean R. *From Famine to Fullness: The Gospel according to Ruth.* The Gospel According to the Old Testament. Phillipsburg, NJ: Presbyterian & Reformed, 2007.

Vanhoozer, Kevin J. *Biblical Authority after Babel: Retrieving the Solas in the Spirit of Mere Protestant Christianity.* Grand Rapids: Brazos, 2016.

———. *The Drama of Doctrine: A Canonical Linguistic Approach to Christian Theology.* Louisville: Westminster John Knox, 2005.

———. *Faith Speaking Understanding: Performing the Drama of Doctrine.* Louisville: Westminster John Knox, 2014.

———. *Is There a Meaning in This Text? The Bible, the Reader, and the Morality of Literary Knowledge.* Grand Rapids: Zondervan, 1998.

VanGemeren, Willem A., ed. *New International Dictionary of Old Testament Theology and Exegesis.* 5 vols. Grand Rapids: Zondervan, 1997.

Veerman, Dave. *How to Apply the Bible: Discover the Truths of Scripture and Put Them into Practice.* Wheaton: Livingstone, 2009.

Veith, Gene. *God at Work: Your Christian Vocation in All of Life.* Focal Point Series. Wheaton: Crossway, 2002.

Vincent, Milton. *A Gospel Primer for Christians.* N.p.: Focus, 2008.

Virkler, Henry A., and Karelynne Gerber Ayayo. *Hermeneutics: Principles and Processes of Biblical Interpretation.* 2nd ed. Grand Rapids: Baker Academic, 2007.

Vlach, Michael. *Has The Church Replaced Israel? A Theological Evaluation.* Nashville: B&H, 2010.

Vos, Geerhardus. *Biblical Theology: Old and New Testaments.* 1948. Reprint, Grand Rapids: Eerdmans, 1991.

Waldron, Samuel E. *A Modern Exposition of the 1689 Baptist Confession of Faith.* 3rd ed. Darlington, England: Evangelical, 1999.

Wallace, Daniel B. *Greek Grammar beyond the Basics: An Exegetical Syntax of the New Testament.* Grand Rapids: Zondervan, 1996.

Waltke, Bruce K. *The Book of Proverbs: Chapters 15–31.* NICOT. Grand Rapids: Eerdmans, 2005.

Waltke, Bruce K., with Cathi J. Fredricks. *Genesis: A Commentary.* Grand Rapids: Zondervan, 2001.

Ward, Mark L. Jr., et al. *Biblical Worldview: Creation, Fall, Redemption.* Greenville, SC: Bob Jones University Press, 2015.

Warfield, Benjamin Breckinridge. *The Inspiration and Authority of the Bible,* edited by Samuel G. Craig. Philadelphia: Presbyterian & Reformed, 1948.

————. *The Westminster Assembly and Its Work.* New York: Oxford University, 1931.

Watson, Thomas. "How We May Read the Scriptures with the Most Scriptural Profit." In Thomas Watson and Samuel Lee, *The Bible and the Closet,* ed. John Overton Choules, 13-46. 1842. Reprint, Harrisonburg, VA: Sprinkle, 1992.

Webb, William J. *Corporal Punishment in the Bible: A Redemptive-Movement Hermeneutic for Troubling Texts.* Downers Grove, IL: InterVarsity, 2011.

————. *Slaves, Women & Homosexuals: Exploring the Hermeneutics of Cultural Analysis.* Downers Grove, IL: InterVarsity, 2001.

Weeks, Noel. *The Sufficiency of Scripture.* Edinburgh: Banner of Truth, 1988.

Wenham, Gordon J. *The Book of Leviticus.* NICOT. Grand Rapids: Eerdmans, 1979.

White, James R. *Scripture Alone.* Grand Rapids: Bethany, 2004.

Whitney, Donald S. *Praying the Bible.* Wheaton: Crossway, 2015.

————. *Spiritual Disciplines within the Church: Participating Fully in the Body of Christ.* Chicago: Moody, 1996.

Wilbourne, Rankin. *Union with Christ: The Way to Know and Enjoy God.* Colorado Springs: David C. Cook, 2016.

Wigoder, Geoffrey, Fred Skolnik, and Shmuel Himelstein, eds. *The New Encyclopedia of Judaism.* New York: New York University Press, 2002.

Wilder, Terry L., ed. *Perspectives on Our Struggle with Sin: Three Views of Romans 7.* Nashville: B&H, 2011.

Wilkens, Steve. *Beyond Bumper Sticker Ethics: An Introduction to Theories of Right and Wrong.* 2nd ed. Downers Grove, IL: InterVarsity, 2011.

Williams, James B., and Randolph Shaylor, eds. *God's Word in Our Hands: The Bible Preserved for Us.* Greenville, SC: Ambassador-Emerald International. 2003.

Wisdom, Thurman. *Royal Destiny: The Reign of Man in God's Kingdom.* Greenville, SC: Bob Jones University Press, 2006.

Wolters, Albert M., with Michael W. Goheen *Creation Regained: Biblical Basics for a Reformational Worldview.* 2nd ed. Grand Rapids: Eerdmans, 2005.

Wright, Christopher J. H. *Old Testament Ethics for the People of God.* Downers Grove, IL: InterVarsity, 2004.

————. *How to Preach and Teach the Old Testament for All Its Worth.* Grand Rapids: Zondervan, 2016.

Zuck, Roy B. "Application in Biblical Hermeneutics and Exposition." In *Walvoord: A Tribute,* edited by Donald K. Campbell, 15–38. Chicago: Moody, 1982.

————. *Basic Bible Interpretation.* Wheaton: Scripture, 1991.